Looking for my Footprints
A guided journey through the inner landscape

Lynne Catherine Walker

Printed in Victoria, Canada

Cover design: Maria Galenza

A cataloguing record for this book that includes the U.S. Library of Congress Classification number, the Library of Congress Call number and the Dewey Decimal cataloguing code is available from the National Library of Canada. The complete cataloguing record can be obtained from the National Library's online database at:
www.nlc-bnc.ca/amicus/index-e.html
ISBN 1-4120-2593-1

TRAFFORD

This book was published on-demand in cooperation with Trafford Publishing.
On-demand publishing is a unique process and service of making a book available for retail
sale to the public taking advantage of on-demand manufacturing and Internet marketing.
On-demand publishing includes promotions, retail sales, manufacturing, order fulfilment, accounting and collecting royalties on behalf of the author.

Suite 6E, 2333 Government St., Victoria, B.C. V8T 4P4, CANADA
Phone   250-383-6864   Toll-free   1-888-232-4444 (Canada & US)
Fax   250-383-6804   E-mail   sales@trafford.com
Web site   www.trafford.com   TRAFFORD PUBLISHING IS A DIVISION OF TRAFFORD HOLDINGS LTD.
Trafford Catalogue #04-0421   www.trafford.com/robots/04-0421.html

10   9   8   7   6   5   4   3

My flesh and bones,
In their journey through the desert,
Make a quick stop here
And leave a little warmth from the palm of my hand
A bit of rhythm of the heart.
The ancient image is far away
But you are still there waiting.

Tell me
Did I stop here once during a previous existence?
I find myself looking for my footprints
Left during a cycle of birth and death

I can see now
That all of us
Since the beginning of time
Have been flowing at the same speed.
Together with four cypresses today
We have stopped for a moment
To contemplate the wondrous trip

Although this calm blue sky has been here a million eons
It is only to me now that this blue sky
Has just been born.

Thich Nhat Hahn

This book is dedicated to those heroes and heroines

whose voices, *poetic, wise and true*, grace these pages

thereby transforming the word into the way.

Contents

Sunday pilgrims

An introduction to the inner pilgrimage

It is Sunday.
      Sunday, in the Western world, has traditionally been set aside as a special time to enter another dimension, to create an opportunity for soul reflection through quietness, time in nature, prayer, family life. A day when, at least until recently, the commercial world of having and getting is deliberately laid low. Properly understood then, Sunday is the foundation day of a cyclic rhythm, one which can be thought of as the intersection of time and eternity within us. On Monday, in tune with the moon of 'moon-day,' movement begins again. We take up our place in culturally determined patterns of doing and living.
      In this spirit and on this particular Sunday, as well as for one Sunday a month for a year, a group of ten men and women who could mostly be described as 'middle aged,' pack up an assortment of belongings into vehicles and drive outside of the city in which they live, to a small village on the edge of the *Canadian Rockies*, for a day of guided inner reflection. They will do this once a month over the next year as participants in a group called *Innerscape*, which, as a result of my own personal inner pilgrimage in 1997, will provide a framework for looking carefully and deeply at the Sunday questions. These are of soul finding, of purpose, of spiritual practice and religious questioning. Some may seek healing from physical or psychological symptoms, of a life lived with vague dissatisfaction as a race or a struggle, as survival but without meaningfulness. Many have reached a crossroads in life and wish to contemplate the next direction. All of them, all of us, want to be well and happy. We want to live more fully with the clarity of knowing who we are. We want it to be said of us, *"She is her own person," "He is his own man."*
      These few would be called pilgrims in another time and they are not alone in their search for what is sacred in every day life. Indeed,

books, talk shows, gurus, workshops, techniques on soul searching and self healing from both East and West abound in such profusion that the choice is often overwhelming. As are the statistics of a troubled people when, in the first year of this century, according to IMS Health Canada,[1] 32.8 million prescriptions for anti depressant medications were filled in Canada. This figure represents a 45% increase over the past five years. Furthermore when any of these prescription users quit taking the medication 80% again become symptomatic. Of those also engaging in some form of therapy only 25% of them relapse.

Whether the short term solution is a pill, a workshop or psychotherapy it is fairly obvious that we, in this age of brilliant technological achievements, are not well. However, what is less frequently understood is that we are not well because we are not whole. The word holiness derives from the word whole and means bringing the personality back to a state of wholeness, which involves retrieving the missing parts or faculties which are lacking and restoring them to a dignified place. An old fashioned term for this dislocation is, 'heresy' and we are in heresy when we are out of balance. *The balance which Sunday aims for, is the balance between heaven and earth.*

C.G. Jung, one of the great inner explorers of the 20th century, said that our most important life work is the relocation of the center of gravity of the personality from the ego to the Self. In practice this involves a vastly expanded view of who 'I/me' is. Over the course of the next year, an intentionally focused year, group members will enter a guided and sequential inquiry for seeking their soul path, for restoring hidden aspects of ego,(I/me) for redeeming this ego, and for recognizing the inter-dependent nature of Self.

Problems are not something we have but something we are. What it takes for one to re discover wholesomeness is not the same as for another, especially so within the diversity of cultures in contemporary life. *We can no longer rest assured in prescribed prayers to the one true God,* when He/She carries multiple names, meanings and addresses. With regard to my own profession of psychology, elevated in this century to the status of a new religion, James Hillman has made a timely argument when he declares that, *"We've had a hundred years of psychotherapy and the world is getting worse."*[2]

I do not wish to disparage what are significant therapeutic interventions in various modalities, to alleviate distress by providing places to rest, to be heard, to be touched, to be understood. Any place where we are encouraged to ask the question, " How actually am I at this moment?" and ring that question around with some space, a genuine interest, and a willingness to wait, has value. Especially so in the computer age where we are flooded with vast quantities of telephoned, televised, tele-transported information without the possibility of really understanding any connection, least of all with ourselves. It is no wonder that there is despair in the jungle of networks and time already spent. The voice of Orestes, an explorer of ancient Greece, may throw us a lifeline when he says, "human life begins on the far side of despair.

"How am I?" is a crucial point of departure for journeying. It is not, "How do I think I am?" nor, "How would I like to be?" but, "How am I, now?" It cannot be properly answered from the judging intellect, nor from reactive emotions, but more from a unified attention to body/mind/instinct in the now. If I cannot be present I cannot change and to 'be-here-now' is not that easy.

Everything in me pulls away-everything that is, except the tentative sense that I am somehow in exile here and need to return to where I came from, to the wholeness of being that calls me from sleep. When I am silent and still to allow that call to be heard in me, for that is part of my essence. I have a chance then to become what I am. In my subconscious being I seem to know that my life depends on it.

James George [3]

Sunday group participants have volunteered for exile of a deliberate nature. At least on this day, they dwell outside of time, cycles, place, country, belief and belonging. Voluntary exile to find one's authentic life, is a classical theme going back a long way, recorded, for example, in Homer's, "Odyssey" from the thirteenth century. Today, I write in a kind of exile from modernity on a small island in the pacific northwest, a place which found me with certainty, as well as initial disbelief, at a time of depth in my own journey. To go on an inner journey or an outer voyage, involves a condition of complete simplicity, which may cost "not less than everything," for release of attachment is one of its conditions.

Where exile means to be outside of place, ecstasy means to stand outside of oneself. On this Sunday journey both are made possible. As we symbolically travel outwards (from the city) so we dive in and down. This may be a rather perilous, lengthy journey if we commit ourselves to the unfolding mystery. It does not necessarily yield quick results. We may be uncertain, are quite likely to trip up, but as *Joseph Campbell* was fond of saying, *"Where you stumble and fall there you discover the gold."*[4] Nevertheless, it is wonderfully supportive to be in the company of others in such an undertaking of unknown possibilities. What is required is an openness of attitude, flexibility, and a willingness to surrender to the serendipitous.

There are years for questioning and years for answers. To be traveling as spiritual pilgrims is to have reached a time and place for serious questioning. This is gardening of the soul, at times spade work, to find the treasure of psyche, the mystery of being, and the wholeness of a balanced life.

> The rose
> was not searching for the sunrise,
> Almost eternal on its branch,
> It was searching for something else.
> The rose
> Was not searching for darkness or science,
> Borderline of flesh and dream,
> It was searching for something else.
> The rose
> Was not searching for the rose,
> Motionless in the sky
> It was searching for something else.   R. Bly[5]

This is a journey _of_ Self (where Self is thought of as a vastly expanded 'I') not _to_ Self. To say this is to begin at the end but it is said now to demonstrate that there are no answers other than those within. *Krishnamurti*, a 20th century prophet, constantly maintained that, *"truth is a pathless land,"*[6] There is then no prescription for seeking Self, other than in an increased sensitivity to the here and now of life. It is said that the purest expression of Self is the knowledge of one's soul path, and the most important experience to be had, the knowledge of expanded consciousness. *What do we mean by soul?* The word is used often these days, but also remains elusive in definition, perhaps rightfully so.

The words *psyche* and *soul* are frequently used interchangeably, the former being more modern and less ambiguous. Psyche belongs to physicality, as the mental aspect of physical life. It is thought of as dealing with the head. Those, like myself, who have a professional title which begins with "psych" are colloquially known as being in the 'shrink' business. Shrinking heads in this day and age is perhaps not a bad concept! The same professionals do not usually advertise the cure of souls, that is more likely left to priests, gurus, and metaphysicians. So, *psyche* has come to have a 'working' definition, *soul* less so. *Soul* is more of a symbol than a concept and as such *makes meaning possible*. It allows events to become experiences and experience involves wholeness.

Anything soulful is communicated with depth of feeling, passion, suffering, beauty, truth, goodness, love. Its concern is definitely religious. To speak of loss of soul is to be outside of oneself, unable to find meaning or connection. It is a condition of being 'not there,' of loneliness, alienation, a kind of deadness to experience or feeling. In short, a state of depression.

The problem of finding soul burns as no other issue, for, without some sense of soul there is a vast confusion of moralities, uncertainties of action and decisions taken which are logically sound, but not psychologically valid.

James Hillman[7]

Embarking on soul seeking is to look for something which, ironically, has never been lost but is hiding in the place we least expected to find it. However much of a paradox the end may be we can only start from where we are with current perceptions of loss, of something missing, and genuinely commit to the search. All wisdom traditions have exemplified such pilgrims' journeys as necessary, and all have indicated the perils of such journeys. What is initially sought may change and the location of searching may quite likely be contrary. What looks up will drop down. What begins on the outside will find parallel on the inside. What is found to be enlightening may initially appear as a darkening. As travelers into the land of psyche it is initially prudent to have, as well as companions, a map, a guide, a reliable home base and faith. For tools we shall need both a *lamp and a sword*. The term for this process is *individuation* - discovering the uniqueness of yourself, finding out first what you are not, and then, what you are. Individuation relates to wholeness.

*Listen to your interior intelligence, take it seriously, stay true to it,
and most important of all, approach it with a religious attitude.* Jung [8]

One gets to be whole only by working with the particular circumstances of *your* life, not by evading or trying to rise above it. In dealing with depression, (lack of wholeness) the mistake is often made of repeating futile attempts to 'repair the old mother,' to restore her, rather than gathering up the pieces and moving out into the deep unknown of oneself.

This journey need not involve metaphorically struggling through brambles, thorns and dense forests, with no sense of ground, although there are those, including myself, who have traveled solo along converging pathways of psychological, meditation and yogic disciplines. Maps are to be found nowadays for each of these routes but they can be contradictory and confusing. It is helpful to have an explorer's guide, a synthesis, in this case, one which is inclusive of Eastern and Western directives. Personally, I see that I have been, actually still am, along with many of the 'baby boomer' generation, my own experiment. Perhaps such a mythical life represents the modern version of the hero/ heroine's journey. For me it has involved an adult life of looking, trying out, reading widely, traveling, going to the guru, leaving the guru, listening, synthesizing, dwelling with. With the questions, "Who, how, what is this 'I' which is 'me'?

The '*Innerscape map*' represents a slow synthesis of that which holds true in my own experience, as well as through time, culture, wisdom teaching and gender. There are others I esteem greatly, pilgrims of our time, to whom I am indebted for their courage by example, and for their sane and verifiable evaluations. I have personally learned much from people such as C.G. Jung, Joseph Campbell, Thich Nhat Hanh, Jiddhu Krishnamurti, Vimala Thacker, Ken Wilber, Toni Packer, Joko Beck, Pema Chodron, Mary Oliver, James Hillman, Stephen Bachelor, Robert Johnson, Helen Luke, Sharon Butala, Virginia Wolf, Robert Bly, Marion Woodman. These and others who have been, or are, seekers, continually and respectfully inform the work of our own momentum. What is crucial, is to understand that *personal journeying is the only means of making sense of other's proclamations.* One must be prepared to make one's way through personal mapping information of symbol, dream, myth, insight, synchronicity, which speaks directly to the individual soul's code.

Being an inner pilgrim requires a reliable enough center and a firm enough seat to face into the painful, stumbling, wobbly places which would normally cause us to defend, by reacting against, or giving up. The pilgrim's agreement is to go willingly wherever the journey leads, thereby arriving in 'heaven,' which is not a special place but a special moment, *any moment in which we are free from suffering*. These moments increase along the path.

Wise leaders agree that an inner journey takes us on a descent into the mess and muck of life. This is the spade work of discovering orphaned aspects of soul, hidden behind and beneath false assumptions about self. Redemption is that which follows, as expanding vision of what is intelligent and possible beyond 'my' concerns.

Innerscape is about as far from escape as one could get. It is here, now, looking and listening, experimenting, filled with curiosity as self meets symbol and symbol engages Self. At these illumined places in the interior landscape energy is liberated, memories are released along with their twin gremlin, suffering, and wholeness is restored. Parts of the inner land which may have been a waste land, especially in depression, may grow green and juicy and ripe again and thrive.

The potential for the Sunday pilgrims is this: *for each participant to rediscover their own soul's pathway and thus wholesomeness of body, mind and spirit*. The treasure is an individual 'blueprint' which will orient further life decisions and conditions. Last, and most importantly, this work is not exclusively about transformation of a personal 'I', for, just as what is done to the rivers in *South Africa*, or the air in *Alaska* affects the whole world, so too, knowing and caring for our selves, properly, has a ripple effect which contributes to a saner and more compassionate planet.

The various components of the *Innerscape* quest represent an integration of my own life explorations in the inner wilderness. This life long interest, study, one may even call it a compulsion, culminated in 1997 as a personal sojourn or gift to myself, as, "*fifty days for fifty years of living*."I knew it was time to take stock, I knew that I must travel both backwards and forwards. It occurred to me that a myth for guidance was perhaps needed but I did not know which myth. There was a poetic voice that spoke directly in saying "*redeem the time, redeem the unread vision of the higher dream*," and so I began.

"*Looking For my Footprints*," travels firstly through journal extracts from my solo quest, then follows the current year long group of ten men and women as they gather together the tools, establish the foundation, sort their seeds, study a myth and encounter progressive levels of conscious awareness as personal questioning and self expression. Their awakening takes place through creative process, ritual ceremonies, sacraments, symbolic expression, myth study, yoga, meditation and dialogue. The reader is invited to participate, as armchair pilgrim, in the here and now sharing of this journey of Self discovery.

1

fifty days for fifty years

When we no longer know where to turn, our journey has just begun.
At that crossroads a voice calls to our pilgrim soul. The time has come to
set out for the sacred ground—the mountain, temple, ancestral home-that
will stir our heart and restore our sense of wonder. It is down the path to
the deeply real where time stops and we are seized by the mysteries.

Cousineau[1]

Tracking soul and psyche for the best part of half of a century
had resulted in quite an accumulation of assorted literature. In my
collected library were books from East and West on psychology,
metaphysics, religious teachings as well as the 'baby boomer's' trade
mark, 'self help' guides. The list was long, in the case of some classics it
was still inspirational, many author's suggestions had been useful at one
time or other but currently the shelves of information left me feeling dis-
heartened. This feeling resonated with a previous call from *T. S. Eliot* who
asked of the modern age, *"Where is the wisdom we have lost in
knowledge? Where is the knowledge we have lost in information?"*

Down Alice's proverbial rabbit hole I had tumbled, into a hall of
mirrors, viewing my-self from abundant angles—excitingly and dreadfully
competent in each view. But which was me? Would there be one more
book of truth to be read? From the West, plunging to the depths of
psyche, from the East, coolly observing the non-self. What to do? Should I
return to psychoanalysis, pray to God, go to a sweat lodge, a vision
quest, a shamanic journey to retrieve lost parts of myself, or follow my
dear friends along the dharma path? At times, I envied those who were
able to believe the truth of one view but I had seen with practice that
beliefs evaporate under the spotlight of direct awareness and scrutiny.

Meanwhile, the foundation felt to be shifting, dreams were vivid,
synchronicity abounded, the heat of menopausal fire seemed to parallel

flashes of 'knowing.' I was approaching a landmark age of fifty in unprecedented times and I knew something was up. I must begin with the questions, travel within, return, review, take stock. The decision was, *"Fifty days for fifty years"* Fifty days of journeying, using outer travel as metaphor and invitation to inner questioning. A time of challenging and provoking, of recording this *Grecian journey of palengenesia* (being reborn each moment.) Instinct said 'the homeland,' so I decided upon a six week trip to England, the home of my birth, as well as religious and sacred sights. In the presence of these, I felt that I had a chance of being re-inspired. Perhaps *there* dwelt the God or Goddess of my own myth the one which could take me further. I was wisely encouraged by *Rilke's* words to the young poet, *"The necessary thing is this: solitude, great inner solitude......"*

More challenging, for me were the six remaining days spent alone in a tent, in the Alberta wilderness but that is to get ahead of the tale. Crucial companions were favourite poets, who are best remembered, not read and luckily quite frequently remembered me.

> One day you finally knew
> What you had to do and began,
> Though the voices around you
> Kept shouting their bad advice—
> Though the whole house began to tremble
> And you felt the old tug at your ankles.
> " Mend my life! "each voice cried.
> But you didn't stop you knew what you had to do,
> The stars began to burn through the sheets of clouds,
> And there was a new voice which you slowly
> Recognised as your own, that kept you company
> Determined to do the only thing you could do—
> Determined to save the only life you could save.
>
> Mary Oliver[2]

Many years earlier I had read and admired *"The Hero with a Thousand Faces,"* by Joseph Campbell. From its unconscious resting place it was guiding this sojourn, which was indeed an initiation, although I didn't consciously know that at the time. A heroine's journey of transformation requires divestiture of the old self by withdrawing from everyday life. It carries the responsibility of return from the depths with knowledge, which must be put to use to redeem time and society. It starts with 'The Call,' which usually comes from a big mistake, like climbing the ladder of a wrong profession, or giving your heart to the wrong person. Because of this disaster you are rendered vulnerable and available. In this state of mind you more readily make connections with allies, unlikely people, ideas, different perspectives. Through these new connections, you cross the threshold toward something larger. Here you make new discoveries, to be brought back eventually to your life context. This is to take a mythic inner journey.

Setting out in this heightened state of consciousness for a soul journey, a quest, I was primed to look carefully, listen attentively to everyone and everything which crossed my path. Conscientiously, I chronicled experiences which arose from within and without. Through the reflective act of writing I allowed the serious questions to emerge, as a sort of inner dialogue.

.... *Fifty years, a half century of life loosely contained in this gently folded skin, felt as a multitude of threads of memory. Now inside the belly of a great steel bird, lifting off so gracefully given its many assorted bodies, all trusting implicitly in the miracle of flight.*

The city disappears as a sea of orange lights arranged like a mosaic upon the darkened prairie. Whatever has been left so freshly, so lovingly with a tear is already the rummage of memory. It relinquishes to the moon in the window, which promises to never be left behind. She is full, luminous, in a clear sky with not a cloud. This emptiness, is perhaps symbolic of the pregnancy of things yet to be born. Inexplicably I feel grateful.

Excitement is buzzing on board as a party of high school kids from a small prairie town, take their first trip to Europe. The young woman beside me has eyes like the moon as she is temporarily reborn with the magic, the wonder of first flight. She quickly settles back into the requisite cloning of adolescence, the initial moment of awe, of all-oneness, put away (but not forgotten), in favour of the 'Tragically Hip,' clamped to her ears to soothe the exigencies of cramped sleeping quarters. This is clearly not for me, a trip, as it is for this school girl and for many others, but rather a gnostic quest, a pilgrimage. There is an alertness hovering behind exhaustion, a determination not to miss anything, inner/outer, all-one today.

Such a night flight across the ocean is boarded as passage from

one geography to another. It is a profound symbolic movement from participation in a relatively fixed human drama, involving a key player who is always, 'me.' The gendered and conditioned 'me'. She who lives an ordinary existence defined by calendar time, a homeland, a people, a family with 'our story,' its own beliefs, habits, local identities, affiliations, professions, etc. This 'me' is a kind of mask, a persona who reflects the categories of its curriculum vitae, of its biography, of failed loves and successful accomplishments, of health, sickness and eventually, death. The mythological world enters by upsetting the agreed upon story such that in the descent to a symbolic life there is possibility for a different kind of ascent. 'She' becomes connected to the more-than-I, to the universal world of symbol, beauty, meaning which endures beyond the time and space of 'my' life span. Life becomes expansive rather than contractual, a mystery rather than a predictable repetition, a call rather than an answer. In flight I was to feel this as a door opening with invitation.
.... *In the time it takes to drink a hot milky cup of tea at Heathrow terminal I become British again. Home, history, pure enjoyment, the temporary solution to everything is in this cup, in its presumption, and the "there you are luv" that gave it to me. A perfect hello, a soul greeting.*

♧ *Question: Do I have a natural affinity with this cultural life? The one I was born to, the one which called up this body, this country of origin, with its milky tea, social anxieties, safety concerns, particularly conditioned customs?*

The first condition of any journey is the setting out with trust. This journal entry is replete with the sensitivity to environment, the literal as well as metaphoric lift off and flight. A time where 'I/me' is shaken up by removal from familiar habits and customs. Travelling time is redefining I/me in the here and now, especially in transcontinental flights. Because of these special conditions there can be a collecting of Self with a heightened sense of the extraordinary in the ordinary. Even a cup of tea! Metaphor and synchronicity abound as attention is fine tuned and the richness of the archetypal (powerfully symbolic) world is revealed, lending enormous strength to the undertaking. All this can and does, happen without any conscious understanding. What I recorded through writing was a stream of consciousness, a waking dream, which, as I was to discover,often revealed its significance much later.

Return to the familiar was both warming as well as shocking. The cultural code, unlike my own more experimental one, is of a life rooted in tradition. Going home is always a challenge and I would quite agree with *Robert Bly*, who says that we become about ten years old by the time we have taken off our coat and sat down at the family table. Many long held negative attitudes which were 'forgotten' reveal themselves again for scrutiny. I thought that after living far away for decades that 'I' had changed yet now was discovering that all depends on circumstances! Do we ever cease believing that our parents will do the changing for us? I had unending faith that the outer home would somehow magically replicate the inner home, which I longed for, but that hope was hope for the wrong thing.

♋ *Question: Where is my true home? What kind of home has Christianity provided?*

.... Today I have arrived at a new home at the Gaia house convent Buddhist retreat centre. It is quite beautiful but that is irrelevant as I am blinded with self interest, greed and covetousness. I want the best blankets, the best view, room, meditation, space, cup, spoon and ridiculously on and on. I presume the worst and set myself up for being miserable. This is a familiar 'shadow'(unconscious) pattern of 'wanting', my own and my generation's.

♋ *Question: What do I really value? How culturally conditioned am I in this regard?*

.... By the second day I am more settled. My chaotic, disturbed mind has responded to order, routine, silence, in quietening and calming. I am no longer required to respond to empty conversation, to respond at all to anyone. There is freedom in this. Birdsong is overwhelming from dawn to dusk. The walking path is graced by an unfurling magnolia tree whose white and pure fingers open to greet the morning sun. Shiny, brilliant green leaves are open everywhere along the hedgerows. I gazed at a grey dove and laughed at the antics of the rooks in the rookery.

In the   afternoon I chose to do walking meditation in the

churchyard. There, I was drawn to explore a rather hidden corner of the graveyard where I found a Celtic cross in stone, overgrown with moss and covered with primroses. The cross, protected by a great oak, is at the edge of a bluff overlooking the entire valley. I was stunned by its beauty. At first, I could not easily read the old inscribed names covered with moss and lichen but then my eye made out 'Walker.' Curiosity was piqued. I scrabbled away at the covering, to reveal the grave of, "Mollie Forester Walker," dead now some 80 years. I thought about her life and the slender threads which link us all through name and gesture, place, time and circumstance. Finding Mollie with her magnificent Celtic cross linked me to her in a way beyond comprehension. I was deeply touched. Her cross, now my cross, will remain in deep memory as a symbol of connection, beauty, love, life, death and continuity.

♙ Question: Why did this symbol call me? Why was I drawn there and then?

As a result of silencing the activities of monkey mind, with all of its constant chatter, the symbolic world has a chance to reveal itself. There are potent images appearing from the world, from nature, from the weather, from the flavour of the day. I had a sense that a message was being conveyed through my time with the Celtic cross and grave, though it could not yet be understood fully. It had appeared in silence and out of the vastness of the collective unconscious.

> Consciousness, no matter how extensive it may be must always remain
> the smaller circle within the greater circle of the unconscious as an island
> surrounded by the sea; and like the sea itself, the unconscious yields an
> endless abundance of living creatures, a wealth beyond our fathoming.
> Robert Johnson [3]

On this journey the more serious my intention, the greater the spaciousness, the more persistent my sincerity to look and see, the more the universe responded.

> A sign is a sign and when you know it's a sign, that's enough, It's not something
> you go looking for, it has to come to you. That's what signs do, they come to
> you,........ there is a moment when you can know something, it is a silent
> thunderous thing.
> E.L. Doctorow [4]

♧ *Question: Am I mindful enough to recognise the symbolic communication of the moment?*

     The signs which showed up along the path were by no means all pleasant. In retrospect it would seem obvious that in order to be born anew as a heroine there would inevitably have to be a date with death. My opportunity arrived at my second retreat which included a formal practice of meditating on death.

.... I was out of sorts all day after waking from disturbing dreams. So, it was somehow fitting that this would be the day for the Tibetan meditation on death. By the time 2:30 pm came around I was ready to die and perhaps did in some inexplicable way. I could barely stay awake, was almost falling off my cushion, not just normal sleepiness but, "I have to sleep and now." It would not pass. Then I became very cold, and imaged my friends' (now dead) mother sitting next to me, and then felt as though all the blood had drained away. Finally the bell rang. Thankfully, I returned to my room to lay in the sun, wrapped up in two blankets. I fell into a deep sleep, from which I awoke an hour later feeling wretched. After eating an apple I immediately fell back to sleep for another hour. Upon awakening from this sleep, my feeling was calm, centred and exceptionally present. I went downstairs and ate a normal tea of bread and jam, which tasted like the best food I had ever had. I walked in the garden and felt that it was paradise. Later, walking outside, looking at the stars, it was as though I had never seen them before. These events spanned about five hours but all seemed to be in one now. I have no explanation for any of this but kept thinking of a quote from James Joyce, "Being in the present one watches the future tumble into the past"

♧ *Question: What is this?*

     Prior to this retreat time I had been reading the myth of *Demeter* searching for her daughter *Persephone*, who was dead in the underworld. Clearly I had much to learn about the important things in life. I had asked questions and the answers were coming at me, through me and around me, as a great teaching about the value of this life. What I was shortly to learn and dramatically, was that life is gained, life is lost, and between, lives 'I,' a fragile, yet great privilege indeed.

.... *Dream: I am with my friend's mother (the one from the death* meditation). We are awaiting the police, for her husband died and she is being questioned, held on charges because he was dead a whole day before she reported it. I sit holding her hand, feeling sorry for her, outraged at the legal implications, which I am sure will now prove her guilty, not innocent. We are sitting on a bed when the police arrive. I am protesting her innocence when they show me that she is bleeding from both ears, as was her husband, the implication being that she too is dying from this. I become frightened, as I am still holding her hand and feel sure that this now includes me. We are all dying. The authorities have now become uninterested. Later I am trying to get away from an entity which is much greater than me. It wraps itself around me as a huge, terrifying presence I know that I am done for. Just at that moment I see a window. The lace curtains at the window part and a little girl looks out briefly but I know that she has seen the presence.Now, there is now hope for my life. I awake feeling frightened, knowing that the presence was death and that the girl looked death in the face and that she, representing life, won. End of dream.

After awakening and breakfasting, I set off for my usual walk. I saw a bird which had been rather elusive earlier in the week. I heard her very distinctive sound like the rattle of a dry engine. Later, I identified her as a kestrel and stopped to get a better look. Suddenly thud! On the grass next to me landed one of her babies which had fallen from the nest. Stunned,, I realized there was nothing I could do, without creating more of a problem, when thud, right at my feet, another one! This time both the mother and I were upset. She was flying around frantically, calling. The little one fluttered, then lay still. I thought of picking it up but decided that would create more shock and terror, so I walked on to collect myself for five minutes or so and then walked back. I found the little ones gone but the mother still calling and flying around. I thought that I perhaps heard them in the trees but as the mother was frantic I decided to leave. I looked down to find one perfect little baby feather, which I assumed was for me.

I left shaken, knowing that I was totally out of control in the midst of life and death. Seeing the fragility, the vulnerability, the tremendous effort it takes to bring forth life and how easily it is lost. I said a blessing for the little birds and, whilst walking past the cross, said one for Mollie-in-her-grave.

Another day, much later on in the journey I was to have another lesson along the same lines:

Early one morning whilst at Brockwood Park I was walking down the lane in the crisp air, as yet unwarmed by the sun. There was not a soul about, only fields extending endlessly to the horizon. Suddenly, on the road before me were two partridges, dead, and freshly so, lying side by side. I was stunned but calm, thinking, "Oh, this lesson again. What are these birds telling me?" I knew, by now, that journeying involved a deep reckoning of the parameters of 'I.' This pilgrim 'I' had no choice but to look deeply into life and death. Later that same evening I chose to watch the tape "The Seer Who Walks Alone," chosen because I had wanted to see a film about Krishnamurti, not a taped talk. Unknown to me, this turned out to be his last filmed talk about death and beginnings. However, I had my own revelation looking at and being with the dead birds, seeing the bodies whilst life in all its richness of birdsong, sun, leaves, goes on. Life passed into and through those birds just as it does with everything.

> I could die peacefully,
> without vengeance or despair,
> because I know life is made of death,
> being is made of nonbeing,
> all is interdependent,
> and you and I, we contain each other.
>
> Thich Nhat Hanh [5]

There was a freedom gained in seeing this, as well as the beautiful feathers left for me by the birds, as a reminder. C.G. Jung says of spiritual pilgrimage and death:

On a lonely journey, or spiritual pilgrimage it is most common for the initiate to become acquainted with the nature of death. But this is not the death of a last judgement or a trial of strength; it is a journey of release, renunciation and atonement, presided over and fostered by some spirit of compassion.[6]

The meeting with the pheasants was my last encounter with death for a number of years and there were no more dreams. The deep and profound encounter with symbol had penetrated me to the core and has remained.

> Death comes with his impressive scythe and says
> "You should be afraid of me"

I look up and ask
" Why should I be afraid of you?"
" Because I will make you dead.
I will make you non existent.'
" How can you make me non existent?'
Death does not answer.
He swings his impressive scythe
I say, ' I come and go, then I come again, I always come back"
" How do you know that you will come again?' Death asks,
I know because I have done that countless times", I say,
" How do I know that you are telling the truth?'
" Who can be the witness?", Death frowns,
I touch the earth and I say,
" Earth is the witness, she is my mother".
O my Beloved, touch earth every time you get scared,
Touch her deeply
And your sorrow will melt away
Touch her deeply and you will touch the deathless.

Thich Nhat Hahn[7]

During the entire journey there were many opportunities presented for turning the time into a trip, a holiday, or for exciting and at times most enticing opportunities. As I was attuned to warnings from the mythic world about 'fool's gold,' I was able to see that the seduction of stimulation, or the needs of others could, if I let them, entice me away from the true gold. A compassionate response is natural but not to the extent of taking me, at this particular time, from my purpose.

Quite early during my stay, due to an odd set of circumstances I went to an interview and there was offered a hard to come by place in a one year program of *Buddhist* studies. This was sorely tempting as it was being directed at that time by two of my most respected teachers, as well as being in a glorious part of *Devon*. My mounting excitement that day would have had me signing there and then but something restrained me. It said, *wait* before committing. Upon taking one last walk through the enchanting garden before leaving, a tiny person, (or was she a goblin, a fairy?) jumped out from behind a lilac bush, startling me, but quite unperturbed and without solicitation of any kind, said "You won't like it here in the winter, it's grey and gloomy and rains all the time. It's not everything you might think it is." With that she skipped off and out of sight! I don't believe I said a word such was my astonishment. I shook my head and took a photo of the lilac tree to prove that it, at least, existed.

It was enough, as well as that quiet voice within and a vaguely disturbed feeling in parts of the old building, to see that it would be wise to decline and continue onwards without distraction. Robert Johnson says about these experiences:

It is an audacious notion to put forth in this age of science and wilful determination that one's existence is somehow inspired, guided, even managed by unseen forces outside our control. Whether called fate, destiny, or the hand of God, slender threads, (such as being in a particular place at just the right time, meeting someone who steers you in an unforeseen direction) are at work bringing coherence and continuity to our lives. Looking back, it is clear now that my path has always been managed by some benevolent fate.[8]

Later, at the *Krishnamurti* centre, I was to be approached by no less than four people with regard to travelling to India to meet a teacher, *Vimala Thacker*, who intrigued me. Indeed, one day, whilst walking on a country lane, I met a gentlemen who, without any particular solicitation, withdrew an address in India from his jacket pocket as a point of contact for me. Again, I was ready to pack my bags and go. However, another of those exquisitely peaceful evenings in the grove (a very beautiful park belonging to *Krishnamurti*) clarified the necessity of saying, "No." I did visit one remarkable cathedral, *Salisbury*, and spent considerable time there alone, soaking in the atmosphere of *Christianity* embedded in a context of humanitarian advocacy for *Amnesty* International. I was drawn into contemplation of the walking nun who graces the entrance to the cathedral precinct. However, that experience of tourism, as well as reflecting on the sacred well and abbey at *Glastonbury*, was enough. I did not need to go to every cathedral and sacred sight. At this time I did not want to be distracted by a trip with a friend to a stately home to watch the making of a movie, nor get involved in the Arts community, nor the active British dialogue group community, despite my considerable interest. Knowing my enthusiasm for these kind of experiences and a tendency to scatter myself quite thinly, due to curiosity, the power of the inner life during those six weeks was remarkably strong. Or, to put it another way, I was not easily dis-empowered by the usual enthusiasms and provocations.

What *was* needed, for *full- fillment*, were plentiful experiences in nature, in beauty, in quietness, simplicity and solitude. This may have to do with an introverted temperament but more than that, a depth of conviction in sensing where my *sorting* had to come from. It was *from the inside not the outside*. There are times for doing a plenty but this was definitely a time to keep re-selecting being. I believe that this experience altered a long standing pattern and has ultimately determined an entirely new approach to living. I made a number of journal entries along the lines of the following one, showing a deepening appreciation and contentment with the simplicity of living close to nature.

.... Tonight I could have walked forever along the beach and into the sunset, where sea laps the shore and gulls circle. This state of extended being, wholeness, is deeper than anything I have previously experienced. I have been drawn, rather surprisingly, to the Christian tradition over the past two to three weeks. I could not have predicted this. I seem to know it without having to learn it. Is that archetypal? Also the symbols, such as the Celtic cross, the golden communion chalice, the stone font above the water course, are beautiful, mysterious and calling for attention. My interest in the symbolic generally has had a huge re awakening on this journey.

♧ *Question: Where do I feel most content? Under what conditions does my spirit soar?*

Within sight of return to Canada this disturbing question of the life I now intended to live, returned. It became even more intense and unsettling as the time approached for departure. Inevitably in life, decisions are made to live somewhere but I sensed then and now realise, that we can push ourselves along in a pragmatic lifestyle that simply does not feed the soul. It was a challenge at this time to stay with the intensity of questioning and not prematurely rush to imaginary solutions.

.... I spontaneously decided to take a three hour boat trip to a remote island out in the Atlantic ocean, the Isle of Lundy. This turned out to be a magical little gem, and served to deepen my questioning around home, 'holy days' and living a simple life, within a world gone increasingly mad for progress. The island is remote and tiny. I walked all around it in half a day going from the tranquil floral east side with wonderful bird song and perfumes, to the wild Atlantic cliffs of the West with wheeling, calling gulls. Wild ponies and sheep abound there, as do a very few resident

inhabitants who live in simple stone cottages and are connected to the main land only three times a week. During the last hour of my short excursion I talked with a delightful woman who ran the village store, listening to her story of how she ended up living there and wondering to myself, "How do such people do it?" I mean, actually make that decision, the one that the rest of us may vaguely think about, before submitting once again, to the unrelenting daily regime of modern urban existence. The return journey was a special, timeless, ocean crossing in which I sat outdoors in the sunshine communing with water, wave, and seagull, deeply present, yet also watching the background movement of thought as past/future: wanting/aversion.

♧ *Question: How to return to a life of simplicity?*

The last phase of my British quest was spent at *Brockwood Park* the home of the *Krishnamurti* retreat centre. For a number of years, I had been drawn to K's writings and had visited the *Krishnamurti* centre in Canada. I was intrigued by his insistence on life beyond ego preoccupations but often found his manner of speaking abstract and difficult to understand. Nevertheless, the utter sincerity of the man, a sensing of truth in his words, kept me willing to explore further. The place that I found myself was indeed a retreat in the truest sense of the word, with tranquillity permeating the atmosphere. Being left alone to read, write, view tapes, or reflect and meditate was the order of each day with a coming together of community and visitors over meals. The flavour of these was definitely meaningful inquiry. It was indeed the best of circumstances and timing for me, for it allowed me the time and space needed to digest all of the experiences encountered to date. There, I was introduced to the work of *Vimala Thacker* with whom I found an easier resonance than with the writings of *Krishnamurti*, although he was her mentor. It was because of her that I was encouraged to continue to find my own way on this religious quest.

Through clouds of suspicion, indifference, humiliation, life moves onward. Wither? I know not. To respond to everything around is fulfilment. To walk austerely through pain and pleasure, beauty and ugliness, joy and sadness of life, is living in silence in inner stillness. This spontaneous movement of silence is meditation.[9]

This was the most theoretical few days of the entire fifty days and as such was highly valuable in bringing together personal experience with guided consideration. As a result of this contemplative time, my understanding of what I was about deepened considerably. The questions I had invoked were coalescing into one central question.

♧ *Question: How to be alone (all one) in the world, living by and through one's deepest value?*

I had observed different ways of living and being, including those belonging to my own past, predetermined through familial and cultural conditioning. I had observed where, when and how I felt to be at ease. I had watched the guidance of the collective, the synchronous events, the symbolic threads. I knew that upon my return I needed to seek out my true home, as both dwelling and place in the world. I needed to place my faith. I needed to live my own truth.

.... *On the train, I am leaving this country of my rebirth, acknowledging again how this inner work is my true path, is my life. How right I have felt to be here doing this and to be inspired by heroines and heroes who are also following their path of truth. I have often wondered at the faith it has taken to get myself here. The planes, trains and automobiles, crossing oceans, arrangements being made with fruitful uncertainties of tomorrow's unfolding.*

.... *On the plane re-reading, re-viewing, re-collecting, re-filling myself with wonder, and inspiration. It was, all in all a fantastic pilgrimage into Self. Despite some apprehension about return, I largely feel confident, ready, quiet. I am satisfied.*

Not withstanding the heart warmth of friends and family, and the garlanded front door which I returned to, I bumped, rather than glided, back into the confines of the familiar and everyday. I had changed, but this particular landscape had not. I had arrived where I started, and saw the place for the first time. Of course all places have their own beauty, we need only perceive with attuned eyes and ears for it to reveal itself. However, one can only be home, when one feels to be 'at home,' and I saw that here I did not feel to be 'at home.' Nowhere is this made more clear than in the myth, *"The Monster of the Deep,"* which *Helen Luke* loved to tell toward the end of her life.(See appendix).

Maintaining the inner beauty and meaning of the journey, whilst patiently waiting for the next phase to reveal itself was a significant challenge upon returning. I still did not know when I would take the remaining eight days of the gift, but the actual fiftieth was a couple of months away and I began to make rather elaborate travel plans to share it with others on the extreme outer coast of the Pacific West Northwest. The intervening months were spent quietly, returning to work, walking, asking of the wind, the weather, the secrets of the sacred.

> Not I, not I, but the wind that blows through
> A fine wind is blowing the new direction of time
> If only, most lovely of all I yield myself and am borrow
> By the fine, fine wind that takes its course
> Through the chaos of the world   DH Lawrence[10]

Living quietly provides opportunity to become aware of the life in things, not only things of beauty but in the ordinary items of everyday living. In our life long impatience we miss much. I had now refined my capacity for *attending* and had begun to practice it in a way that previously I had understood only fleetingly. Quiet and ordinary times of day, of circumstance, I now re-discovered were full of meaning, even though the larger questions did not have obvious answers.

Four days before departure for the big birthday trip, everything fell through and I mean everything! The complexity of planes, boats, helicopters, weather and mis-communication left me unbelievingly watching the best laid plans unravel. I was not meant to go, another death and an emptiness of a kind which I had not felt for a long time. Still stunned, I was driving on the freeway performing an errand when I spontaneously pulled off and found myself in the parking lot of "Camping Village." An hour later I was stuffing purchases into the trunk of my car, looked up at the magnificent sunset to the South West. I knew that my time had come to 'follow the sun' for the last of the promised days of pilgrimage.

> The world has crystallised into vivid focus. And you respond. You hold your breath or fall into reverie or spring to your feet, according to the day or the mood, there is a continuous sense of being one with the rhythm of all life and all time.   Colin Fletcher[11]

This fiftieth non- event was an inauguration into the Greek concept of *amor fati*, the love of one's fate, which means accepting the life one is summoned to, not the life envisioned by the ego. It is a heroic submission to the Gods; not my will but thine.

> The love of one's fate is, finally, the affirmation that the gods are the gods, and that our task is to respond to their will, wheresoever that road will take us. To take such a road......will lead one to abundance   James Hollis[12]

Embarking with enthusiasm, on this final solo trip into the south western Alberta wilderness, was *not* what I did. Indeed, this outdoor wilderness camping adventure was a far greater challenge for me than taking an aircraft to England. However, I did set out willingly, with faith, food, my animal necklace as talisman (a practise I had adopted many years ago when travelling in the wilderness) and with one myth. Echoing Helen Luke, I knew that it was only by facing fear, thus giving a fundamental consent to insecurity, that we may hope to experience freedom from anxiety.

The most difficult letting go came with the realisation that I would, contrary to all cultural expectations, be quite alone for my fiftieth birthday, a fact which I accepted had been orchestrated by powers greater than mine.... To trust, to let go to this, the mystery, which unfolded.

.... *What about birthdays? Often a culturally conditioned concept of celebration which usually involves food, alcohol, excitement, going somewhere, often expensive, enviable, and with others. Well, mine was now to be none of that. It took some reconciliation to let go of the should, could, if-only's, then packing, heaving my camping gear, food, warm clothes, hiking boots and bike into the car. A three hour drive to the south west brought me to a remote campground found along the evening sun's path, many miles down a dirt road and looking promisingly empty.*

A huge thunderstorm heralded my arrival, hail stones like marbles as I sat and watched and wondered. After it cleared, I and three deer figured out how to erect the new tent along with inner judging voices around incompetence. Old programming needs new love. I felt that the deer were there for just that purpose, as gentle friends. Eventually, I did get organised, ate quickly, walked and sat by the river. "Aha...I can breath now." Darkness fell as I sat contemplating the stars, drawing safe comfort from my camp fire and then falling into a deep timeless sleep.

Morning was cold and clear, sounding with the call of raven, the chatter of gopher. After a hasty breakfast, I drove to a jewel lake further to the west and sat in silent timeless time, by sea green water. Feelings of loss settled into wind born ripples. Artemis is present I thought, as I touched my animal necklace and picked up a purple daisy. Looking down I found a perfect, heart shaped little rock which I released to the depths. In a state of mind which swirled like the water, I remembered another daring pilgrim of this century, D.H. Lawrence.

> The space of the world is immense,
> before me and around me,
> like a soul in a boat on
> very clear deep water....
> Seeing myself isolated in the universe,
> And wondering what effect I can have.
> My hands wave under the heavens like specks of dust
> And are floating asunder.
> I hold myself up and feel a big wind blowing.
> So much is there outside me, so infinitely
> Small am I. What matters if I beat my way minutely ,
> To be lost immediately?
> How shall I flatter myself that I can do anything in such immensity?
> I am too little to count in the wind that drifts me through.[13]

The common denominator of my previous travel and this one was in awareness, in listening, in attention. I find that this is more possible when alone beyond the many sounds of human discourse, the redundancies of language. Constant stimulation requires constant chatter, all too frequently, a patter of meaningless cliches. My realisation at this time was that the freedom I sought was, in part, the freedom from the modern conditioned patterns of living and doing that get in the way of real listening. How much of human life now relies on food, booze, entertainment and endless chatter? Are these the very things which are making us unwell, deadened, depressed? To relinquish these few items from the agenda, if only for a short time, is unthinkable for many but at this time for me, a true joy. Sitting quietly alone, all -one, I was free.

.... Later in the day, as I returned to my canvas domed soul home, more thunder clouds rolled in causing me to I retreat indoors with a lantern, cozy from the downpour. Looking out an hour or so later, a double rainbow arched gracefully over the meadow landing right in front of my doorway. I had been presented with the pot of gold two days before my fiftieth!

.... Morning, earth steaming, evaporating the downpour.Oh what a smell! A butterfly landed on my leg during my meadow yoga, then settled on my sweater for a long time. A creation of brown and black speckles, green hairs along the body, now with wings opening and shutting toward the sun's radiance. When folded the wings are nearly heart shaped. What an exquisite, delicate companion this day had delivered.

I was learning to take my cues from whatever appeared in front of me knowing that in this heightened state of awareness nothing is by accident. So, like a butterfly, I did a bit of wandering here and there, dipping into the myth which I had instinctively brought along, taking a little from here depositing it there, realising that this is how the butterfly does it, this is how the soul does it. My eye and thoughts kept reflecting on the tale of the "The African Necklace," (see appendix) until I understood that it wished to speak with me. What I did not yet know was that it wished to live me. The story is an African tribal/village story, in which the value of a woman's femininity, symbolising her soul development, is displayed through the quality of her necklace, created during the course of her passage from girlhood to womanhood. In the tale the heroine is tricked into parting with her necklace, her Self symbol. She goes through the grief of loss, takes a descent journey to look deeply into herself, and returns with a newly honed identity, symbolised by a new necklace.[14]

.... The river called me early, by a remembered verse by John O'Donahue, as well as the hot day,

> I would love to live like a river flows.
> Carried by the surprise of its own unfolding [15]

.... Setting out along the river bank, I had decided to find the ubiquitous waterfall at the end of the valley. About three kilometres along the parched dry stream around a bend in the river, I came upon, a small but very deep green pool, shaded on the north side. By now I was so hot that it took little thought to strip down and dive in. Cold, naked, down I went. Not once but a number of times, surfacing and descending, alone and daring, reaching into the fathomless below until, at depth, the old woman with her green slimy hair, spoke. She spoke about surrender, trust and compassion, about this amazing world of beauty and spirit, about a life to be lived to the full. She offered a promise of enduring protection. Later laying in the sun, returned now to the normal world, it was all a dream which I had only last night read about,... or was it?

If over explanation separates us from astonishment, I was, and still am, content to be astonished. If there had been any doubt about being 'on my thread' it was now dispelled. I had seen that the risk it took to blossom was being rewarded, a reminder that 'amor fati' is, after all, even amid defeat and confusion, a form of love. To love one's fate is to embrace the loathsome woman of the deep, kiss the suppurating wounds, accept the ignominy of defeat, yet to somehow find that one has been blessed.

.... The first thing to be noticed on the fiftieth day was clear blue, not a cloud anywhere. The first thought, "So the second half will be about clarity, seeing clearly." And so the long awaited and unplanned for day unfolded in an extraordinarily, ordinary way. Not at all what I had expected. By now a seasoned pilgrim, I should have known better than to have expectations. I had in mind to climb, as high as I could, and early, before sun and people showed up to the highest easily accessible summit of the Kananaskis range. There, at 9,500 feet, I enjoyed a perfect peach for breakfast amidst unparalleled solitude and splendour. It was a time both all-one as well as lonely. Walking up and down alternately rejoicing in what was and regretting what was not, both in step with each until, upon descent, I was just walking on no particular summer's day. In 24 hours I had been to the heights and to the depths both literally and metaphorically.

On the drive back I promised myself an ice cream treat at the highway gas stop. As I went to the glass counter to pay I looked down. There, in the case, were three beautiful Indian, beaded necklaces. No others, just those. One made out of jade and porcupine quills drew me. I quickly found out that they had been traded the previous evening by some native people who had no money for gas! And so, my birthday gift walked out of the myth to be lovingly placed around my neck, on the very day of my half century milestone. All else forgotten, I realised the enormity of the revelation of the past two days as the myth was now living me, confirmed through external symbols such as this. Eating my gourmet camp fire celebration meal of pasta and wild mushrooms, I recognised a state of grace at the heart of the mystery; that in the willingness of these fifty days to be lived by reality (at depth), I had gained the immediacy of reality, of this perfectly ordinary/extraordinary moment. Something far more intelligent and unified than I had taken up the living and the telling of this tale.

..........the gate which leads you to this state of mind, in which you live so close to your own heart that you no longer need a language. It is utterly ordinary. It is what you are already.......there is no skill required. It is only a question of whether you will allow yourself to be ordinary, do what comes naturally to you, and what seems most sensible to your heart......and not to the images with which false learning has coated your mind.

Helen Luke[16]

The governing symbols in myths are archetypal, that is, expressing 'primary possibilities' of psychic reaction. C.G. Jung was convinced that the unconscious somehow links up with the structure of inorganic matter to bring about what we term significant coincidence or synchronicity. Such an event is a meaningful arrangement of inner psychic and outer facts. In living out the myth, these chance events in the wilderness appeared. Due to quietening of the discursive mind as well as an openness to the emergence of the archetypal energies, it seems that the world is able to reveal itself in totality. This is far more than we are normally able to see.

One sometimes feels that the unconscious is leading the way in accordance with a secret design. It is as if something is looking at me, something that I do not see but that sees me....... But this creative aspect of the psychic nucleus can come into play only when the ego gets rid of all purposive and wishful aims and lets go to a deeper, more basic form of existence. The ego must be able to listen attentively and to give itself without any further design or purpose.

C. G Jung.[17]

.... After a gourmet, evening campfire meal with two deer for company, I sat later on precious earth, looking up at a million dollar view of golden, sunset bathed mountains. Now that is a birthday to remember! For desert, I had an urge to walk barefoot into that golden light, feet devouring lush green grass. Sitting under a tree, looking down on my empty chair way below at the edge of the meadow, no human anywhere, I 'saw' everything whole and complete. "So here it is," I

thought, "the birthday symbol is none other than my own empty chair!"
(For many years after the Buddha's death an empty chair was used as
the symbol to represent 'Buddha-nature'.)
.... Quietly by the fire, evening settles on this figure of a lone woman,
sitting just here, just now, always, never. The fire crackles, the river flows
in the valley, deep pools are filled with wisdom, this body breathes. No
one to think up complications and the sunset is magnificent.

I felt this to be the end of the journey even though two more
days remained out of the promised fifty but perhaps they would appear
later, or perhaps not at all. Nothing of nature ever fits into perfectly
appointed categories of time. My learning was completed, not with 'now
I have the answer' but with a circular symbol of magnificence, an
abiding revelation. There was also trust, that if I returned to doing what
comes naturally then all would unfold as my, and only my, destiny. It
had been necessary for me to walk in compassion, with my own failures
and sorrows, to stay alert, to remain connected to context, to read and
breath archetypal truths, to lick the wounds of painful sores, to embrace
death and loss, to be reborn, sanctified from the heights and the depths.
To know that I would never fear being alone. It now remained to
exchange the old necklace for the new and to follow the directions for
leave taking.
.... On the last day, one of peace and completion, (of a cycle of
setting out, death, all-oneness, and now resurrection) the loose threads
had come together in a woven fabric. I meditated in the sun and then sat
for a long time with feet in cold running water, thinking of the descent to
the goddess, all of it speaking now with meaning and necessity as a
result of this journey. By early afternoon, thunder clouds appeared
again, a signal that it was time for departure. I packed leisurely, readying
to leave my protected home. Out of respect for the sacred, as well as
gratitude, I thoughtfully chose and left behind, a rock, shaped like a
bird/fish. Walking one last time to the river I gave back to the waters of
life, a small rock shaped like a woman. Poised on the precipice, warm
from my hand then cooled in those waters, it was claimed by the river in
remembrance of this epiphany. On the way home, stopping briefly at
'my' lucky gas bar, I found a beautiful key ring with a beaded mandala
design. I accepted this last gift as the key to the road ahead.

Slowly, calm as sky, rooted as earth, fluid as a mountain stream,

I made my way back, knowing on my own pulse what *Meister Eckhard* had previously only intimated to me in words,

> Wisdom consists in doing the next thing you have to do.
> Doing it with your whole heart and finding
> Delight in doing it.   James Hollis [18]

Within a few weeks of returning I was invited to lead a women's group for one year. The request was to help these women to find a way to, "get to know themselves better." As a result I was able to reflect on, then work out, some ways of symbolically approaching the key elements of my own inner journey. These could, in symbolic form, possibly provide a map for others. Included were suggestions from respected wisdom teachers, practices which they considered essential for the integration of body/mind/spirit, along the hero's/heroine's path. The outcome has been seven years of dwelling with other self appointed pilgrims through the *Innerscape* one year guided pilgrimage into Self.

23

2

Building a foundation

The High –priestess of the ancient world
has been silent for fifteen hundred years now.
Many writers recorded her words and oracles
All knew her first motto: *"Know thyself."*[1]

It is Sunday. A Sunday for collecting and centering.

The day cannot decide upon the season, although the leaves are many shades of bronzed shedding. It is time, after a summer of anticipation, for the group of pilgrims to cast off the garments of the familiar, to travel westwards to a higher elevation and the proximity of winter's barren branches. People arrive early, others arrive late, one who lost all time today. Our habits, mistakes and defenses precede us, are packed in the basket, along with journals, pens, wonder, nervousness. The room is warmly yellow and inviting.

Elements of East/West wisdom teachings, integrated into personal learning following my own quest, had slowly distilled into components, ones which I found essential to the 'work' of inner pilgrimage. Means and ways of addressing essential questions were worked out to fit into the format of our gatherings as well as the constraints of people's every day lives. Specific approaches to *'questioning through experience'* have evolved over time and with feedback but the foundation of proper inner attention remains the same for any pilgrimage:

Conditions of the quest as vulnerability, waiting, an instinctive decision, a stated intention, risk, then movement.
Trust in intuitive questions, in synchronous responses, in silence.
Faith in the reliable ground of home, of the sacred.
Wonder at symbolic appearances.

intensive re-examination! It is also most helpful to see each other in truth, for we learn much from seeing in each other what we have not yet been able to claim or release in ourselves. It is a step by step process taken with careful consideration, what one may call a religious attitude, one which extracts meaning from everyday life. Defeats and disappointments are especially instructive. Nothing actually compels us to find meaning which is perhaps why many who live habitual and unexamined lives feel depressed. We simply feel better when our lives are more meaningful.

> "Meaning makes a great many things endurable-perhaps everything."
>
> C.G Jung [5]

For this reason, symptoms are to be welcomed as a starting point for questioning. For, to find possible meaning in suffering, is the first step to its release. It is not a question of wanting to know why we suffer, rather asking the symptoms to reveal their deeper symbolic significance.

> Symptoms humiliate..........Cure of symptoms may but restore the ego to its former ruling position The humiliation of symptoms is one of the ways we grow humble-the traditional mark of the soul
>
> James Hillman [6]

Once symptoms are seen as symbols then healing of the soul is never far away, for healing most frequently 'just happens.' It is represented on the outside by some form of symbolic transformation, for example, in my case, the 'old' necklace being replaced with the 'new' one. There is a quality of letting rather than trying in this attitude to questioning, as well as healing. It is not a matter of curiosity, which can lead to narrow introspection, but rather being openly contemplative, as in taking a long and loving look at what is there.

To encourage this as attitude and process I encourage active forms of symbolic meditation through drawing, creating, for example personal renderings of the great Self symbols, the *Tree* and the *Mandala*.

The Tree of Life

> The Tree refers to the life of the cosmos at the macro level and the life of the individual at the micro level. It's source is rooted in the ground of being and it's fruit the treasure which man set out to find, but few obtain.
>
> Roger Cook [7]

The *Tree*, is an ancient, mythological as well as natural symbol. Curiously, it is one of the first symbols drawn by all children everywhere, regardless of circumstance. (Baker 1982)[8] Often referred to as *The Cosmic Tree*, it is an image which has been seen as representational of our path of evolution by many religious traditions. C. G. Jung saw *tree* as a symbol of the psyche, where the self is felt to be in a parallel process of growth. This process he named *individuation*, whereby we become more wholly ourselves, much as the acorn does in its gradual ascent into a mighty oak. So this longing for growth is felt metaphorically as upward and outward like branches and downward into roots.

All tree images are perceived visually as a vertical axis, known in cosmic terms as the *axis mundi* (world axis) which passes through three zones, the underworld, earthly world and the sky world. Today, we live in an individualized culture, therefore it is most useful to consider the *axis mundi* as 'soul center,' including but not limited by I/me. James Hillman defines depression as,

"The world-soul's sickness, announcing its despair through me."[9]

In ancient literature, a *serpent* is often associated with the lower aspects of the *tree*, containing and responding to the moon and *Great Mother* cycles of birth and death. *Eagle*, is associated with the upper tree, in possessing aspects of freedom from earthly constraint. The *Tree of Life* and The *Tree of Knowledge* appear in Genesis as myths which have powerfully shaped the evolution of the Western psyche. According to Jewish mythology, one only arrives at the Tree of Life by finding a pathway through the Tree of Knowledge. The Tree of Life appears on all Islamic carpets, calling earth bound individuals to seven levels of prayer and worship. In kundalini or chakra yoga, now popular in the west, the body is thought of as possessing an 'axis,' which is the spinal column. The life force, which travels along energetic pathways or meridians, was traditionally imaged as a serpent laying coiled at the base of the " spinal tree." The aim of yoga practices therefore was, and still is, to arouse this sleeping energy such that it rises, passing through the *chakra* centers to the crown chakra and transcendental dimensions.

There are numerous available interpretations of '*chakras*' which can be confusing for the seeker but what all do agree upon is that the difficult ascent of the body's 'tree' can be imaged as a twofold path, reflecting human polarities of masculine and feminine, mundane and spiritual. As we develop through different qualities of experience, referenced by ascending chakras or energy level frequencies, we have the possibility of bringing about balance, a union of opposites in which a breakthrough in consciousness is experienced. Suddenly leaves sprout.

The motive of the twofold path, imaged in the East as intertwining serpents, has been demonstrated at the molecular level, a few thousand years later, as the structure of the DNA molecule, the code of life. The spiral motif is an archetypal model for the process of physical, psychological and spiritual growth. In the Western tradition it appears as the *Caduceus*, the staff of *Hermes*, healer of souls, messenger of the Gods, and master of the hermetic art of alchemy (the forerunner of modern psychology). This symbol is to be found on medical prescriptions for, among other curatives, antidepressants!

C.G. *Jung*,[10] saw a direct correlation between this alchemical or *kundalini* transformation and the more modern idea of individuation, becoming more fully and wholly who we are. After examining thousands of dreams, his own and others, he realized that the image of the *tree* most often appeared in people's dreams at critical periods when there was a need for a supporting image of growth and integration. This image spoke and healed in a way that many well meaning words could not. *Jung* understood that our earth living context of trees speaks to us continually as a reminder of the three parts of ourselves, unconscious source (root), conscious realization (trunk) and supra conscious liberation (crown of leaves, flowers and fruit).

It is for these reasons, rooted in the mythological, psychological and spiritual dimensions, that we begin the *Innerscape* journey by contemplating and rendering as image, a personalized tree. This first activity, both in process and product, reveals much about inner tendencies, habits of mind and doing, in approaching this task.

.... *When I first went outside to draw my tree. I walked around it a couple of times, looked under and between the branches and just kind of studied the way it stood. Then I sat down beside it and looked up at it from a different angle. After a couple of minutes, I seemed to be rooting with the tree. It was a fairly cool day when I drew my tree, but the sun was shining, I could almost feel how the tree felt, with the sun shining on it, soaking up the warmth, before the winter season is upon us. When I* started to draw I had no idea that I had that much creativity in me. I live out in the country and there are trees all around us but I have never really taken the time to actually look before.

.... Drawing my tree was a lot of fun. Since then I have been thinking a lot about trees. As I started to draw the main branches I realized I needed to make the roots stronger, deeper, or else my tree would fall over. Down deep there are rocks, in the way sometimes, but the roots either go around or embrace the rock, or are sometimes stunted. Coloring in the trunk, I felt a lot of movement and flow, upwards and downwards. This tree is a big one, tired and in need of a rest. I feel content as I color, it makes me think of the spectacular Fall colors. I love my tree it waits with hope for Spring to come. It has helped a family of robins safely raise their young.

The Mandala

In the seventeenth century *John Bunyan* wrote his still famous book, "Pilgrim's Progress," which was depicted pictorially as a circular movement towards an inner center. Heaven was to be found at the center with many pitfalls along the path of reaching that very center. Among the many mythological representations of Self, from diverse cultures, the enlightened one or seer is represented in the center of a circle divided into four. *Jung* used the word *mandala* (magic circle) to designate structure of this order, as a symbolic representation of the 'nuclear atom' of the psyche whose essence we do not know. Some aboriginal groups, for example *Native Americans*, experience the inner center directly as who they are. Native leader, *Black Elk* says,

Everything the power of the world does, is done in a circle. The sky is round, and I have heard that the earth is round like a ball, and so are all the stars. The wind in its greatest power, whirls. Birds make their nests in circles, for theirs is the same religion as ours. The sun comes forth and goes down again in a circle. The moon does the same and both are round. Event he seasons form a great circle in their changing and always come back again to where they were. The life of a man is a circle from childhood to childhood, and so it is in everything where power moves.[11]

Other communities use the *mandala* motif to restore a lost inner balance. For example the *Navaho Indians*, by means of *mandala* structured sand paintings, heal a sick person by bringing them back into harmony with the cosmos. We are familiar nowadays with the amazing sand *mandalas*, constructed by the *Tibetan monks*, beautiful and precise constructions which are used to consolidate the inner being, or to enable both creator and observer to become centred. The monks use their temple *mandalas* to recreate order when there is disturbance, as well as to bring previously unspoken possibilities into existence.

Magnificent examples of *mandalas* are found in all great cathedrals, for example the magnificent rose window of *Notre Dame*. They are there for similar reasons, to conduct the soul/psyche away from external life and its secular concerns inwards toward God. Architecturally, towns and cities were, from the middle ages onwards, formed around the center which was symbolized in the church or cathedral. This central location was to encourage people to remain simultaneously aware of both the periphery of life ('me' in the world) as well as the living reality of the Self, or the life of, "God in man." The soul life.

There is a tendency to assume that a point or place is an identifiable center, whether it be of a town, an orange or a circular artistic creation. However, the point marked as center is, of necessity, larger than the true center. No matter how much we decrease the central point, the true center is at the center of that, hence smaller yet. The circumference is that line around the center which is at all points equidistant from it. But since we can never know the length of the radius, it may be said of any circle we can imagine, that our *mandala* is larger than that. It is 'smaller than small' and 'bigger than big.' This is why the *mandala* is the symbol of the *Self*. It has the qualities of the circle, the center and the circumference, yet, like the *Self* it is more than any possible definition of these qualities. Whatever name we give to that which dwells at center, God, Goddess, Self, Spirit, Deity, Delphic Oracle, Great White Buffalo, Atman, Tao, it is always smaller, yet more than we can know or imagine. An ancient quote attributed to St. Bonaventure sums it up as, "God is a circle whose center is everywhere and whose circumference is nowhere."

The fact that the *Tibetan sand mandalas* are destroyed on the fifth day emphasizes that the process of approaching center is the important factor, not the realization, which is an impossible goal. In the contemplation of *mandalas*, because both center and periphery are unified as a visual gestalts, there arises a feeling of inner peace, a sense that life has again found meaning and order. Generally roundness, wherever it is found, suggests a sense of wholeness, completeness. Enough has been said to show that a simple circle with a center has enormous integrating power.

There is something in the human condition that we may call the nostalgia for paradise. By this we mean the desire to find oneself always and without effort at the center of the world, at the heart of reality"   Albert Low[12]

Pilgrimages to find this center are often fraught with difficulty and obstacles, both in journey and approach toward an ever disappearing goal. Once engaged in a *mandala*, the relationship of periphery and center is not a simple one. In much of our daily inner discourse we quite unconsciously place ourselves at the center of the world as in 'my story,' the events which are happening to me. Less easy, is to place ourselves at the periphery where someone or something else is at the center such that myself is an observer-participant. The interest of the *psychoanalytic school of object relations* seeks to understand the protective strategies of the ego when viewed from one or other of these two 'positions.' The less developed place asks the question, "What has the other done to me?" (therefore, how will I protect myself from the harmful other?) The second, asks "What have I done to other" (therefore, how will I compensate?) Depending on age, circumstance, maturity, we will all oscillate between these two modes of being in the world. The third possibility, suggested in *Eastern wisdom discourse*, is the collapse of both aspects, with the realization that there truly is no self separate from other. This is the '*Great Teaching*' from the East, leading us in our own inquiry and meditation practices, to the ultimate question, the one I began my own quest with, "What is Me?" This has the effect of stretching the quoted *Delphic Oracle* "know thyself" to the limit of paradox.

Religious practices of the human race are designed to maintain and restore the power of the centre through ritual, ceremony, prayer, contemplation. Because of the unifying power of the One, the antagonism inherent in the two centres, me-as-centre, and me-as-periphery, is laid to rest.   Edward Edinger[13]

One in whom this paradox has been unified, is the one at the place of the thousand petaled lotus, (the seventh level of energetic balance) or the one who has been released from the suffering of 'meness,' thus, united with divine energy. This is the goal of all traditional spiritual pilgrimages.

The mandala is the major symbolic expression for the experience of being an individual. Such an image emerges spontaneously from the unconscious at times when all the grand and terrible implications of being a unique indivisible lonely monad are beginning to dawn on the individual The experience which the mandala symbolizes is by all evidence the most central and fundamental fact of human existence   C.G. Jung[14]

The *Innerscape* journey, as far as possible, is taken on experience and less on theoretical concepts, for it is more effective to 'get it' from creating, living, looking, walking (as labyrinth) one or many *mandalas* than it is to track the words about it. The making of a personal *mandala*, as well as coloring in a number of specific *mandalas* holds healing potential for disturbances. These activities have the capacity to allow one to dwell with both center and periphery. We are moved outside in, as well as inside out, meanwhile dwelling within a sacred container. It also shows us that we are all unexpectedly capable of original artwork!
.... *Drawing and coloring my mandala was a lot of baby steps. I never thought I was creative before but my inner voice was saying, "Yes, you are."the making of the personal mandala proved to me that I am!*
.... *The mandala was a very interesting process. I started out nervous and apprehensive as I am not very artistic. The fact that I analyze everything to death made it more laborious than it needed to be. The most interesting part was my "family" section which I thought would be most important but ended up absent because I just couldn't decide on what to put in it. It gave me a lot of trouble and I kept coming back to it. Eventually I decided it wasn't meant to be in my mandala, reaffirming this as a year to focus on myself—very enlightening!!*
.... *The mandala process was spectacular. I dove right into it and just kept going. I came in with some ideas and none of them went on to the paper. It all just flowed for the whole month I drew and colored. I didn't want to finish and left the fire to the very last, taking days to contemplate and study fire before coloring. I finally finished and felt so proud that I drew something so cool!*

Myth Study

> The man who thinks he can live without myth or outside it, like one uprooted, has no true link either with the past, or with the ancestral life which continues within him, or yet with contemporary human society?
>
> Joseph Campbell[15]

Everyone knows that *myths* aren't true. The word in general usage means exactly that, a *falsehood*. It is because of the scientific methodology of our era that we are able to dispel, for example, ancient biblical stories. Ones such as woman being made out of a man's rib, all of us being kicked out of the garden of paradise which we may only return to after long and tediously prescriptive behaviors, a baby being born from an unfertilized egg, a man living inside a whale, all the *animals of the world being packed into a boat for a few months.*

It is not only our western tradition that has these enduring stories. Indeed, they were preceded by millennia of human existence and paralleled in all cultures. The curious aspect of this is that the same themes in different disguises, determined largely by immediate context, have been going on for as long as we have. In spite of us knowing the fabrications involved we still routinely tell these tales, such as the nativity, to our children and love them! Worse, governing bodies of men throughout history have ordained ruthless persecutions for the sake of sustaining these myths as fact. It is happening today in the middle east, much as it happened in the western world for a thousand years or more. There were those ancient Greeks who, as rational scholars, already knew that the earth was round not flat, who already knew that our planet revolved around the sun and not the other way round. They also knew that there were many more species on the planet than would fit into an ark. They died for these 'heresies,' whilst the myths were sustained. Why then would we now not only preserve but revive the telling of these tales?

Joseph Campbell, devoted his distinguished career to looking at that question, writing significant works as a result of exhaustive anthropological study on man and his mythology. In his book, *"Myths to Live By,"*[16] he tells us that it is through the understanding of the nature of our psyche that we can find a frame of reference for these enduring myths.

When these stories are interpreted, not as reports of historic fact, but as merely imagined episodes projected onto history, and when they are recognized as analogous to like projections produced elsewhere, China, Egypt, India, the Yucatan; the import becomes obvious, that although false and to be rejected as accounts of physical history, such universally cherished figures of the mythic imagination must represent facts of the mind.[17]

As initiation of his life work, Campbell's exploratory questions were, "Who invents these impossible tales? Where do their images come from? Why, though obviously absurd, are they everywhere so reverently believed?"

They (myths) speak not of outside events, but of themes of imagination. And since they exhibit features which are universal they must in some way represent features of our general racial imagination, permanent features of the human spirit, or, as we say today, of the psyche. They are telling us, therefore, of matters fundamental in ourselves, enduring essential principles about which it would be good for us to know if our conscious minds are to be kept in touch with our own most secret motivating depths. [18]

In "The Cry for Myth," author and psychoanalyst, Rollo May, looks more closely at the link between human psychology and myth.[19] He finds that myth is essential to maintaining mental health and relieving neurotic guilt and mental anxiety. He gives as example, the time in ancient Greece when myths were vital and strong, then individuals were able to meet the problems of existence without personal struggle. All myths were a vehicle for discussion of beauty, truth, goodness, and courage as values for human life. Unfortunately, people nowadays rarely turn to myths for making sense of their inner world, consequently are alone with their demons, or else, turn to psychotherapists to somehow magically disengage this lonely inner fight.

Whether we go to the latest movie, opera, ballet, or theater, we will find myth, for mythic symbolism is at the basis in all resonant art. This represents more than a pleasurable experience, an evening's entertainment. Myth reveals a process of thought, man's response to the universe, his fellow travelers and his separate being with a purpose. The protagonist in any myth is an archetypal character, expressing in a highly graphic, charged, dramatic and energetic way, our own ways of doing and being which at times hold us in their unflinching grasp.

Myths are permanent because they deal with the greatest of all problems, which do not change because men and women do not change. They deal with love, with war, with sin, with tyranny, with courage with fate; and all in some way or other deal with the relations of man to those divine powers which are sometimes to be cruel, and sometimes to be just.   G.Hyatt[20]

A philosopher of the nineteenth century, *Schelling(1856-91)*, set about uncovering the transformations of consciousness throughout history from the earliest beginnings of mankind. Of particular significance is that he based his stages of transformation on the history of mythology. By means of detailed studies *Schelling* arrived at a crucial insight, namely, that *the inner development of the myths and the process of their emergence in the course of history, reflected and embodied the inner spiritual development of man.* It was C. G. Jung who took this work further, showing that *myths are archetypes of psychic experience, present in us all and from the beginning of mankind.* It takes, he said, only a pertinent and related experience in our lives to reactivate these archetypes.

An image is to be regarded as archetypal when it can be shown to appear in identical form, and with the same significance, in the documents of human history.["21]

C. G. Jung, Joseph Campbell, Rudolph Steiner, Robert Johnson and others, have made significant contributions in this century by alerting us to the necessity of viewing our individual lives from a historical and communal perspective. They have repeatedly emphasized that our *mythological heritage is one of our greatest treasures* and that the psychic life of humans disintegrates when we loose it. We are still drawn to great dramas like *Hamlet* because they are mythic. They represent the existential crises in everyone's lives.

Plato, recommended that all education should begin with myth telling rather than mere facts or so called rational teaching, a value still practiced in *Waldorf* education with children and in *Innerscape* with adults. The premise being that it is attention to the 'what' of our lives, not the how, which offers us the possibility for contentment. In his critique of the technological era, poet *Archibald MacLeish* asks what has happened in the twentieth century when,

.....we are deluged with facts, but we have lost or are losing, our human ability to feel them. We know with the head now, by the facts, by the abstractions. We seem unable to know as Shakespeare knew who made King Lear cry out to blinded Gloucester on the heath, "you see how this world goes," and Gloucester answers; " I see it feelingly"[22]

In having the opportunity to identify with heroes and heroines we are able to connect with our own hidden aspirations, hopes, dreams possibilities and meaning. Similarly, when we discover that our experience of fear, disillusion and futility is more than a matter of personal dismay, that it is shared by all people, then we become reassured that there are ways of dealing with the archetypal problem.

Myth stands in relation to mankind in general as a dream does to the individual. A dream shows the individual an important psychological truth about himself. A myth shows an important psychological truth that applies to mankind as a whole. A person who understands a dream understands himself better; a person who grasps the inner meaning of a myth is in touch with the universal spiritual question life asks of all of us.
Robert Johnson[23]

During the year's preparatory reading, many group members have now read or re-read a myth for the first time since childhood.

Previous groups have been all-women, which means that we have had opportunity to study a myth about feminine development, "The Handless Maiden." This story is especially relevant to growing up in a patriarchal culture in which father-knows-best as well as the negative consequences of wanting what we don't have. The central character of the myth sacrifices her hands (the capacity for independent living) but courageously uses this betrayal to set out on her own journey, trusting in the goodness of others, in synchronicity and in the wisdom of being drawn toward her own evolution. As testimony to the power of the unconscious and being 'lived by a myth,' one woman fell on ice and injured her wrist after the very first reading of the story. The result was that she was incapacitated, in much the same way as the heroine, for seven months. For that period of time she lost the use of her dominant hand, her 'doing' capacity. It was a costly lesson yet invaluable, as she learned much during that time.

"The Maiden King," a myth about the reunion of feminine and masculine, has been chosen for the present mixed gender group. The story addresses a loss of meaning, which we have discussed as being evident in contemporary life and sustained by our 'forgetting.' Robert Bly, as a modern day story teller, sorts out for us the archetypal images and metaphors of the tale, as well as showing comparisons with other stories from other traditions (this story is of Russian descent), whilst Marion Woodman focuses on the realm of the unconscious. She relates the psychological maturing of the hero in the course of the myth, which is us, as serious inquirers. Myth can be thought of as the supporting beams of a house, invisible but necessary for the maintenance of stability and the integrity of the whole culture. Similarly, the structure of this story may provide that function for the group as they engage in the often painful and unsettling work of recovery of their inner sleeping selves.

Meditation

> Though one sits in meditation in a
> particular place, the Self within,
> Can exercise its influence far away.
> Though still, she moves everything everywhere.
> Katha Upanishad 2.21[24]

Regular silent reflection during pilgrimage is important as a balance for activity and a chance for reflection on present conditions. A simple *meditation* practice can be done anywhere, anytime and requires no equipment, no prerequisites. The number one cause of all depressive illness is mental fatigue and it is a commitment to daily meditation practice which most successfully reduces this fatigue. Anyone who sincerely sits quietly, without distraction, remaining aware of the breath and the *stillness behind movement* for say fifteen minutes, a couple of times a day, will find their mental outlook refreshed and calm, even more so than after a long nap. This is by no means the purpose, or intention of meditation but it is one of the most essential and astounding side benefits as an antidote for our cultural malaise. Simply put it reduces anxiety and allows insight into the root cause of anxiety, for it is primarily an anxious state of mind (too much to do, too little time to do it in), which leads directly to cerebral overload and exhaustion.

One therapist told me that she finds the greatest resistance of all in trying to have people look at their schedules with a view to deleting items. I wonder what would happen if we asked the soul about the day timer, or the palm pilot? *How does soul find accommodation within the day?* Is there time for dreams, daydreams, quality time with others, for time in nature, for time off?

To my mind, there is clearly a place for the skills and knowledge acquired during........solitude---knowledge about the solitude, it's significance, its imaginative richness, its relation to death, and its education in love. Also the value of staying with tough stuff in a time of the fast fix and the quick buck. There is a place for the strength of character and subtlety of insight that the investigation of interiority produces. I call this psychological engagement, "soul making"...

James Hillman[25]

    Daily personal practice forms the foundation for all other aspects of inquiry as well as re balancing the action/being equation of living. Without settling the active mind true questing is impossible for the program elements will remain at a level of intellectual curiosity which does not open the way to direct knowing or insight. I do not insist on, or even recommend at this time, rigid adherence to traditional meditation paths or religious devotional practices. Rather, trusting that 'truth is a pathless land,' and pilgrimage intensely personal, I suggest that each person find their own way to spend in contemplative silence on a daily basis. What is important is to set aside the time consistently making the necessary effort. Walking slowly in nature, sitting quietly in a chair, watching a candle or a sunset for focus or a more elaborate seasonal altar, sitting in the bathroom with a candle lit and the door locked, all may provide a sacred space, a small piece of heaven, where 'I/me' becomes the listening receptor for Self, and the soul's activity is expanded. If this is done sincerely, then it will bring about a new life time habit also a sense of what is possible, by creating a space in busyness for stillness.

Sit down in this circle.
Quit acting like a wolf, and feel
The Shepherd's love filling you.
At night, the beloved wanders.
Don't take pain killers.
Be empty of worrying.
Think who creates thought!
Why do you stay in prison
When the door is so wide open?
Move outside the tangle of fear thinking.
Live in Silence.
Flow down and down in always
Widening rings of Being.

Rumi[26]

.... *"This may be a dumb question, but why is silence important. Why do we do this at all?"* This is a good question! At the time it was asked, quite spontaneously, I pointed to my little topaz cross on the altar and said, *"That symbol shows us why."*

Only in this kind of deliberate quietness are we able to gain insight into how our lives may be out of balance. *Robert Johnson* says we are in *heresy every time doing and being, heaven and earth, are not balanced in our lives.* The symbol of the *celtic cross* (a tree and a *mandala*) pictorially shows us the balance of the *doing/being horizontal polarity* and the *matter/freedom vertical polarity.* The center of the cross and the circle is where we dwell when things are in balance as we experience wellness, happiness, freedom. It is also important to understand that *silence of mind is not the same as a failure of speech* and does not lead to this. We can, and will, during the course of the *Innerscape* explorations, take a thoughtful look at patterns of speech and its redundancies, but for now, we are intentionally choosing to cultivate the opposite, namely absence of speech. This does not mean that we become increasingly unable to express ourselves, but that we now have silence as a possibility, a chosen state with its own purpose, which will be revealed by the willingness to give it a go.

Sitting comfortably, with the spine erect to facilitate complete breathing and alert relaxation, meditation practice involve attending to the breath as it enters, passes through, then leaves the body. Simultaneously being aware of changing sensations in the physical body, and mind. The words *awareness* and *attention* are used frequently to encourage the group to deeply enter into exactly what is going on in the here and the now. This does not mean that we strive after awareness, for it is not something to get, have and use. *You don't seek awareness, you simply are aware.*

Whilst the West does have a contemplative tradition currently enjoying a resurgence of interest, it is from the East that we have, in the past two or three decades, learned about meditation states and possibilities. One cannot read any of the instructional literature without coming across the word *mindfulness.* Simply put, *this refers to the capacity of present attention to maintain clear and stable observation of a chosen object,* whether a visualized image or some aspect of one's own body/mind. Mindfulness is to be fully present in 'what is,' without getting overly involved in content. This stable, clear state of witnessing, involves developing and training an easily distracted mind, the one that is generally preoccupied with habitual programs, associations and commentaries about, 'I,' me' and 'myself.'

In order to train the mind we practice by sitting still, breathing, watching and returning again and again to what is here and now without any further add on. Slowly, one realizes that the mind need not be thought of as a container that gets constantly filled up but can be experienced as an open possibility where something more may take place. As we rest in this quietly reflective state we begin to discover that our identity is deeper than we had supposed.

This sounds fine but after a couple of sitting periods as well as a silent walk outside it becomes apparent that this practice is far more difficult than the simple instructions would indicate. All this talk of clarity when most people are just caught up in being high jacked by the next train of thought. How to get to the place where thought does not constantly tug the observing mind unwittingly off on some new pathway? A train, I find, is quite a useful metaphor. Unpacking, can be done many times at many train stations! There are other strategies to assist in letting go of habits of mind, of adhesion to content, of a tendency to augment content, which masks over the perennial quiet presence and depth of being that is the constant backdrop of mental activity. As this latter tendency grows with familiarity then these strategies for dealing with distracting mental content can be dropped, as a steady mind state unfolds.

Normally the life of a North American is driven by restlessness and acquisition, all of which keep us moving and often well ahead of our-Self. This practice is a significant antidote to that generalized state of doing, doing, doing. At first it feels odd, uncomfortable and at times very painful because we have poor posture from too much chair sitting. It helps to learn to realign the posture in yoga. Besides a physical disability for sitting still, awareness reveals that mind and body are constantly shaping and responding to each other. This is good news as releasing stresses and tensions held in the body will simultaneously loosen the mind. If you follow either body or psyche far enough it brings you to the other. This has huge implications for the treating of somatic complaints, from headaches, to terminal illnesses.

When a frog is put
On the center of a plate
She will jump off the plate
After just a few seconds.
If you put the frog back on again
She will again jump off.
You have so many plans.
There is something you want to become
Therefore you always want to make a leap,
A leap forward.
It is difficult
To keep the frog still
On the center of the plate.
You and I
Both have buddha nature in us.
This is encouraging,
But you and I
Both have frog nature in us.
That is why
The first attainment
Of the practice-
Froglessness is its name.

Thich Nhat Hanh[27]

Hatha Yoga

Know the Self as lord of the chariot,
The body as the chariot itself,
The discriminating intellect as charioteer,
And the mind as reins

Katha Upanishad 3.3[28]

A daily *hatha yoga* practice of physical poses chosen to systemically reflect the current psychological inquiry is the remaining foundation for inner pilgrimage. Some people have never been to a yoga class so are challenged, initially, by participating in a full weekend of yoga. This initial workshop is designed to re balance all seven energy centers in the body. It sounds like a lot but much can be done at a simple level, for stretching and opening the body does not need to be complex *in order to be effective*. With the use of some well chosen support props most people are able to 'do' everything. Much like art work, those who believe themselves to be incapable of this, find themselves pleasantly surprised, even amazed, by the benefits.

.... I came to yoga angry and upset with someone, I was at the end of my rope, but the yoga settled me down a lot, so that I was able to find a prayer. I have an inner voice that says I am too fat for yoga which set me off feeling depressed.....but I did feel a lot better after.

.... At first, on Friday and Saturday I didn't notice anything all that significant but Sunday was quite different, I don't really know how to describe it. There was a definite energy shift with the heart chakra work. I felt sad and grumpy for a couple of days, I also came home thinking that I was exhausted, but couldn't sleep. Seems that I was totally relaxed and did not know it.

..........Time became irrelevant. My mind did not wander from the activities I was involved in. I started out apprehensive, as my yoga is only at a "beginner's stage."On leaving, my body was weary, but strong. My mind was clear and I definitely had a smile on my face.

.... I found yoga amazing. It was exactly what my body and spirit needed. I was shocked at the amount of stuff I hold in my back, shoulders and neck and found the poses there to be intense. I definitely need to work on improving my posture, not surprising that constantly living in the future and always striving are habits that I'm currently de-programming.

By definition, the word yoga means to balance and what is being balanced is matter and spirit. Along the horizontal axis, what is brought to balance is the left side and right side, traditionally associated with feminine and masculine, or moon and sun. This is the root meaning of the words "ha" and "tha." As well it is important to consider balance of front and back. In Western culture we are frequently ahead of ourselves, rushing toward the future, resulting in a sense of being ' all at the front.' We have thoroughly embodied the great discovery of the past century, acceleration. The body thrusts forward,(to meet the next goal) with the result that the back is compromised, leading to middle age 'back' problems. Students are reminded to move with awareness, in the back of the body, to walk forwards as though walking backwards, to pull thoughts to the back of the head. This results in a whole new take on life!

All yoga asanas or postures are practiced for equal amounts of time on both sides of the body. A short experiment shows where lateral preferences are, so that practice may be readjusted to emphasize the non dominant side. Without exception, all yoga poses are designed to bring about a *balanced and open relationship between ground, breath and spine*. The *spine* is the first structure that forms inside the womb, legs, arms etc arising from the spine. In a baby it is soft and supple but as we age it often becomes stiff and inflexible due to years of resisting gravity using strength without flexibility. An ancient yogi from Israel wisely taught that, "You are as old as the flexibility of your spine."

Many spines shorten due to stress and constriction, increasing the effects of gravity, as a result the spine does not 'flow' when in motion. Exaggerated areas develop as a result of compromised movement and habitual holding patterns. Associated with this is a blockage of the related energy center, to be seen visually as an abnormal curvature of the spine. The deliberate elongation of the spine as well as a compensatory backward suction, help to resist the ravages of age and life. When standing correctly, as practiced in the foundation mountain pose, there is a feeling of liveliness, as energy flows unrestricted through the spine, perhaps for the first time in a long time! Because of the space created especially in the center of the body, the breath is also able to flow more freely, contributing to a sense of energy and well being.

Mountain pose symbolizes stability and cessation of movement. The base of the pose is firmly established as connection between feet and earth, the center of the pose is stillness in the sacrum (the back of the belly) and the upper body experiences a sense of expansiveness. All other poses are a variation of this pose therefore the *mountain* is worthy of constant attention to bring about an equilibrium in these crucial parts. If done correctly, it is the pose par excellence for uniting feet, ground, spine, breath and the crown of the head. The same principles may be practiced upwards, (mountain pose) downwards, (headstand) sitting, (stick pose) and laying down (corpse pose). Always in stillness.

Asana means 'to stay,' 'to be.' The *sacrum*, a strong triangular bone at the belly region of the spine, means sacred bone. As it is the center of gravity of the body and therefore of the Self, the place of rest and the seat of all instinctual life, it is considered *sacred*. It is made up of five bones and five is the number of the moving/changing human being. Because the *sacrum supports the upper spine*, we are able to walk upright with all the consequences of that view of the world. It is wise indeed to walk with a perpetual awareness of this center. As it is focused on and stretched with the yoga poses it will tingle and become vitally alive.

A preoccupation with mental complexity, our modern malady, has led to a paucity of roots, connection to each other and to planet. The outcome is an inner instability and a sense of being 'up in the head.' By dropping down into *standing repose* we metaphorically sink into the level of the collective unconscious and into our personal and collective past. Standing still, therefore, has an effect not only of calmness but of also releasing psyche's shadow materials. The more we are able to drop down into the body and out of the grip of the head, the more the spine is able to elongate and come into proper alignment with the *axis mundi* of the world. Like a wave, in yoga we drop down in order to lift up. We *feel the support of being held from below, which is the standpoint of faith.* From this standpoint one can experience lightness and freedom in the upper body. The union of these two opposites is the state of yoga.

There are many possible variations of these simple foundation poses in which the flexibility of the limbs, the muscles and the joints is challenged gradually, to open as petals of the thousand petal flower, symbol of the pilgrim's goal. Each month *Innerscape* participants practice a different group of yoga asanas, designed to open and balance the appropriate energy centers. Always the focus is on attending to grounding, belly, spine and breath. The poses are comfortable, often supported with props as needed and as challenging as the student is ready for. The goal is to practice each day if only for short periods. The rewards over a year speak for themselves.

Practice transforms us..... we become more beautiful, our faces change and our walk gains elasticity. Our way of standing is steady and poised, our legs are firmer, and our toes and feet spread out, giving us more stability. Our chests expand, the muscles of the abdomen start to work, the head is lighter on the neck. To watch these enchanting changes is amazing.......A different life begins and the body expresses a happiness never felt before. These are not just words, it really happens.

Vanda Scaravelli [29]

45

3

Sorting the seeds

His life had been confused and disordered,...
but if he could once return to a certain starting place
and go over it all slowly, he could find out what that
thing was.

F. Scott Fitzgerald[1]

It is Sunday. A Sunday for trust.

It is early November with a light snowfall already. The season, with a Northern feel, is conducive to a state of introversion for questioning personal history and sorting memories. Each month the inner work naturally conforms with nature's trends and seasons, as they constantly inform soul life.

A short ritual of lighting a central candle creates the transition from secular life to sacred gathering. This is followed by passing incense for cleansing smoke, a *Native American* tradition for clearing the energy field. Similarly, honoring the four directions realigns bodies and the group as a whole with the earth's polarities/ seasons/ elements/ magnetic energies. Wherever a group sits together in a circle a *mandala* is formed creating an entity, a symbol, which is whole and more than the sum of its parts. This *ritual* emphasizes the transition from a collection of individuals to a group, for this day. There is a quieting of the buzz of social contact as we collectively drop into the 'other' time of ritual space and silence, punctuated by a few inspirational poems and readings.

Yoga poses for this month are appropriate for and reflective of, winter darkness. Resting poses, as well as a joint freeing series, are designed to open and free all of the joints as well as the spine. Such a practice gives lots of opportunity to befriend the body again and get to know where there is stiffness, tension, numbness or a few aches and pains of age and holding patterns especially in the joints and vertebrae. As the exploration of *Soul's Seeds* involves delving backwards into the conditions of birth it is a useful time to give attention to the back of the body. I suggest about five minutes a day laying on the back on a blanket with legs up the wall. This position allows the whole weight to drop into the back where it is well supported. In this simple exercise, which is calming and restful, (an antidote to busyness) we are able to feel each place of the back making contact with the floor. The sensation of awareness in each vertebra is reinforced, to be reawakened any time when standing, sitting, at a desk, in the car. Gradually, these simple practices can result in a great change in awareness of energy restriction, or flow, as it relates to postural integrity.

The Soul's Code

The role of *myth*, in providing a reliable guide to inner pilgrimage and patterns of behavior has already been established. What will be addressed in the *Seeds* inquiry is the particularity of *personal* mythology which has been encoded in a number of ways, some acquired from parents leading to physical attributes, propensities etc. We are all familiar with hereditary patterns which, to some extent, determine the story we live out but we are less familiar with the details of context which surround and dwells in us deeply, from the moment of birth if not before. Nor are we often aware of, or receive truthful feedback about, the energy we 'give off' to others and how that is perceived. How we are perceived determines the presence and absence of interactions which ultimately determines our lived idiosyncratic story.

Usually we think of our biography as a developmental sequence, as the parents we are born to, the place we are born at, the language we speak, all part of the mix. What comes out is a rather conditioned version of *me*. The moments of decision when we do, or do not, take a course of action can seemingly change the story, sometimes irrevocably. It is, however, possible that our lives may not be simply developmental, where one thing leads to another but rather predetermined or coded, just as an acorn is coded to become an oak tree and not a dandelion. *Fate* derives from the Latin *fatum*, meaning to speak in the sense of something spoken or decreed by a God.

The modern world engages in a terrible heresy in assuming that everyone is born like a blank page, assuming that the experiences of life form our character. That is half true. The other half is that each person is born with a mythology built in. This personal myth determines much of our experience of life, and it is extremely important for a person to discover and understand his or her fate. Life is easier if we cooperate with that myth rather than continually pull against it.   Robert Johnson[2]

Being happy with the life which you are called to live is an important factor in the individuation process but, far from loving our fate, most modern people are racing to change it, for the better, yet that better thing may have an unforeseen price, *depression*.

Loving one's fate in the end, means living the life one is summoned to, not the life envisioned by the ego, by ones parents or by societal expectations. The love of ones fate is not fatalism, resignation, defeat or passivity. It is an heroic submission to the gods—not my will but thine-which leads to the blessing of a life lived as it was meant to be lived.
                                                        James Hollis[3]

Becoming the being that is set in motion by one's acorn is the quest of the inner pilgrim. This is seldom a comfortable ego gratification but rather an engagement with life whether the ego cooperates or not! The word *character* means, 'marked or etched with sharp lines,' such that character is most often built out of wounds and scars that may be viewed as the initiation into our adult and mature life.

In following the soul's call we accept both our demons and angels who express themselves as the character who occupies me. The task before us as pilgrims is to find out about and then allow the becoming of the Self we are intended to be. Many wisdom teachings promise us that, *"the soul knows who we are from the beginning."*

Your song
 a wished-for song.
go through the ear to the center
where sky is, where wind,
where silent knowing.
put seeds and cover them.
blades will sprout
where you do your inner work.   Rumi[4]

.... *How do I, my myriad of thoughts, select the ones which convey my very being? I try, but resist, my other life always calls upon my time. I am forever pulled to be the pleaser, the performer the perfectionist, the perfect person for all others except myself. I must pull myself out of this pattern. I need to cocoon and be patient. If I am not allowing time for the seeds to fasten in my life, how can I grow if I am too busy moving mountains, how can I grow if the sun cannot find me? Be still, the seeds are asking, be still. I have walked with my ragged being and discovered a shadow side. I can only go inward.*

In investigating the seeds of our acorn, the soul's code, we become, for a short while, detectives, looking at how each individual has and is, interpreting these determining factors of his or her fate. It is as though we are 'reading things back to their origins and principle,' their archetype. Michelangelo called the acorn images, the *imagine del cuoer*, the image in the heart and we are suggesting that this image is the determinant of one's life script. This means that things which happen to us in the course of time, (which we have called development) are various actualities of the image. In other words *we are images in the seed before we have a biography.*

We *feel* that the unconscious/ the universe/God leads according to a secret design. It is felt as if something is looking at me, something that I do not see but that sees me and communicates, if at all, through a 'feeling/knowing.' To grow into Self more fully is to trust the totality of the psyche. As we gain trust then gradually a more mature personality emerges (one who knows themselves) which, by degrees, becomes more effective and evident to others.

Is the word the work
Of someone who tills the blue field,
Unearths its dark plenitude
For the tight seed to release its thought
Into the ferment of clay?
Searching to earth the light
And come to voice in a word of grain
That can sing free in the breeze,
Bathe in the yellow well of the sun,
Avoid the attack of the bird,
And endure the red cell of the oven
Until memory leavens in the gift of bread?

John O' Donahue [5]

If the soul's code may be considered to be the footprint of essence, then we are now hunters looking for these footprints. Those which are present as faint traces left behind, as in sand, encoded in a way that may reveal itself to us. So where will we look?

Firstly, we are privileged to be in a group of others whom we do not know, who can simply look, look freshly, and share the truth of what they see. Each of us holds around us an energy field of emergent qualities, sometimes unmistakable, such that it is easy to see why one person is a loving mother, this one, an engineer, another one, an intellectual. These surface manifestations are fairly easy to track, less easy are the deeper qualities, the quality of being which may, or may not, find representation in actions taken. When we know little about each others action lives, the soul's qualities may often be more readily perceived and, under the right conditions, shared. There is a possibility, then, of recognizing something true and essential which was known only peripherally before.

Name as a Soul signature.

"A name is sacred and must be treated as such".

Sobonfu Some[6]

Shortly after birth, if not before, most of us are given at least two names. Generally we do not think about this much, unless our names do not fit us well or when the inevitable female dilemma of marriage and possible name change comes around. Women who remarry may have a number of different last names during the course of their life such that they cease to be linked ancestrally in any identifiable way. Similarly for children in step families. Men usually have only one and so remain connected to the patriarchal line of their fathers. If this line goes back far enough without change the name may quite obviously refer to something significant about one's ancestors.

Primarily in our culture, our *names* are used as a sign, as a way of identification, both personally, familiarly, and until recently, ancestrally. In some cultures the *second name* links you to mystical dimensions, to context, such as animal, mineral, botanical. For example, in *African* tradition the first name is chosen to map the life purpose, the second to link you to these contextual and sacred dimensions. Because your *naming is a serious and mythological* undertaking it is both found and introduced slowly and through ritual to the community. So in these more thoughtful, soul related cultures, the name is less a sign than a symbol.

A name is chosen to match the child's purpose in life. The name should be strong enough to defeat fate and help the child overcome all the milestones in life. When deciding to give a name to a child, it is very important to listen to what the child is saying. To have a name put on you is a huge responsibility. If the name is not appropriate the spirit can crumble under its weight.

Sobonfu Some[7]

In ancient times, according to Egyptian beliefs, the *name* was a living part of the person as much as the body. In essence it was the carrier of soul. This view was shared and perpetuated by most cultures in some form until very recent times. The name was a vitally important part of who a person was. Because this name was so significant parents would go to elaborate lengths consulting oracles, noting place, season, geography at the time of birth. Or it may be chosen as a harbinger for parental expectations. Naming a child after oneself (one's own unfulfilled aspirations and projections) was and still is, common. Anyone who has been named after someone else would be wise to study that person and family perceptions of that person!

Is it possible to 'see' the expression of soul qualities through the personality called up by our own and other's perceptions of our name? With the help of experts from three ancient metaphysical systems, still in use today, the *Kabbalistic Hebrew* alphabet, *Numerology*, and the *Norse Runes*, we are able to understand the derivatives of sound and language which make up the root symbols of our names.[8] There may also be other aspects that can be discovered through tracing genealogy or appearance of name in place and history. For example, I discovered that my name first appeared in the *Doomsday book* of 1281, in a reference to place as 'Aqua de Lyn.' This place name came from the old English word 'hlynn,' meaning a *torrent*. These days my torrent may have necessarily slowed down to a broadly flowing river, but nevertheless this energetic quality has been present oftentimes in my life.

Sounds and syllables of names, as with all words, are rooted in more ancient symbolic aspects of language. These are of particular archetypal significance. That is, there is an energetic implication in hearing the sound of ones name, moreover, the first name is a word which we probably hear more than any other word over the course of a lifetime. *The name which we "wear' affects us in more ways than we think.* Its combination of letters and phonetic sounds produces textures and layers of significance which can provide the hidden meaning of the whole word.

In the *Kabbalistic, Jewish* mystical tradition the twenty two *Hebrew* letters are all decreed to contain a kernel of mystical truth. The letters correspond to twenty- two paths that connect with the *sephirot* or nodes, (cf. *chakras*) contained in the mystical Tree of Life. The idea is that by understanding the meaning of letters and number correspondences, the spiritual seeker is offered a pathway from which his or her life originated. Because the kabbalisitc tree is represented head down, the numbering of the sephirot is a reversal of the numbering of the *chakras*.

For example, Lynn contains *Lamed* (driven/just), *Yod* (energy),*Nun* (introspection)and *Heh* (observer/control). Putting these together as interpretation suggests a naturally shy individual who has much inner strength and is not as frail as she looks. She feels things passionately but is reluctant to speak about her feelings. She is very good at keeping secrets. Those who know me would not disagree!

An ancient alphabet originating from the year 200 C.E in *Northern Europe*, is now commonly used as a tool for name analysis. This is the *Futhark* (named for its first two letters, like alpha and beta in our word alphabet) which is often referred to as 'Runes.' The symbols of the runes, usually carved onto stones or wooden tiles, are both pragmatic as well as mystical, things such as thorn, cart, torch, hail, ice, harvest, Yew tree, womb, war, necessity.

The runes are usually read and any twice occurring symbols or the most emphasized sound takes on primary significance in interpretation. Lynne read backwards then reads as, *Nauthiz, Nauthiz, Eihwaz, Laguz.* *Nauthiz* is interpreted as necessity, need, constraint. *Eihwaz* is a yew tree, *Laguz* is water, lake, ocean. This is a revealing exercise and a reminder of an ancient value linking world, language and meaning. There is something inherently satisfying, I would even say redeeming, in finding in ones name a symbol of a Yew tree and ocean as in my own example. Rather than going for other's interpretations I like to stay with the symbols and allow their special meaning for me to be revealed, sometimes over time. In this way these symbols can be treated in the same manner as dream or mythological symbols that is, in allowing the deeper aspects to come to the surface as personal insight. What we can do is to hold the image as a question with purpose.

As physics continues to confirm that things in the world are more intimately connected than previously thought possible, the idea that a *name*, a *birth date* or a *place of birth* can influence a person's life script and fate, is becoming more feasible. This idea of a deep existential connection amongst all things simultaneously allows for the possibility that our given name is fundamentally correct for us and that other's perceptions are resonant with the truth of that name. If a person cannot at all find this resonance it may be that the strengths and power of the archetypes of that name have never been activated. Knowing this and opening that gateway may have a significant effect. Only after these possibilities have been assessed should one actually change a name, or better, find a derivative of the original name by which you could ask to be called. This close scrutiny of name gives some a push to be done with an 'old' name, to take the plunge and rename oneself. This is an action which should not be taken lightly and requires some thought over a period of time. It is said that it takes at least five years to grow into a name.

.... *I had always used a shortened form of my name rejecting my full name as too formal, associated with my father and authority figures. When I discovered the meaning and strength in my full name I decided that it was time to risk living up to it. What a revelation! I noticed that contemplative and introspective showed up a few times in the seeds materials. It is right in my name. I have always relied on a practical approach but now I want to look more at inner time with myself.*

.... *I changed my name a few year ago from a childish form to my full name. I feel more powerful now, and what stands out is strength. I like my name more now.*

Personal Number As Soul Signature.

Many Greek philosophers were interested in the mystery of *numbers*. An outstanding thinker of the early Greek period, was Pythagoras, who claimed that numbers were sacred and that ' all things are numbers.' He was a religious leader, a mystic, a pure mathematician and an astronomer. Most people have heard of Pythagoras as the father of geometry but less so as the father of numerology, expressing the notion that numbers not only possess meaning as a measurement of quantity but also have an intrinsic meaning. Pythagoras postulated that everything in the universe emitted a certain vibration, depending on its distance from the center around which all things revolved. These vibrations, sometimes heard as sound, referred to as the music of the spheres, were also seen as affecting the life of an individual influencing their destiny and character. By knowing the numbers of a person's birth their destiny could be discovered and embraced because each number contained within itself a vibration of musical significance. So, for the Greeks, the sound of one's name, as well as its condensed numerology, plus time and place of birth, were all considered highly significant to ones soul path. Mathematicians have found even greater justification for the Pythagorean hypotheses, finding that the deeper one looks into the way the universe works the more mathematical one finds the cosmos to be. Numbers are foundational to an understanding of the precise way that the universe behaves. C.G. Jung maintained that numbers are archetypes of "order which has become conscious." He believed that numbers are both qualitative and quantitative.

Another and simpler way of working with the concept of numerology, besides the Kabbalistic method already discussed, is to find the correspondences of the numbers of one's name with our own alphabet, and on the basis of a simple calculation find the holistic number associated with your name. This can be done for a single name, a whole name, or a name one is contemplating. The same process can be applied to one's day, month and year of birth to provide another idiosyncratic numerical equivalent for the time of birth.

Time and Place of Birth as Soul Signature.

After a discussion of the qualitative aspect of numbers it is not too difficult to consider that the time, date and place of birth may not be an arbitrary, meaningless, chance event. The conditions of our birth may indeed "be such stuff as dreams are made of," therefore less than our inflated beliefs but more than a chance phenomena.

Astrology, is a study of the meaningful interaction between the stars, planetary cycles and events on earth. To find archetypal meaning in the connection of one's birth with the cycles of the planets is to concur with a view that everything is interconnected, in a constantly shifting and dynamic relationship, with the cycles of the cosmos. These cycles have geometric, numeric, magnetic and energetic relationship with each other and with us. We cannot stand outside of a living system for *we affect it* and are profoundly affected *by it.* This perception adheres to the *Greek* concept of *kosmos.* The *Greek* mind was the most compelling and sophisticated attempt at coherent thought in the ancient world, permeating down to modern Western culture and awaiting the confirmations which are now possible. The *Greeks* were the first to see the universe as a question to be answered, they established a dynamic tradition of critical thought to pursue the quest. Out of their quest was birthed the *Western mind,* with its passion to understand and penetrate deeper truths.

Ptolomy, another Greek scientist, is credited with placing both astronomy and astrology on an equal, yet differentiated, footing. For *Ptolomy* and his colleagues *astrology* was regarded as a useful science, a study of how specific planetary positions and combinations coincided with specific events and personal qualities. He noted that astronomy dealt with abstract mathematics and calculations of celestial movement, while astrology applied that knowledge to the more unpredictable arena of human activity. While acknowledging its inexactitude *Ptolomy* and his era saw that it possessed a rational foundation and firm principles of operation, and it worked! It was taken up enthusiastically by a people passionate to understand their universal connections. Astrology was regarded as the best method for interpreting cosmic influence and then aligning ones life with it.

Sun and *Moon* correspond to the cycle of day and night. On the basis of this rhythm early calendars were established and interpreted as hours, days, months and years. There are *twelve cycles* throughout the year and these are what are referred to as the Sun sign of ones birthday.[9] These *sun signs* are named after the ruling planet of our solar system nearest to the sun, for that date. They are also related to the four elements, earth, air, fire and water which are universal archetypes with specific associations. Going beyond our solar system, astrology can also take into account *fixed stars* which are suns in their own right, some are far larger than our own sun. Due to the remoteness from earth of these stars they appear as stationary, which is why they are called fixed stars. Their influence is relative to their strength which is calculated by their brightness. There are many historical references to fixed stars from *Babylon, Egypt* and, most famous of all, guiding shepherds and wise men to attend the birth of *Jesus*. As the *fixed stars* are essentially the same as our sun they possess a magnetic force field which has influence upon our own sun and solar system.

These influences may be individually profiled (with the assistance of expert information)[10] as, *Sun sign at birth* and the *element* associated with it; the *fixed star*, if any, which was present in the sky at that time; and the movement of the moon, or more specifically the *position of the moon nodes*. More precisely the *moon nodes* are not planetary bodies but symbolic representations of points in the heavens. They are formed by the intersection of the orbit of the moon with the ecliptic, the apparent path traced by the sun around earth as measured by the backdrop of the fixed stars. The point at which the moon in its orbit, touches the ecliptic as it moves into the *Northern* and *Southern* hemispheres is called the *north node* and *south node*. Symbolically, the ancients represented the nodes as the two heads of a dragon, as well as two tails of a serpent (*kundalini*). Because of the archetypal aspect of the Sun, the south node is related to individual will or purpose, while the north node is related to the soul path, destiny. Like the soul, a part of the moon is always hidden from view. The south node is about where we come from, and the north about where we are going. Traditionally there have been twelve periods to consider but the system we use has been worked out in greater detail for forty -eight periods, each of which is presented as a detailed personal and named path of destiny.

The *Seeds* work of inquiry is, without doubt, the most information heavy part of this inquiry and needs time. The darkest winter months provide an incubation period for these 'facts' to be assimilated as meaning. We are quite naturally drawn to that which holds meaning for our own predisposition. In itself, seeing that which we are drawn to, also that which we are not, speaks volumes about our ancestry, our heritage, and our soul's longing, as well as sometimes, to our resistance.

.... I found the work with the soul's code to be very affirming. I have been exploring work of self awareness for many years now, but have not been exposed to astrology, numerology, naming, and the wheel of self perception. The information from these sources confirmed much of what I have already discovered about myself. I found the accuracy and relevance of the descriptions to be uncanny. I recall having a recurring dream in childhood, one of the lake at our cabin being drained, and me being able to observe its contents. This suggests to me, an early desire to delve into deeper and more profound levels of existence. I liked curling up like a seed in a ball. I had flashes of intuition this way, because of slowing down, listening. It's hard to be a seed , patient, quiet, waiting, allowing things to be, without feeling helpless.

Archetypes of the Tarot as Soul Signature.

The *Tarot* is a symbolic map of consciousness, an ancient text, first appearing in Europe in the 14th century, pictorially presented as seventy - eight archetypes of inner and outer experiences which are prevalent in human life. The word tarot likely derives from the ancient Egyptian word "*ta-rosh*" meaning the 'royal way', which perhaps links to the idea of dream symbols being the 'royal road' to the unconscious. Tarot symbols and dream symbols have much in common. It is for this reason that the picture cards are such a useful tool for connecting to the inner world and provoking intuitive guidance. In contemplating the images one is able to visualize what 'walking the mystical path with intuitive feet,' may look like. Drawing a card-image is personalized to the inquirer, reflecting only their own attitude, focus and state of consciousness. It is a symbolic imagery tool, like the,"*Monster of the Deep*" story,(appendix) it shows you where your chosen soul 'home' is for the present moment.

Tarot cards are divided into the first 22 cards which represent "*major mysteries,*" and the remaining 56 cards which represent the "*lesser mysteries.*" These 56 cards are divided into four suits, each suit has 14 cards ranging from one to ten, plus four court cards-page, knight, queen, king. The 16 court cards represent, through their symbolic images, various stages of personal or spiritual maturity. The remaining 40 cards depict personal experiences, gifts and challenges in the areas 'governed' by each suit. Each of the suits can usefully be thought about as a family story told backwards from the *King*, who knows the whole story due to maturity, to the *Ace*, who also knows the whole story without knowing it, and all those in between, who are at various stages of learning the story.

Pentacles or discs, tell the story of a wealthy family and the temptations and possibilities afforded them by the luxuries of wealth and the merits of hard work. It is about the strength of our ground or faith in this life on earth. It represents our ability to manifest what we want in the outer world in arenas of health, finances, work, creativity.

Swords are pictures about our thoughts. They tell the story of our mental problems experienced as grief, difficulty, conflict, capture, rescue and the desire for revenge. Also the thought and wisdom needed to dispel the illusions created by ego and separateness.

Cups tell the story of the search for companionship and the path to happiness. They represent all the emotional states from satisfaction to disappointment, anger, fear and inertia. They describe the development of mature feelings to be used for guidance on the journey.

Wands tell a story of the division between traditional and new ways. They discover that harmony and progress are best served when the old and the new work together. Theirs is a story of the maturing of the spiritual life, representing vision, and insight.

Visual information through scene, activity and characters is conveyed in the cards. There are a number of different artistic interpretations of the tarot deck with a wide range of artistic license but with an integrity of representation of symbolic meaning. The original deck, the Rider-Waite,[11] is still one of the most obviously *psycho-mythologically symbolic* in aspect and therefore the one I choose. There are a variety of symbols embedded in each picture which are designed to activate Self in intuitive response. *The best use of the tarot is to affect our own perceptions and to stimulate a dialogue with the unconscious.* Indeed, looking at a tarot card is much like pictorially reading a myth, or engaging in a dream sequence. At that level they bring together ideas not necessarily linked by logic, so that we cannot easily articulate this language and yet at some level we 'know' what is meant. In this manner everyone is the first expert in the understanding of their own cards.

Major Arcana cards, of which there are 22, are seen as a depiction of the great archetypes of myth, history, culture and representational deities. They may be used, by means of a simple calculation, (adding the date month and year of birth then reducing to the lowest possible number) to determine the *personal archetypal image of one's life soul path*. The *'Life Soul Path,'*[12] represents inherent potential and purpose in this lifetime. It provides seed information about the central and enduring theme of our personal myth. As each birthday arrives a number may be calculated in a similar manner for that particular year of this life time thematic journey. This represents the Growth Path or particular focus of energies for that year.

One woman found that she was able to make use of the attributes of 'The High Priestess,' her soul path archetype, in guiding her behaviors through some difficult family scenarios. This was new for her and she found it both possible to call on these latent energies within herself and to see the difference in outcome.

.... *A thorough description of my character, The High Priestess. She sits up on her throne way above all her kingdom, not easily accessible and prefers it that way.*

.... *The Fool was my tarot guidance archetype for this month. I can see myself in so many ways. When I quit my job in the fall so many people thought I was crazy especially when I didn't have another one. That's when I decided to take this course, like jumping off the cliff. I still don't know what's ahead or where its taking me.*

.... *My soul path is The Hermit. As soon as I heard that I was stunned. Suddenly everything made sense, as everyone finds me to be just that, myself included. It is the archetype of the wise person which I am now living.*

.... *When I first picked the Tower, I felt like running out the door and heading for home. I was shaken and thought something horrible was about to happen. However I calmed down and realized that it was about things I needed to let go of in order to move forward in my life. It has been an intense time ever since of sorting and getting rid of.*

Native American Animal as soul Signature.

Because our gatherings are held on *indigenous Native American* lands, as well as the fact that those born in Canada's north have ancestry here, I think it wise to include as a further possibility for determining the soul's code, archetypes drawn directly from this *tradition*. In the shamanic practices of Native culture, the shaman would both use and 'find' the guiding animal totem for each inquirer. The energies of this particular animal are thought to be drawn to and reflective of that person and influence the behavior patterns. The animal's habits may well be reflected in the persons preferred home base, in daily rhythms, eating patterns etc. In the *Shamanic* religious tradition it is thought that the animal lends 'power' for that person to draw upon. Some participants of *Innerscape*, because of their affinity to this land and its people, have been very drawn to the notion of *animal guardians* and have chosen to visit one of the local shamans. Others, whilst respecting our friendship and co-contextuality with animals and birds, do not have a particular archetypal affinity, to this as religious/mystical path of knowledge. The purpose of pilgrimage is to find *our own* path with heart and meaning, by way of a return to the archetypes of our unconscious choosing. These are different for each.

To keep this simple, at the Seeds meeting and once more at the seventh meeting, we draw from the Animal Medicine cards, in the same way as we drew the tarot card, *intuitively*. The animal which shows up can be both intuitively contemplated and consulted in the guide for its symbolic message.

.... *I was astounded when I picked a deer from the animal cards as the day before I had seen a deer in the city outside my house (which hardly ever happens), his leg was injured and he was searching for a way over a chain link fence. I feel that both the gentleness of the deer as well as the injury are asking for my attention.*

.... *I've really enjoyed getting to know rabbit. I've perked up my ears to 'what you resist will persist,' and, 'what you fear most you will become.' Yikes, that's me! It's the fear which paralyzes. It's suggested that I feel my fears moving through the body and into the Earth. The key here is letting go. I need to work with "Burrow into a safe place and realize your fears until it is time to move again."*

Each year, the *Innerscape* group as a whole seems to have adopted an animal guardian name, no doubt, carrying significant implications for the group as a whole. These names show themselves early on, usually as a synchronous connection for me with the animal or bird itself as I contemplate the people who will compose the new group. This year an owl flew ahead of me as I walked along a forested path, thinking over the forthcoming year. A small owl, unusual to see on a sunny morning, landed and perched overhead, half hidden, carefully yet silently calling my attention. So, Owls this group became.

Let us now follow the journey of the Owls, the quiet, hidden, disappearing owls, the nesting owls, the burrowing owls, the surprisingly wise owls, the ones who patiently wait then pounce for food, then retreat. The ones who call on behalf of all of us, "Whooo, Whoooo.........am I?"

4

Where is home?

In this very hand is the power to open or to close.
Let the wanderer return to his starting point.
I find myself all alone at this crossroads
That offers both opening and closing,
Mounting and descending.

Thich Nhat Hanh [1]

It is Sunday. A Sunday for faith.

Sunday morning early in January promises sunlight on mountains, pristine air outside of the city, unseasonably warm and with little snow. My Tibetan bell, an archetypal voice from antiquity, is rung, to create separation between secular and sacred time. It's potent and clear voice announces, *"Wake up, pay attention, something important is about to happen."* A reverberating resonance quickly dispenses any muddy energies which may be hanging around the eleven gathered bodies.

Yoga poses for the month's practice are grounding, standing, foundation poses, designed to reconnect the feet and body with the earth, to create strength in standing with firmness and balance. Everyone has been prompted to take a good long look at their feet, walking without footwear this month is encouraged, as is paying attention to the way in which feet touch the earth.

Take your shoes off and walk with me, in the soft grass,
On the smooth stone, warm sand, cool soil.
Your feet can be a simple prayer.......
The naked earth loves nothing more than the naked touch
Of your naked foot on her naked Self.

By Felix[2]

.... *I never realized how frightened I am when standing. I feel my toes gripping the mat as soon as I lift one leg in tree pose. I don't trust the ground beneath my feet, don't trust my sense of balance. Reaching out and up is hard. I want the root to be in touch as I struggle to trust that I can stand by myself.*

.... *For a month now I have been walking barefoot, spreading my toes reaching into the earth, it reminds me every time —to be in the moment.*

.... *I have become aware of roots growing out of my feet as I walk, run and stand among the beautiful mountains. I have more awareness of thighs, fear of moving forward. I am 'talking' to the muscles in the roots to ask them what they are protecting me from.*

During this Janus faced month we will re- look ('reconnaitre' – to know again) at *childhood*, the foundations of life, relationship with home, parents, the particular exposure of cultural and familial conditioning. Our exploration is seeded by reading the myth, *"The Maiden King,"*[3] as well as watching together a video series on the myth, led by *Marion Woodman* and *Robert Bly*,[4] in conversation with their own particular group of explorers.

In this first part of the myth, *Ivan*, the hero, has lost his real mother, (real is positive in mythical language) and is presently being manipulated by his stepmother (step is negative mother), as well as his unwitting tutor. His father is absent much of the time. As every character in a myth is viewed as a part of oneself, the opening sequence of the myth raises the question of how we carry the inner representations of negative and positive aspects of parents, as well as the effects of education. While these inner figures are much influenced by early learning, they are constantly being reshaped by experience. How do these internalized figures influence adult behavior? How is our true Self shut down early on, as a result of not being received and mirrored, either at home, school or work?

Current inquiry is around ways in which we 'go to sleep,' perhaps quite literally or through the use of addictive substances in order not to feel the pain of this betrayal of our own true nature. In the myth the tutor sticks a pin in Ivan's neck resulting in instant sleepiness. It is an enactment of betrayal, the 'sleep' which follows indicates that the inner feminine of hero *Ivan* is relegated to unconsciousness. When the shadow is unconscious she (or he) cannot emerge, therefore *Ivan* cannot take action, nor follow inner directives, nor integrate his own energies. In the tale, "The Maiden King," the beautiful 'anima' woman, is representative of an aspect of his own character of which he is as yet unaware. In men this other is referred to as the anima, in women, the animus.

The anima in a man and the feminine in a woman is what brings things into reality. A man may have the most marvelous fantasies about women, about having a 'wife' and yet when it comes to achieving this he may be lost. The feminine is what carries them out, just as a man generates a child but the woman brings it to life. So, if a man's anima is dead, if he has no relationship to his inner femininity, then he may be the greatest idealist in the world, and have marvelous plans to reform the world situation, but when it comes to putting them into reality he will be at a loss.   Marie L Von Franz [5]

As we ended our myth evening the feeling in the group was deeply thoughtful, with a readier sense of the inquiry of this month, re-finding that source of shadow energy which was and now is, habitually closed off, left to slumber in the deeper regions of psyche. Following this evening I had a rather profound dream which I felt had been stirred up by the myth study. I associated it immediately with long ago, childhood perhaps, but I really did not fully understand it. Nevertheless, I felt that it would influence the present inquiry.

.... *Dream: I am at the edge of a forest with a group of people; we are on a journey together. One person hears or sees a 'bear' and fear passes through us. I see that it is beneath us and coming very close. At first, I too, am frightened and preparing to run, but then look more carefully, as the creature is by now directly beneath me, and see that it is not a bear. I am amazed to see that it is a huge, lumbering creature, with extended quills coming from its long snout and neck. It must be twenty feet long and round like an elephant. It is so big and so ancient that it has shrubs and small trees sprouting from its vegetative body. I feel enormous sympathy for its ungainliness, for its endurance. There is a sense of urgency in the group and we plough deeper into the forest. I come across a large depression in the ground, and assume that this is where the creature sleeps. There are beetles scurrying all over the earth at this spot and it smells not too good. I turn and see another depression in which there are three grey transparent skeletons of elephant like creatures. I assume they are the remains of a kill, but then their heads begin to move, their long trunks swaying, even though they have no insides left. They are as ghosts. By now I am quite unnerved* and run from the perceived threat of danger, as does everyone else. I grasp the hand of a little girl, thinking I will find her parents later, and we travel on together coming to a deserted shanty town where I meet an old friend who was one of my early spiritual teachers. By now I am also carrying a baby, which he carries for me. We go into a coffee shop and I finally relax, but not for long. We must go to meet the others. I would have preferred to stay there, in the warmth and safety, but rouse myself. We arrive at an old Mexican building, which has an empty, open restaurant. I feel uncomfortable when I see terrorist type people in a room. I turn and exit quickly through the open restaurant to find my friend on the street, with baby and an older woman whom I know and respect greatly. The others are apparently lost so we will go on together to re-establish a community. Our group comprises the little girl, who is part of me, the (individuated) man, the baby, and the wise older woman. I feel calm and prepared.

Firstly fear, then faith, is the background feeling tone of this dream. These are the feelings which cause the foundation of the personality to either crumble or strengthen. Briefly put, *fear* is the expectation that something bad will happen, therefore requires vigilance and defensiveness. *Faith* is the expectation that something good will happen, therefore requires nothing further and results in relaxation and optimism.

.... I realized this month how often I worry and that worry is another form of fear. I am no less afraid to discuss what a big deal this is to me and lo, the sky has not fallen in and no one has ridiculed me.

.... I didn't realize the extent of my fear. Now, I stand. I stand and focus on my feet. My feet find the earth. The conversation goes on. I listen through my feet. I buy new shoes. A period of feeling grounded, stable, happy. What happens to topple my stability? "Black smoke with my mother." I feel guilty, but I speak my truth. Bargains, the co-operative daughter; the good daughter; the friend; the therapist...I break a bargain... I see my own rigidity, how it affects the mothering of my children. I don't cringe, it's where I was at. I am doing my best job in mothering. It's where my mother was at too.

We shall look carefully at the antecedents of fear and its converse, faith. Pema Chodron, a leading Buddhist meditation teacher, challenges us to work with fear by courageously moving into it and thereby becoming released from it.

We must do ourselves the ultimate favor and finally get out of the nest. That this takes courage is obvious. That we could use some helpful hints is also clear. We may doubt that we are up to being a warrior in training. But we can ask ourselves this question; "Do I prefer to grow up and relate to life directly, or do I choose to live and die in fear?"

Pema Chodron,[6]

Elephants are solid stable creatures who move deliberately, heavily upon the earth. Their joyful wavy trunks seem to inspire, to possess a life which is greater than the bondage of matter or even physical decay. Lighting the central candle I notice that I have chosen a floor covering which has elephants parading around the perimeter. A single white elephant with seven trunks is the central symbol of the traditional *Muladhara* or *chakra 1 yantra* (a pictorial representation of the energies of the first *chakra*).[7] He wears a collar which represents our false bondage to matter, he is white which symbolizes divinity in matter and his seven trunks represent the seven aspects of human nature which prevent us from seeing clearly. The first of these is fear.

Beetles scurry around on the ground feeding on what is in front of them, perhaps dead and decaying things. Their range of vision, of possibility, is small. They are survivors keeping safe in their carapaces. As such, they symbolize the condition of living that is bound by a restricted personality, by anachronistic traditions, by limited belief structures, by an armored, rigid body. They are victims of their conditions limited in initiative, movement and action. This is comparable to the life of one who has been 'stuck in the neck with a pin,' at an early age such that any form of sleep and stasis is preferable to life, joy, and innovation.

This peculiar archetypal dream creature has the feel of a *Great Mother*, a *Kali*, a *Baba Yaga* of the deep. Awesome to behold, ugly as all get out, but with an obvious need to be approached properly, with empathy, with humility, with the right question,

> Kali, be with us.
> Violence, destruction, receives our homage.
> Help us bring darkness into light,
> To lift out the pain, the anger,
> Where it can be seen for what it is.
>
> May Sarton[8]

Kali is an Indian deity equivalent in awesome power to the

European Baba Yaga, generally a reference to the same energies we speak of these days as *The Great Mother.* The word *'kali'* is the feminine form of the word time, so *kali is time.* She is most often depicted with skulls dangling from her neck, parallel to the *Baba Yaga,* who happily, playfully even, gobbles up humans. So is the nature of time. These reminders help us to be less attached especially in considering the nature of matter, of things, of people, which all too often we misread as being with us forever. The power of this huge being is the power of burning forests, hurricanes, giant redwoods, and the galaxies. *Bly* comments that we seem to feel quite a reluctance in encountering this large one, the one who is the dark mysterious side of the good mother.

'Baba,' in Eastern Europe, means revered grandmother or *Holy Teacher.* Dealing with her means that we have to be in touch with our own life force or that we find it very fast. As *Woodman* says "her ferocity does not allow for 'namby-pamby' behavior." The *death Goddess* does exist. Parts of us die each day, and we meet her in every situation of loss; lost jobs; lost relationships; lost youth. So long as we are hostile to her she is hostile to us. This means that we must wait, approach with reverence and be prepared to stand under the unwanted experiences until they are redeemed. A dream 'baby' is significant of a born again Divine child, one who is radiant with light, intelligence and love. The baby is wise. With her presence there is an optimism such that out of the dark places of our investigation new life may be born.

Mother is in the room today. She is present, whether we like it or not, in her awesome aspects, as giver and taker of life. All cultures from recorded history (perhaps with the exception of the early *Christian* patriarchy prior to the *Mary* cult of the Middle Ages), have honored her with ritual, celebrations, sacrifice, as well as symbolic images, painted and crafted as deities representational of the particular idiom of that time and culture. Consequently, there are many faces of the *Great Mother* symbol and many names. We honor these today as a set of pictures of the Goddesses from multi-cultures. People have also brought a picture of their own personal mother to set beside the Goddess Mother. These highly evocative images are simply to be beheld in the context of our inquiry, without words or speech. The unconscious responds to the presence of image as an invitation to reveal both shadow and light qualities, to be recognized in dream or synchronicity.

To open this particular window of the inner world (it could, in Eastern terminology, be called a 'chakra 1' window), we must reconnect with 'mother' energies, both as remembered, as archetypal and as internal aspects of psyche. Women and men hold this archetype quite differently for growing up female is a very different process than growing up male. The task of the *female child* is to become *like* her mother and to become mother, whereas the task of the *male child* is to *differentiate* from mother and until very recently with Western cultural norms to become *anything but* mother. Like it or not a woman is destined to become her mother. One of the hardest tasks in therapeutic work is to get a woman to see how she is *like* her mother, even though that may have been consciously resisted. That is not to say that women cannot transcend the limited possibilities of their mother's psychology but the path of growth is most definitely transcend by inclusion, not by way of exclusion.

Men, may need to dig deep to find internal nurturing, receptive, life sustaining and creative, positive mothering aspects. Men are easy pray to moods of repressed anger, toward the felt bondage of women's potential power over. 'He,' has been culturally indoctrinated to throw off any feminine attributes as though they may overtake and devour his masculinity. For the less aggressively testosterone driven males, passive procrastination may be the manifestation of anger and fear toward the *Great Mother*, who is seen as taking up residence in his nearest and dearest. With these complexities lurking many men resort to their preferred style of 'going to sleep' on the issue, including one or more escape modalities. These range from the proverbial body behind the newspaper, to the beer drinking TV sports fiend, to the always busy work-aholic and all manner of drugs, world wide web, and entertainment.

All of us, men and women, have our preferred methods of escape from the grip of our anxieties and fears; shopping, food, phone calls, gossip are perhaps preferred female varieties. Some of these things are ostensibly harmless in themselves but, when habitual, may be used as escape from insecurity. Ultimately we become chained, like the elephant, to the very feelings from which we attempt escape and which only grow stronger by being ignored.

It takes determination to ask the right question of the feelings, such as, "What was that about? Where did that come from? When did it begin? What does it really express?" The unconsciously held energy is thus redeemed into consciousness, available for growth, for mature integration. In myth, as well as in the above dream, one must travel deep into the forest (or out into the ocean) for this redemption to take place. The usual caution is to not look back, for if you don't go forward determinedly the past will suck you under.

It is important that awake people be awake.
Or a breaking line may discourage us back to sleep.
The signals we give: yes, and no, and maybe should be clear,
For the darkness around us is deep.

William Stafford[9]

One man made a moving, honest recognition of the source of not doing, of his procrastination. He placed in the center, a figure of the old hunch backed *Baba Yaga*, carrying her burden, which quite dramatically emphasized his insight. One woman commented that when she found herself regressing emotionally she would image the warrior yoga pose, which would instantly give her strength and courage. Another was visibly moved as well as liberated in deciding to omit her family from her personal *mandala* drawing: *"Finally I am doing something, which is only about me,"* she tearfully told us. In this difficult choice she was also re-balancing *Mother archetypal energy*, from its usual stuck place. Simple, thoughtful sharing revealed both humor and profound questioning. Each speaker was gifted with nine perceptive questions to take away and ponder.

The central act of transformation in fairy tales, in psychotherapy and in achieving personal wholeness is asking the proper question. It is the key to the secret doors of the psyche that lead to awareness and healing. In the legend of the Holy Grail if the knight on his quest fails to ask the right question of the fisher King, keeper of the Grail Castle, then the Grail Castle disappears, the Fisher King remains wounded, and the knights journey continues.

Marie Louise von Franz[10]

Sharing a communal lunch in sacred space and silence is a ritual of celebration of the Great Mother as provider, and for the group together, a communion in the spirit of the Tao.

Feasting is the flame in midwinter that kindles the fire
And strengthens the community [11]

This feast, like all acts of communion, connects us in spirit, one to another, and to the bounty of *Earth* as mother. With home baked bread and wine as symbols we understand directly the connection of matter to spirit which is our birthright. The concept of incorporating the god or goddess by taking in symbolic food is a most sacred ritual in most religions. In passing shared foods we engage in the ritual of eating, smelling, tasting, connecting to the *Great Chain of Being*, which, in its many energy aspects has served to bring the food, in its present form, to our bodies. Thus, we thoughtfully serve and care for the physical body, as the matrix-home for mind and soul.

.... *I took more care with eating this month, and it became clear that a lot of it was motivated by fear and discomfort. I tried to chew more slowly, to savor the food I was eating and to prepare more of my own food.*

The last part of this Mother honoring ritual is a solitary walk to find a personal way to root and ground, to touch the earth.

> To know the Earth on a first name basis
> You must know the meaning of river stones first.
> Find a place that calls to you and there
> Lie face down in the grass until you feel
> Each plant alive with the mystery of beginnings....
>
> Nancy Wood[12]

One group member related deeply to this exercise, realizing how much being healed by the earth meant to her especially as her mother had died early in her life.

.... *I have now realized what it is that I seek in my wanderings through nature. I used to follow cow paths when I was lonely as a child, today I still like to follow paths-waterways and hiking trails that lead to beauty, stillness. I know how much healing takes place with the time I have to just be in nature. Sometimes as I walk home from work I stop in a park and practice just being with Mother Earth's energies.*

Appraisal of Mother includes her in archetypal form as the *Great Mother* of life and death, of nature and the planet which is our collective home. Also, as personal mother whose body was our first home and ultimately as the mothering principle established in our personal interior space as a result of encounters with the previous two. This mothering, nurturing, containing principle, has powerful antecedents in the dependency of childhood, so it is to samples of childhood stories that we look

It is not difficult to find in both modern and historic literature many examples of the effects which parents have on the fear/faith foundation for living. A few selected passages from contemporary sources illustrate the outcome of cultural and familial conditioned patterns of defensive living and believing. Such ways of living are designed to ward off fear and uncertainty but their effect is to penetrate innocence as the symbolic 'pin in the neck.' At times, these are stories of abuse, at other times neglect, and ambition. The cost is the same, a *denial of one's soul life.*

There is a confusion in children which often lives on, between the archetypal and awesome power of 'Mother,' the giver and taker of life and one's own mother, who is more than likely a well meaning, loving, but confused human. When the former is superimposed on the latter then the persona of mother is vastly inflated, along with her admonishments and coping strategies. A child first learns the mother language of hint and nuance prior to verbal language, such that he/she frequently acquires a kind of artificial, rehearsed persona, designed to 'fit in' with the perceived requirements for mother's attention and care. The degree to which this runs contrary to intuition of the truth is the degree of eventual suffering. Such a split lives on into adulthood, and is present to some degree in each person in the room. C.G. Jung reminds us that;

Whatever aspect of reality we split off from awareness will continually be presented to us by life. And more often than not it will come to us as fate—an unwanted and feared intruder. The more energy we have used to suppress it, the more powerful will be its re emergence in our lives. [13]

.... *Forgiving my mother has always seemed more difficult than anything, so difficult to be around, but this month I tried to develop more empathy with her, realizing our similarities. Mother has passed on some demons to me but it is my choice what I do with them. I wouldn't be on this journey if I hadn't had the push of needing to battle the demons.*

Margaret Laurence's novel, "A Jest of God," was a groundbreaking piece of Canadian writing in the sixties. It opened the possibility of viewing *dark places relating to mother, home and the psychological imprisonment* of victimization, a guilt which extends long beyond childhood. The novel's main character, *Rachel,* is still living at home with her mother at age thirty-four, living in her home town where she is suffocating. She is chained to the subtle manipulations of authority figures as well as cultural conditioning. This mythical theme is identical with that in, "The Maiden King." The main characters are a heroine who is asleep, an absent father, a negative self serving and unconscious mother, a traditional patriarchal educator and a seductive man, asleep himself. Here is an excerpt from the mother/daughter relationship.

" Where are you going Rachel?" Are you going somewhere?
" Yes." I should have told her before, I know. "I'm going to a movie."
" Oh, what on? Maybe I'll come along."
" I mean I'm going--- with someone."
" Oh I see. You might have said, Rachel. You really might have told me dear."
" I'm sorry mother, I just......"
" You know how glad I am dear when you go out. You might have mentioned it to me that's all. It's not too much to ask surely. After all I do like to know where you are, I would worry otherwise."
" I'm sorry."
" Well it's quite all right dear. I shall be fine here all by myself. Don't you worry about me a speck. I'll be perfectly all right. If you'd just reach down my pills for me
" As long as I have them handy, in case anything happens. I'm sure I'll be fine. You go ahead and enjoy yourself Rachel."
I can never handle this kind of thing properly. What's behind it can never be brought out. She'd only deny and be stricken and wounded. Maybe she really doesn't know what she is saying. She half convinces me all the same, because its true that something might happen, and then what?
" All my fault. [14]

Like the mythical *Sleeping Beauty*, as well as *Ivan*, *Rachel* is silenced in the throat, in expression, by a weapon so tiny it is invisible yet powerful enough to sever thought from feeling. Later in the book Rachel claims her own life through sexual awakening. Fate presents her not with the new life of a baby but with a tumor lodged in the place of her own regeneration. She has the tumor cut out, then dares to speak to her uncomprehending mother, stating the insight which will liberate her:

" You want me to say, no of course it hasn't been a strain, and of course I want to stay here, and I'm sorry I ever brought up the subject, and we won't discuss it any more. But I can't now, I can't do that."
" Rachel, you are not yourself. You're not talking a bit sensibly dear. I just don't see what you're getting at."
" I'm sor...I mean try, try to listen."
" That's terribly unfair of you, Rachel. You know I always listen, dear, to everything you want to say. I have ever since you were a small girl. I've always listened."
" But have you heard?"

72

Such stories make for harrowing reading with a sense of the heaviness and inevitability of destruction of soul life. The victim/heroine is like an ant scurrying around her mother living a life of constricted view until her own unconscious fantasy manifests as a real sexual encounter. This is ultimately a betrayal but nevertheless constellates sufficient energy for exorcism (of the metaphorical tumor) to make movement possible. The ancient Chinese wisdom teaching of the *Tao*, as well as the more modern approach of *Pema Chodron*, helps us to understand that misfortunes, failures and disappointments in life are all "manure", in that something so repugnant when stuck to your shoe can be so important in contributing to growth and the sustaining of life.

If we understand the importance of manure, we understand that nothing is truly wasted. Everything can be useful if correctly applied. Therefore even the bad things in life may become fertilizer that will help us grow and become strong.[15]

It is no less than this internal chasm, this forced in-authenticity, the separation of Self and pretend self which we are investigating on the way of the inner quest. The pain of this often remains unconscious yet it engenders *profound suffering which may be experienced as depression, externalized as violence, anaesthetized with substances, or somatacized as illness. In fairy stories this energy of the dense Mother archetype appears initially as dark, dangerous and threatening, as she is in dream life (including my own dream.)

The old petrifying mother is like a great lizard lounging in the depths of the unconscious. She wants nothing to change. If the feisty ego attempts to accomplish anything, one flash of her tongue disposes of the childish rebel. Her consort, the rigid authoritarian father, passes the laws that maintain her inertia. Together they rule with an iron fist in a velvet glove. Mother becomes Mother Church; Mother Welfare State; Mother University; the beloved 'Alma Mater.' We unconsciously introject the power inherent in these archetypal figures, which, in the absence of the individuation process, remain intact at the infantile level.

Marion Woodman [16]

"The Joy Luck Club," is a synchronous story in the form of a novel by Amy Tan, also made into a movie. When films are well done, as this one is, they can provide a powerful means of connecting with mythical themes. This particular version is about four mothers who were raised in the old milieu of Chinese traditional values (like any tribal system). They weave harrowing tales of bondage and escape from cruel circumstances, where girls were chattels. One girl was given in an arranged marriage at age fifteen to a *'puer'* boy-child/man, who lacked both potency and initiative. She was able to use the gift from her own more individuated mother which was, "to believe in who she is," to liberate herself from this rule/ role bound superstitious family. Using her power of observation she manages to trick the old matriarch, trapping her in the web of her own beliefs.

This film wonderfully portrays the triumph of the human spirit, when *one knows who one is*. Both redemption and hope for the *Promised Land*, in this case *America*, are central themes of the tale. As always, the Promised Land is not to be found 'out there', nor in the next generation, nor in hope or expectation for, *"hope, is always hope for the wrong thing."* The four daughters (and one son) must all struggle through their own suffering in trying to live up to their mother's unrealistic hopes. The story is an accurate portrayal of false self performance, along with true self struggle, although this generation are much quicker to find and risk speaking their "No," albeit with attendant guilt. The 'American' daughters find their own compassionate voice, not through escape but by a more accurate inner perception. That this can be communicated between mother and daughter promises further liberation. It speaks to a huge leap forward in the evolution of consciousness. It is interesting to note that the one male in the story is able to resist the mother's manipulation. He stands up to the shadow sides of his mother and his wife. In him we are given a brief view of the prince carrying both the lamp of consciousness as well as his cutting sword. His most moving words to his wife are, *"I'm listening."* Thus he represents the evolution of the masculine.

The most obvious point about traditional customs and beliefs is their impenetrable nature. They are not available to discriminative thought, to the feeling function or to questioning. These energies are chained to the density of matter, the weightiness of history and monochrome vision. It is as though all possibility of movement has been fossilized. Cultural context has a huge influence on the norms of family life inviting in its members capitulation or rebellion, depending on the degree of fear. It would seem that if fear is not vanquished then we are doomed to replicate our parents' choice along with their lack of individuation, by repeating patterns. Even when we know something of these patterns and seek to avoid them we may find, years later, that we have repeated them. Especially is this true in the area of intimate relationships.(See chapter 7)

.... *I discovered in my meditation practice that underlying my negative thinking was fear, also that being with 'this bully fear' for a short while caused the internal war to diminish and creativity to emerge.*

Only by concerted effort to sort out the specific nature of our personal programming can there be hope of change, of new choices. Alternatively we may set about a life of overcompensation. If mother was blocked by fear then we compensate by risking everything. If the parents were impoverished then we tenaciously, perhaps at great internal cost, pursue abundance. Wherever we say, " I will be anything but my parent," then we are still controlled by that parent. We cannot change past events but we can change their role, the effects of the programming on our lives, and how history plays out anew. It is not easy.

> Fear and lethargy, the twin gremlins which sit at the foot of our bed
> each morning, each wishing to nibble away resolution and desire.

The primary task of escaping the past, through attending to myth and dream, is to see what images psyche carries.

> ...... the more one can align the world of conscious choice with the indications of the unconscious, the more one will feel a sense of personal harmony, whether or not one's choices are supported by the collective environment.
> James Hollis [17]

The Tao tells us that in surrender to Self we will meet the gods, which are none other than the holiest aspects of our own mind. Trust in this inner wisdom will dissolve fear, " *the gods will direct you forward to the very border of reality itself.*" Standing at this border we become afraid of losing what we think is our identity, of being destroyed but only in crossing it are we born to the new life which awaits us. This is a way of saying, "*feel the fear and do it anyway*".

In rounding out our kaleidoscopic look at 'Great Mother' it is important to realize that anything which ends in '... ism' is also an aspect of sanctioned view, doctrine, position, and belief. Too frequently we are willing to trade our own inquiry, our own archetypal wisdom, for the security of adherence to this *"mother knows best"* sanctioned view with its unchallenged claim to truth.

When sacred symbols of any tradition are alive they speak directly and anew to each individual, to be resonated with and understood. For example, reproductions of the *Willendorf Goddesses*, from 7,000 years ago still elicit awe, in recognition of the creative manifestation of the sacred female form. Or, an ancient *Celtic cross* found in old English churchyard, as on my own quest, moss covered and yet speaking to me directly in the immediacy of now. Too often in modern times these symbols have been reduced or hidden, in favor of wordy conceptual doctrines and spoken dogma, lists of things to be remembered rather than energies to be directly experienced. It is exactly here that the '..*ism*' takes over.

If, when the individual is thrown back on himself through the loss of a projected religious value (e.g. mother as Mother Church) he is able to confront the questions of life that are posed for him and may be able to use this opportunity for a decisive development in consciousness....
E.Edinger[18]

The loss of meaningful symbolic life and its consequences, is illustrated well in *Yvonne Johnson's* story told by *Rudy Wieb*, as the autobiography, *"A Stolen Life."*[19] Yvonne, describes a life of growing up native in an impoverished Westernized era, surrounded by the suffering of a 'just forget about it' alcoholic mentality. There was no longer mother (as tribe), no way of life that either she or her personal mother could connect with, be contained by. There was no way possible, in an overwhelmingly controlling and abusive context, for her to say "No." Those who abused her were themselves abused, robbed of all dignity by the culture, which now sought to control them. This life of appalling self-neglect and exit through alcohol, led Yvonne to the ultimate place of control, one which set a boundary that she herself was unable to establish, a maximum-security prison. It is boundary setting that is a mystery to those who have been deprived of nurturing, containment and safety.

At the *Cypress Hills* native prison, Yvonne was able to reconnect to her roots through the liberation of her *Native American* ancestral archetypes, which she was then able to be guided by, for individuation and healing. By way of defeat and persecution she was ultimately able to redeem that which was sacred to her. She came to know who she was. Thus, in defining herself, she is now able to define her boundaries and protect them with symbol and ritual.

.... *The gift of a wounded childhood is a ticket for the journey. I have analyzed this journey over and over, but it's sitting with myself with compassion for me, and my roots, which is easing the jacket of sorrow from my back.... I have been able now to sort out my tribal values. The ones that work for me and the ones that destroy. At the same time, I have chosen to embrace some of my tribal values, and am proud to do so. It is those ones that burrow their way back uninvited, tug at you when you least expect them, that really bug me.*

A good enough mother is one who is able to mirror. Her behavior allows a child to comprehend themselves clearly when reflected accurately through her eyes, spoken observations, perceptions. This is soul food, every bit as important as breast milk. To be seen, to be visible, to matter. The outcome of mirroring is *Self seeing, Self esteeming. Self respecting.* By carefully contemplating questions of mothering a picture may be recreated about the early years. Whether one was mirrored accurately, nurtured such that one is now self nurturing, whether a victim, or beneficiary of the climate inside the walls of the place which was home. Whether mother nature herself was friend or foe.

Our aim along the way of individuation, is not to linger in history, nor in self-pity, resentment or derision but to look directly, *to learn from and to leave behind, binding memories.* It is necessary to see that the remembered context is now present only in self- centered thought. It is important to ask of oneself, *What myth am I living?* Am I living out my mothers or parents un- lived life, compensating for their fears? Am I in thrall to the values of the herd, which may be at odds with my own soul, but keeps others happy? Am I living out an inner complex which is fear driven? .... *Because of my broken arm, I have had lots of time to look at the fears I carry. The negative obsessing I do inside my head. Normally I would keep busy, on the run, or numb out with wine, but with my sore arm I cannot do either, so I had to look at my thought patterns head on. I made a container, so when I am thinking negative, I write it down and drop it in the box—I have been surprised at how they sneak up on me, and I am trying to nip them in the bud. What I am noticing, is how far back the roots of this go—lots of mother issues surface with this activity.*

Once the dark crutch is de-potentiated then one is ready to find inner strength. Remembering, is quite literally a re-embodiment in the sense that numbed out body parts and senses can be rejuvenated and reincorporated. Whilst this reclamation is taking place yoga practices provide a sense of firm reliability as well as increased sensing function (which leads to self nurturing). Daily meditation practice provides a stability from which to view the full picture.

When we speak of 'home,' we are usually referring to a *house*, a dwelling, A house is ideally a home, to the body/mind of self and intimate others. *What turns a house into a home is a matter of respect, of love.* We look to our home for containment, for safety, for renewal, for the relief of the familiar in a rapidly changing world. Attended to and used properly this is both necessary and comforting. It is important to quite literally feel at home in one's home and we will feel at home if we are both held, nurtured, are there able to attend to our soul life. Are our family relationships unbounded, open, available to change or are they restrictive and deadening? *Does one look forward to returning home, or not? Does one look forward to leaving home or not?* These questions help us to find out just what home is.

The condition of house as home, tradition as home, body as home are all changing and passing. What remains is the 'home' of spirit, that indefinable something which is an integral part of all that is. We may say that its home is Divine. As we grow into our true Selves then home as a place becomes more and more fluid. We may be lucky enough to possess a house as home to return to and gladly at times but that it is not essential. *When faith rather than fear becomes the operative principle in our lives, then we are more and more at home within.* We possess faith that where we are in the here and the now is exactly where we are meant to be, it is right here where the gods are speaking to us. Here is the place of autonomy, even if it is, as in *"The Monster's Tale,"*(see appendix) a hole in the ground!

Can you tell me who has built this house of ours?
And where do you hurry to before your death?
Can you find the thing of true value in this world?

Kabir[20]

5

What is a symbolic life?

Whatever man makes and makes it live
Lives because of the life put into it.
A yard of Indian muslin is alive with a Hindu life.
And a Navajo woman, weaving her rug in the pattern of her dream
Must run the pattern out in a little break at the end
So that her soul can come out, back to her.
But in the odd pattern, like snake marks on the sand
It leaves its trail.

D.H Lawrence[1]

It is Sunday. A Sunday for wonder and awe.

Winter has arrived later than usual. Wet February snow is falling and blanketing as pilgrimage is made to the Sunday sanctuary at snail's pace. Early pink light on the nearby foothills is startling as well as magnificent. I have a sense that this much snow, on this day, is a symbol to be noticed. Of what, or how, I do not yet know but one thing journeying has taught me is to wait. This is a *white waiting*, drawing out a soul response of opacity, spaciousness, softness.

During this month I attended a weekend meditation retreat not far away from the village. In seeking my allotted room I found, as expected, my name but also a picture of *white Tara*, a visual reminder of one's *'buddha- nature'* or *'own true self.'* I was alert for white showing up in any form so this spoke to me as symbolic language with meaning.

Next morning, rising early at first light, I walked into the forest following coyote, rabbit and deer trails, my big snow boots sinking into the night's pristine covering. Joining a snow-tractor trail I trudged along it for a kilometer or two before it petered out although I had not. I knew I was heading for the river as had the night's hunters before me. Crisp morning air, cold flowing ice, river welcomed by blue sky, everything enveloped in a cocoon of silent white magic-beauty. All of this claimed me for its own for I know not how long until my pocket clock announced that I was in danger of lateness for the day's schedule. My pace picked up but the trails did not. Heavy going wet snow, strong legs yes, but still a bit of a sense of "I'm lost" as I circled through bush following my inner directional sense, one clump of trees looking like every other in nature's monochrome landscape.

    'Lost' and 'white' are frequent and synonymous symbols in fairy tale language. To be lost is to be controlled by forces outside of rational self, to not know where one is, or what anything means. It takes courage to stay with that. However, we are told in fairy tale language that, "In lostness there is treasure." At times like these I talk to myself, "Calm down, relax, enjoy the moment, you'll get there, late if inevitable, is O.K." This is a rather familiar pattern, an internal litany, but one phrase stood out. "You need to find your footprints." A moment of revelation, "Oh, I see, I'm looking for my footprints." Isn't that the title of the journey? Then a shift back into dream time, timeless time, as this title lived me.

    .... *I am on a one hour mini pilgrimage. The one who left home is the same, yet not the same, as the one who returns. Having left home, I left that time, fell into whiteness, gained my true and nameless home and now look for the footprints to return by.*

> The past and the future look at each other,
> And the two shores suddenly become one
> The path of return continues the journey.
>
> Thich Nhat Hahn[2]

    This particular morning's sojourn had entered into a mythical dimension in a relatively short time. *Myth teaches by penetrating life in such a way that its spiritual value comes through.* I did find the prints, as well as comfort, ease, delight in replacing my own two feet in my tracks homeward.

    White is usually associated with death as the color of purity of essence, of spirit, the unknown vastness of Self. A bride most often chooses white for her wedding, signifying not only purity and innocence, but more importantly, change. The wedding ceremony is one of few remaining initiation ceremonies in our culture which, through ritual, costume, drama, inebriation with spirit(s) and promises, symbolizes a rite of passage which at the every day level of 'wedding planning' may be entirely forgotten. Nevertheless in its enactment it is an initiation for psyche. The symbolic walk down the aisle declares that the fathering task is complete and the daughter has gained a degree of freedom. Through experimentation with life as a teenager she now has the possibility of knowing who she is as woman.

To understand *white*, as I learned in my own synchronous experience, is to encounter it as an absence of anything certain or definable. Lost temporarily in snow-white with no familiar landscape features required that I acquiesce, surrender and listen to something inner. Most of all *white* asks that I pay attention to the quality of soft, fluid, shape-shifting, something which dazes rational mind bringing one to life in 'another kingdom.'

Like whiteness, *water* is forever changing form and shape. Water is always involved in movement and birth, influenced by the moon and its mysterious tides of coming and going.

> Nothing in the world
> is as soft and yielding as water.
> Yet for dissolving the hard and inflexible,
> Nothing can surpass it.   Tao Te Ching[3]

Water softens the earth and readies it for change. In adolescence there is an unmistakable call of a waterfall at the cellular level. The call of life toward blossoming sexuality, towards bliss. At the mythic level all movement (of psyche) both downward and outward seems to involve water, for, Mary Oliver reminds us that,

> it is the nature of stone
> to be satisfied.
> It is the nature of water
> to want to be somewhere else. [4]

For these reasons it is upon the water that Ivan, our mythical hero meets his 'bride.' He has initially set out fishing with his tutor, fishing for his differentiated self. An honorable tutor would teach by way of assisting and encouraging this fishing-into-Self process. However, Ivan's tutor, having been seduced had deceived him.

The sea represents the vast unknown of the unconscious whose contents may be caught and may be landed. Those fish and sharks and whales are the bridges between the unconscious and the conscious. They are the dreams that we are sometimes lucky enough to pull onto our raft. If we have the courage to ingest these fish –that is bight into them, chew them, swallow and digest them---then their energy enhances our conscious life. Gradually we contact our own creativity......The devils and angels are in our depths.
Marion Woodman [5]

Two group members had quite profound fish dreams during this month and more had water experiences or dreams.
.... *What came were fish at the bottom of the ocean, a mama fish and a baby fish, and a butterfly above. I am scared of fish and the dark depths of water but I now figure that my treasure must lie down there and once I am willing to swim with the fish there will be a transformation.*

The movement of all psychic processes depends on the principle of opposites. There are two mirror sides to everything human, underneath fear there is often a wish, underneath hope, there is unconscious dread, underneath love is the shadow side of hate, underneath gain is often loss. Our emotional life is always under the sway of duality. Life lived from only one side of the polarity is depressing. It takes a great deal of energy to push away the denied aspect of reality. *Whatever aspect is split off from awareness will be continually presented to us by life,* or symbolically in our dreams. C. G. Jung observed that it would most likely come to us as fate, as an unwelcome intruder. The more energy that is used to suppress it, the more powerful is its re-emergence in life.
.... *I recall vividly being terrified of water. It was my father who, for many years, took me to the pool. He would never give up until I learned to swim, so that I am now comfortable in water. He helped me to overcome numerous childhood fears. I remembered him through the collage with a picture of two loons and ducklings. There seemed to be warmth, security and hugging coming up from underneath the page.*

When this woman was rattled this month she found drawing what was at the heart of her confusion very helpful. She produced an image of a half fish, half person, body in, head above the water. She said she had felt like a fish out of water this month, but also a sense of ground which allowed her head to be above the water. Sacrament by water is suggested in these images and a sacrament by water is a baptism into new life. *The function of baptism, never was to put anything into us, but to draw something out of us.* [6] What is drawn out, I believe, is that which has been hidden, coded all along, hiding as our footprints which though faint, when 'seen', are obviously ours. It is a call to 'follow your bliss' and one of the functions of myth is to let you know what can happen when you follow your heart's passion and soul's pleasure.

"Seal Skin/ Soul Skin,"[7] a water story, has many versions from many watery cultures, who, living close to moon and tide are aware of both the water's perpetual call as well as its dangers. In this tale the seal's skin is akin to our *footprint* in that it is both generic but also unique, as personal blueprint. In the tale, a seal woman has come out of the water with her sisters to bask in the sun's rays. She has cast off her familiar skin and is therefore naked and vulnerable. At this time she is deceived in her naivete into committing to a man, to marriage taking on his life, his happiness in the top side world. For a while she is content and bears a boy (spirit) child but then begins to lose her moistness her vitality, her capacity for movement, for change, her own skin. It is only through suffering and longing and the intervention of this spirit child's intuition that she is able to re-find her real skin, the equivalent of our footprints, which will return her to her true home. From thence forward she is able to live and influence both worlds, the top side through the son and the ancestral side through her soul home and the support of the grand father, the one who ensures her freedom. C.G. *Jung* says that *when the spirit becomes heavy it returns to water,* therefore, the way of the soul leads to water. It was the footprints of instinctual wild animals which led me to the river that morning.

In the center of the room on this particular Sunday is a mini fountain as altar, to be used in ritual, firstly to watch, look, listen, and absorb the nature of water as flow, *"filling up and spilling over as an endless waterfall".* Secondly to allow group members, by way of sacrament, to re-baptize themselves by dipping into our sacred water and reaffirming the seeds of their own true Self. The water is a mix of river water and a small amount from the *Glastonbury* well in England. This well in the original abbey gardens has never run dry since its inception in the 2nd century C.E, by the first *Celtic-Christians* who established a church upon the summit of *Glastonbury Torr* in Somerset. Water, which I, along with other pilgrims from around the world, drew from the well at the time of my own quest, has been passed through all of the *Innerscape* groups, as a further symbol of connection to the mutuality of inner life through time, person and place, for, *"running water is a holy thing."* As *Mircea Eliade*[8] says, *"....water symbolizes the whole of potentiality; it is, "fons et origo," the source of all possible existence."* As such, it has always been honored as symbol of the matrix of our becoming. In the book of classical *Chinese Taoist* teaching, the *I Ching*,[9] one of the sixty- four symbolic images for contemplation is *"The Well."*

.....every human being can draw in the course of his education from the inexhaustible wellspring of the divine in man's nature........ The all important thing is that the water be drawn. The very best water is only a potentiality for refreshment as long as it is not brought up. So too with great leaders of mankind. It is all important that one should drink from the spring of their words and translate them into life........the well is there for all. No matter how many come, all find what they need, for the well is dependable. It has a spring and never runs dry. Therefore it is a great blessing to the whole land.[10]

Teachings associated with wells and springs are as perennial as our concept of a heaven. Since the classical period, temples have been associated with wells where those in need of healing were taken to bathe in the waters, which would invoke a healing dream. Until the nineteenth century a well priestess would guide the seeker, on the correct use of ritual with regard to the well. She may also act as an oracle. On May day it was customary for young maidens to seek the name of their future husband from the well. Most dealings with 'the other world' in the *Celtic* tradition were facilitated by a female spirit or goddess. The well was viewed as leading into the womb of the earth mother. At the ancient city of *Bath* in England, the local goddess of the well, *Sul*, was adopted by the Romans for the healing baths named *"Aqua Sulis."*

Many Christian churches were constructed near or upon pagan sacred wells, placing a font for baptism over the sight of the well. A number of old churches in England contain a crypt or grotto which opens into a subterranean spring. This place close to earth and water, is the innermost sanctum, the hidden holy center of the sacred enclosure. In Ireland pilgrimages to holy wells are still made on *St Brigid's* day, the old

Celtic festival of *Imbolc* on *Feb 1st*. Our *'watery'* Sunday gathering is also held very close to this date. The 'soul' possesses a strong instinctual feeling for the archetypal nature of sacred waters. Sadly, respectful ritual nowadays has largely been reduced to the tossing of a coin into a wishing well.

Focused upon a central fountain, watery energies were present in the room on this particular Sunday. The Koran says that, *"the fountain in our midst is like the soul of a believer, immersed in the remembrance of God."* Much like the experience of wandering in an Islamic garden we invite the soul to recognize itself as it beholds water,*"finding animation in its play, refreshment in its rest, and purity in its clarity."*

At the beginning of the tale, our mythic hero, *Ivan*, set out on the water on a fishing trip, just as we do metaphorically when we engage psyche at depth. There, he was lulled into a sleep born of deception before he was able to listen to his intuition, the part of him that 'knew.' His inner feminine (outer princess) sends him a *'letter'* confirming his "knowing," which awakens him to instant and decisive action. He makes a symbolic act of cutting off the source of his bondage as a necessary precursor to claiming his freedom. The freedom to discover who he really is. He then embarks on the way of his 'soul' treasure.

Exploring this theme of buried 'soul' treasure by 'going down into the well,' was engaged by the group as an activity at the symbolic level. They simply drew and colored whatever images spontaneously arose. Mining for buried treasure was, for some, immediately liberating, for others painful memories had first to be negotiated. Drawing is an activity which puts us directly in touch with childhood imagery and is less vulnerable to deception than is language. We spent quiet time spontaneously creating a symbol which was a childhood treasure, a special experience of being connected to something larger, joyful. Afterwards we brought forward into present time, as image, where and what that treasure is now, suggesting a possible root to its retrieval from the inner labyrinth. Retrieving the treasure will occupy the next considerable part of our inner journey. It could be viewed as a kind of re-incarnation. What this vaguely defined concept actually suggests is quite simply, that you are more than you think you are.

There are dimensions of your being that are not included your concept of yourself. Your life is much deeper and broader than you conceive it to be. What you are living is just a fractional inkling of what is really within you, what gives you life, breadth and depth.

Joseph Campbell[11]

Mining lost treasures in this symbolic way was a quiet concentrated process and it took some time to digest the outcome. Some found it to be liberating, surprised at what came out. Others had great difficulty finding anything. One woman just drew a blank, an upsetting lostness, nothingness, much like my 'white' experience, which requires patience and waiting for the depths to open. This poem was appropriate for her as encouragement.

> I have a feeling that my boat
> Has struck, down there in the depths,
> Against a great thing.
> And nothing
> Happens! Nothing.....Silence...... Waves....
> Nothing happens?
> Or has everything happened
> And are we standing now quietly, in the new life?
>
> Juan Ramon Jiminez [12]

Another man visibly moved by this process saw that he had created a rabbit hole down which all of his treasures, such as spiritual calling, love for his father, had slithered. It looked to him more like a wreckage than a treasure until he recognized that the hole now looked quite like a cocoon from which a *butterfly* may, under the right conditions, emerge. One woman had a butterfly in her drawing and a large hairy *caterpillar* which she identified as her lost treasure of possibility from childhood. After spending a couple of days with the image she returned, excited by the transformation of the 'hairy hidden grub,' into the creative color of further drawings, which represented the emergence of her beautiful, butterfly self. Another person relocated a frog as one of her first symbols of transformation, feeling that she needed to cool down in frog style, perhaps bringing on some 'rain' as tears for cleansing. My own image of a *flower garden* associated with my father invited recognition of the gift of creativity. A little girl self had clearly observed this transformation of earth into magnificent flowers to be a miracle, which indeed it was, and still is, as an inherent quality of soul. These moments of transformation along the way enrich the group as shared treasure, and faith in the possibilities inherent in the process.

By example and encouragement, through metaphor or in reality, *it is the father who can, and usually does, take the child 'fishing.'* In my case it was gardening, but still, the treasure must be mined from below and retrieved through patience, effort, self discipline, watching, waiting, observing. It is brought forth from the collective ocean into the personalized world of identity.

.... *Dad was always thinking of ways to save money. Dad wasn't afraid of trying new things. He was a strong stubborn man, but had a gentle soul. I was seventeen when he died but I never said goodbye to him.*

> Sundays too my father got up early
> and put his clothes on in the blue black cold,
> Then, with cracked hands that ached
> from labor in the weekday weather, made banked
> fires blaze. No one ever thanked him.
>
> I'd wake and hear the cold splintering breaking.
> When the rooms were warm, he'd call,
> and slowly I would rise and dress,
> fearing the chronic angers of that house,
>
> Speaking indifferently to him,
> who had driven out the cold
> and polished my good shoes as well.
> What did I know, what did I know
> Of love's austere and lonely offices.   Robert Haydn[13]

There are many mythical themes, including the *Christian* one, in which the hero is on a father quest, going out into the world of discovery or recovery. As Campbell says, *"the mother is right there, she brings you up to the age where you must find your father."* It is important to read this symbolically, for personal fathers may well have failed or seemed to have failed in this fathering task. In this day and age the movement outward may equally be demonstrated by a creative out -in- the- world mother. It is not gender determined any longer but a principle of *mentoring* which is being identified. Mentors encourage patient discovery work at depth, encouraging the soul-carrying symbol toward the light. Therefore, to live the life nourished by the father principle is *"to have lived your own life in your own adventurous way."* [14]

Previously, our inner exploration has rested firmly upon the feet encompassing the frozen- earth winter quality as silent, restricted. Now, as the river starts to flow again, so do the energies which we are investigating. The principle is one of fluidity, movement, change, as well as surprises. What is to be restored from depth, from dormant seed, is often as amazing as that which is held inside a bud. This is rather fragile inner work, what I now call 'white work', and traditionally symbolized as a butterfly yet, at the same time, it is full of the potential of generative life and vitality.

The second *chakra* energy center, the *Svadisthana* is located deep within the belly, held sacred in Eastern traditions as the 'hara 'or center of the vital, sexual life force. The belly can be thought of as a mini ocean which incubates soul symbols at depth, to await imaginative and productive thought. Out of this internally held matrix flows all created form. At the back of the belly are fused vertebrae called the sacrum or sacred bone, upon which all the weight and movement of the spine rests. Suggested yoga poses for daily practice are ones where every movement is felt to arise from the center of this internal lake or ocean. Because it is such a lively place it is relatively easy for everyone to experience the electrical charge of awakening in the sacrum through simple stretching and twisting exercises. Most of these are done in laying or seated positions and there is a gentleness, a dreaminess to the practice.

Seeds of creativity are encouraged to find symbolic and imaginative form, to remain open to the possibilities of expression but without hurried completion. All regeneration requires a gestational period. Hence, the search for buried treasure was initially for many a tentative placing of pencil on paper.

.... *I have now found out that I was very creative as a kid. I found some early grade school reports which said I was a creative individual. I was completely surprised by this, then thought that, from early on I had to help out on the farm, to survive. So, in went "the pin" and "bye-bye" went creativity.*

Mythic symbols operate from the belly, so to speak, i.e. beneath intellectual cognition, as do personal dreams which are similarly a rich source for mining buried treasures. Oral tradition of native peoples are replete with references to dreaming, perhaps the most famous being the prophetic dream images of *Black Elk*. In the *Lakota* tribe for example, there are many references to dreams as well as differentiation of the type of dreams. One type is a common dream, which science labels as REM dreaming, others are what the Lakota consider visionary dreams, which have the capacity to pierce a barrier and participate in another realm that is sacred. Central to their belief connected with dreams is the conviction of the transparency and mutability of all things. For the aboriginal person there is a synchronous existence of various planes of reality, in which both linear time and physical geography are only one level, one that constantly needs attention, for it is still in the process of ongoing creation. This capacity of the native mind to sustain a form for mythological presence in the transparent world, to integrate sacred time and geography with ordinary time and space, gives rise to a coherent view of Self in relation to all things and to others (similar to the Buddhist doctrine of interdependent origination), including those who dwell in the sacred or spirit world. This is the one which *Australian Natives* call, *"Dreamtime."*

For inner pilgrims this is a month to welcome this other worldly language of the night as symbolic images, felt sensations, and presence.

I learned this, at least; that if one advances confidently in the direction of his dreams, and endeavors to live the life which he has imagined, he will meet with a success unimagined in the common hours.

Henry David Thoreau [15]

Dream recall is frequent for some yet for others who may have been less connected to the inner ocean it is rather vague, like a room in which the magic opening of the mirror is missing. No matter how vague or ephemeral, there is usually immediately upon awakening at least a sense of feeling which lingers. If this vagueness is held with intention then the traces of form, like footprints, may suddenly occur, sometimes when least expected. C.G. *Jung* spoke of dreams as, *"letters from the unconscious."*

.... *In the dream my father had built a huge light filled church in the center of his childhood home. When asked how he paid for it, he replied "On credit." I have been mining my own treasure on credit, through reading, and thinking, but without the necessary inner work of remembering and suffering and redemption.*

Many books have been published on ways of interpreting dreams and dream symbols, indeed this fascination, in both East and West, goes back to Classical times. That our dreams perplex us is because there is in us an unmistakable call to something beyond the ordinary, beyond the repetitive rhythm of a fixed identity. It is, therefore, no surprise, given our analytic propensity, that we wish to know what the dream means. Too often book interpretations result in jumping to rational conclusions about that which was not intended for interpretation. Yet we wish to know and so bring the vision down to the level of the ordinary, rather than trying to see how the ordinary partakes of the sacred. A more useful attitude is to 'befriend' a dream.

As I grow familiar with my dreams I grow familiar with my inner world. Who lives in me? What inscapes are mine? What is recurrent and therefore keeps coming back to reside in me? These are the animals and people, places and concerns, that want me to pay attention to them, to become friendly and familiar with them. They want to be known as a friend would.....this is nothing less than kinship and community with oneself.

James Hillman[16]

Listening to dreams is a rich source of soul or Self tending. It is not about knowing the 'meanings' of symbols involved, but more a questing after the wisdom inherent through attending to and being with the images, moods, emotions, context, which remain with the awake 'dreamer who dreams the dream.' In attending our dreams over periods of time it becomes possible to distinguish those dreams which come through the "gate of horn and those which issue forth from the gate of ivory." The former are recognizable by the ordinary and familiar details, the latter more by a quality of ecstasy and which only the word 'awe' can come close to describing.

When any nascent symbolic expression or life force is disrupted from emergence the energy associated with it does not disappear, instead it is relegated to a hidden area of psyche. We are familiar with this idea of a personal unconscious which stores energy complexes. These do not yet have the necessary conditions to be brought forward into life. This area of psyche is referred to as 'shadow,' and it is from this very 'shadow' that we will discover our treasures, sometimes painfully so and sometimes joyfully so. The effect of our culture is to confine much of our feeling function to the shadow. We are simply not given permission to freely and fully express our feelings whether love, grief, attraction, pain. Instead we have learned to pretend that they are not present. Often *shadow elements emerge in dream's disguises.*

Robert Johnson tells us to, *"own our shadow."* He suggests obeying the cultural rules by keeping your shadow out of circulation, but *"do not forget that you have it!"* As cultured human beings, he says, it is necessary to differentiate emotions, otherwise we live at an animal level, but in stopping there life becomes unbearable because one is split. A definition of the word "religion," is to *re-connect,* so that a religious life means putting this split back together. We must also remember that our very best characteristics may have been hidden in shadow because of their unacceptability in the familial, religious, or contextual milieu into which we were born. Currently we are all raised in a time and culture which above all else loves reason, and Johnson warns us that, *"the more extreme our love of reason becomes, the more extreme the shadow will be."*

Great literature has been written around the theme of the difficult work of recognizing and re-integrating shadow. Perhaps the greatest most enduring work of literature in this regard is *Goethe's, "Faust,"* which instructs in the healing of the cultural split. The story is about a great man who had refined his nature to an extreme degree, but had taken no account of the un-lived side of his life (his feeling side), thereby encountering a death-inviting depression. It is the synchronicity of hearing Easter music, (thus symbolizing the possibility of resurrection) that allows him to begin a true dialogue between his rational, pure persona and his devilish, feeling side, shadow. The whole work demonstrates a tempering of the two elements, ego and shadow as they rub on each other, resulting in the evolution of a character who is rich with life and living.

A more modern myth, in the form of the novel, *"Chocolat,"*[17] which has also been made into a film, is about the tempering of two sides of human nature, (the rational traditionalist and guilt driven; the feeling, sensual and pleasure indulgent.) The story takes place in a quiet little village whose "people believed in tranquillity." This was promoted by *"understanding what was expected of you, of knowing your place in the scheme of things and if you forgot someone would remind you"* Through good times bad times, famine and feast the villagers held to their traditions. They trusted in the wisdom of generations past, hard working, modest, self disciplined. We are here introduced to the grip of conditioned "always so" (see Chapter 4). There are a number of scenes in the movie such as at the confessional, which just scrape the veneer of this gentile life. Human nature being more than one sided is always playing at the edges of guilt, for, *shadow wants out*!

Into this community of repression arrives, at the height of a storm, a red, cape clad, mysterious mother and daughter. The new proprietress of the 'Choclaterie,' offends the very proper town mayor by opening her window of sensual delights during Lent. She, though gracious and respectful, does not bow to authoritarian pressure and proceeds to charm, tend, heal, and comfort the villagers real needs and wishes, through her tempting chocolates and winning ways. *Vienne*, the heroine, is both sexy and compassionate, honest and flirtatious, truthful and courageous, an integrated human being. Shadowy characteristics of the villagers hide under the blanket of pretense, include secrets, abuse, drabness, constriction and lack of joy. They are held in check through the concept of sin, therefore they feel guilty about any kind of sensual pleasure which has now appeared amongst them. It would be to spoil the story to reveal more of how it all plays out, but as earth dissolves into water, so water evaporates into hot steam and it takes a symbolic fire to release the bonds of guilt which holds shadow in check. Being a good fairy story, a successful integration is eventually made, ending as all evolutionary processes do, "Happily ever after," at least for a time!

The first 'demon' encountered on this inner journey was one of *fear*. The second 'demon' showing up in the previous story is one of *guilt*. "Chocolat," is a wonderful depiction of how guilt operates to keep certain aspects of human nature, held in the shadow, in check. Those who have been raised in fundamentalist religious backgrounds have been inducted through guilt. Nowhere is this more obvious than in the area of *sexuality*, especially for women. The pendulum has swung wildly during the past fifty years from a, "good girls don't'," mentality, to trendy promiscuity, especially condoned for young teenage girls through glossy advertising. The 21st century as a glitzy western culture is primarily hedonistic in its promotion of the pleasure principal. We are summoned on every side to, *come and get it*." This lust for immediate thrills may rightfully be depicted as pornographic, wherein the driving energies of sexuality are both split off and publicized. Thus seduced by Eros, we are in need of a balancing and collective insight which may restore sexuality to a place of privacy and integrity.

In my many years of counseling women, I have rarely encountered any woman who has fully integrated her own uncontaminated sexual/sensual/ spiritual needs. I purposely link these qualities. In so doing I hope to restore the sense of wider perspective which attends them as collective within psyche. Present culture serves up less guilt than previously but has run the risk of *splitting sexuality off from its counterpart, the life of the spirit,* for it is this, which tempers and hones the raw, driven, demanding energy of life. If honoring of Self grows simultaneously with sensuality, sexuality and reverence, (for Self, other and all of life) then this river may flow unimpeded by conditioned views of what is right, wrong, sanctioned, demanded, or rejected. This cannot be done unless the shadow is seen through and redeemed in the direction of compassion, care and creativity. Those on this journey are committed to exactly that. We can only begin with ourselves.

The Eastern equivalent of 'shadow work' is the liberating and balancing of the energies of the "*Svadistana chakra.*" *Svadistana* means sweetness exemplified beautifully through our heroine's demeanor, as well as business, in the story of *Chocolat.* One woman began her enjoyment of sweetness this month with chocolate. She remarked how grateful she was for permission rather than guilt!

.... *My husband won a box of chocolates on Valentine's day this month and brought them home for me. Now how sweet was that? I also went for a pedicure which was even better than chocolate! Next I painted my bedroom in soft colors. It looks awesome. A friend told me how creative I was, trying different things, it's funny though, because I've never seen myself as that.*

.... *Reading about the Empress was depressing. I feel so far away from that, my depression has taken away my sense of life and gusto for pleasure. I have a lot of, "I used to's." I looked around the house and realized, I don't even have any curtains or decorating or personal touches. I even stopped watering my plants and let them all die this year. The Empress finds joy in life and I have lost it.*

We have seen some examples of what may happen when kundalini energies are misappropriated, as they so frequently are, either through over activity leading to hedonism, or under activity leading to martyrdom and a lack of "sweetness," or juiciness of life. In the East, manipulation of this *kundalini energy* is treated with great respect and care.

Another modern portrayal of an old myth, "The Handless Maiden," is a screenplay by *Jane Campion* for the film, "The Piano." The opening scene leads us across an ocean, through a wet, dark, shadowy world of old restrictive beliefs and traditions, which, along with grief, have rendered the heroine mute. Loss of voice is a frequent companion to loss of instinct. The heroine, arriving on the shore of a new and primitive world, wades through mud and muck, gossip and custom. This she silently shuns, whilst listening internally to the creative voice of her inner lover and sharing the childhood exuberance of her daughter. She is re- awakened through her love of music, her tenacity in claiming her piano, and the man who plays her, as she plays it. Her husband, in name only, is an inhibited casualty of his upbringing, guilty in sexual desire and no match for the unleashing of *kundalini* passion. Sexual energies literally seethe throughout the story, as instinct, as temptress, as natural, as compulsive, as forbidden. Predictably the old puritanical and prohibitive ways do not yield forgivingly or by way of understanding but through sacrifice of that which is most precious. The cutting which takes place is the necessary falling of the axe, the sword (cf. Ivan's tale) which ends the stasis. It terminates the impossibility of ingredients and allows the redemption through which the future may set foot.

> As we live, we are transmitters of life........
> We ripple with life through the days.
> Even if it is a woman making an apple dumpling,
> Or a man, a stool,
> If life goes into the pudding, good is the pudding
> Good is the stool,
> Content is the woman, with fresh life rippling into her,
> Content is the man.
> Give and it shall be given unto you
> Is still the truth about life.
> But giving life is not so easy.
> It doesn't mean handing it out to some mean fool, or letting

The living dead eat you up
It means kindling the life quality where it was not
Even if it is only in the whiteness of
A washed pocket handkerchief   D.H Lawrence[18]

To *"kindle the life quality where it was not,"* is to move out of a fear based stasis (Ch.4) as well as guilt laden compensations (martyrdom) into a life provoking encounter with the Self where *Self is selving*, that is, generating possibilities of meaning, and deepening the experience of life through symbolic acts. These may initially announce themselves as affective moods, especially upon waking, as a shifting evaluative process called feeling, as intuitions supported by synchronous events or the selection of telling symbols, as dreams, as bodily symptoms and unconscious behaviors.

.... *I'm at a point now where I feel that life is on my side. I've wallowed in self pity for years and now I am doing something about it. When I wake up now, I feel rested and in a good mood, where before, I was not a morning person. I feel as though I've been given a second chance to do something with my life, even though I don't yet know what that is. Life can be as sweet or as bitter as you make it. The bitterness drains me and sucks the living energy right out of me. Lately, I choose the sweeter road, and I have more energy than I've had in a long time.*

Finally you have spent
All the energy you can
And you drag from the ground
The muddy skirt of your roots
And leap awake

With two or three syllables
Like water in your mouth
And a sense....
Certainly not yet the answer,
Only how it feels
When deep in the trees
All the locks click open,
And the fire surges through the wood,
And the blossoms blossom
                          Mary Oliver[19]

When one turns away from the inner guru, as we all at times do, then we find ourselves once again looking at life through window of perception. Life will feel bogged down or else rather desperate. To remain attached to the security of sameness, to the old familiar complaints, is to live with a deadness toward risk and change, to be doomed to living superficially. Martyring ones resources in order to 'be good,' or else, defensively falling prey to addictions are swamp lands of this inner terrain, beneath which the Self awaits attention. Such provocative contemplation and appraisal is the one with which we must live at the February crossroads, with the flowing of the waters and the stirring of new growth. These are the questions of inquiry which are to be beheld, suffered and reconciled, in order for the next set of footprints to appear. In snow white water walking we may be fortunate enough to make the realization, along with other pilgrims before us, that:

> The world, I've come to think, is like the surface of a frozen lake
> We walk along, we slip, we try to keep our balance and not to fall.
> One day, there is a crack, and so we learn that underneath us
> Is an unimaginable depth.
>
> James Joyce[20]

6

What is right action ?

She didn't yet know it, but she was programmed to follow in her parents footsteps Most people are. It takes a lot of effort to break the pattern. It costs a lot.

Margaret Drabble[1]

It is Sunday. A Sunday for empowerment.

We have been exploring acquired definitions of self. Acquired in response to early mirroring of approval and disapproval. While most of us say that we want to relinquish these relics of childhood, in practice we almost always resist giving up the familiarity of, "Who I am." The 'false self' remains in charge for good reason for the notion of it being replaced with an unknown is intolerable for most. Both the myth study and meditation practice invite us to dwell at precisely this place of uncertainty and wait.

Immediately prior to this gathering I again had a timely, significant dream about the topic of current inquiry. It was a new night time production of a familiar play, a reminder about relinquishing 'parental' dependencies, in order to gain the freedom to seek one's treasure.

.... *Dream: The scene is a very busy airport where I await International travel. It is a vast maze, there are many people milling everywhere as we move towards the gate and the departure lounge. My parents are in front of me. That is, my mother is immediately ahead of me, she is wearing a yellow jacket. My father, I assume is in front of her, but there is no sense of substance to his presence. I go through the gate to the other side and they are not to be seen. At first I am unconcerned as I begin to search for them they are nowhere to be found. I tell a kindly -looking official about their disappearance, saying, "No-one can disappear just like that!" She takes* me to a side room in which are a few lost and found articles. I pick up a bag containing many lace ribbons. There is one yellow one the same color as my mother's jacket which I feel is important. I leave the room. Next I meet a woman from Australia (down under) who is most pleasant and is telling me about wonderful adventures. She cannot, however, help me to find my missing parents. I realize that I have missed the plane, in any case the plane which I now need to take departs from another airport to another destination. A pleasant woman who has just finished work offers to drive me to this other airport, I tell her that would be too much trouble as it is quite far away, and she kindly says, "Not at all," since she had nothing else on that evening anyway. So we set off.

> I will not mention them again.
> It is not lack of love
> Nor lack of sorrow.
> But the iron thing they carry, I will not carry.
> I give them---the kiss of courtesy, of sweet thanks,
> Of anger, of good luck in the deep earth.
> May they sleep well. May they soften.
> But I will not give them the kiss of complicity,
> I will not give them the responsibility for my life.
>
> Mary Oliver[2]

Bly and Woodman have encouraged us to grow up, to find our own images of an authentic life, to dig through the archeological remains buried in psyche, to seek out fossilized treasures. To be prepared to wait. In the ice bound waiting, emotions have been churned at depth, for some, a sense of disintegration, internal chaos awaiting the ordering of Spring's purpose. Matter is governed by two opposing principles, one of chaos the other of organization. The conflict of these two is the condition of our existence requiring homage to each at the appropriate time. The (re)ordering principle is awaited as a matter of faith. Faith in the purpose of Spring. During periods of instability there is a need for reassurance, something which is often found in poetry where resonant images suggest a community of understanding.

> In this new love, die.
> Your way begins on the other side.
> Become the sky.
> Take an axe to the prison wall.
> Escape.
> Walk out like someone suddenly born into color.

You're covered with thick cloud.
Slide out the side. Die,
And be quiet. Quietness is a sure sign that you've died.
Your old life was a frantic running from silence.
The speechless full moon
Comes out now.   Rumi[3]

   Inner descent calls upon steadfastness at the times when we wobble. One woman to almost call it quits. However, seeing through her own excuses she chose to set out. Instead of staying in the city she stayed over in the shivering village at a warm and welcoming B&B, a haven for her to recollect Self away from the fragmentation of a month in the harried, preoccupied world of too many things too little time. Radiance returned by Sunday, complaints forgotten, she glowed with her newfound freedom acknowledging herself as more, not less than, someone's nurse, someone's wife, someone's mother.

   The myth had by now brought us to a place of crossroads. Often an indeterminate sorrowful place. This place for *Ivan* where the old power of parental manipulation and control had been cut off left a void, not knowing in which direction his treasure lay. By way of his watery visions of the ecstatic he knew that treasures there were but was lost as to direction, nor was there much help or guidance from the outside. It could and often does, mean a time of being lonely and lost since the values one has previously assumed are re-opened for inquiry. Even the questions are initially undefined, let alone the answers.

   Bly and *Woodman* had more to say about dis-empowerment, false images mirrored into us or onto us, like a psychological straight jacket. This 'clothing' is felt to be a second skin, the one we show to the world. The nakedness of authenticity recedes and we wear the prescribed uniform as though it were our own for far too long. A verbal sword, the word 'No,' divests us of power-controlling sources.Left in its place is a hole.

   Dance, music, poetry, writing are helpful activities through difficult times as the inner pendulum swings from anger to joy, from depression to action, from apathy to movement, all the while with a growing sense of being alive. This is what happens when the warrior energy is stirred, the energy to fight for what is precious, one's soul enlivened life. To commit to one's own life's purpose implies strong determination, intention and action. A leap forward from the wallowing in mud of 'falling asleep' where no discipline is required. Provocative questions such as, "What does it mean to give up being a mother? What does it feel like to give up being a mothers' son?" should be asked and asked deeply. Bly lays down a challenge of giving up one's parents-as parents by the time one is 32 years old!

These are fiery words and fire is the element which we embrace at this time. Fire can be conceived of as the sun which gives life to all, or as the personal sun which is held in the central core of the body. It is held in psyche as one's personal value. According to the novelist and philosopher, Ayn Rand, happiness is found when one lives according to that which one truly values. The famous characters of her novels demonstrate the possibility of fearlessness wedded to integrity which gives purpose and meaning to an individual life. It is this essence which Ivan seeks in his time of wandering and questioning and not yet knowing the right way to proceed.

> I see a light but no fire.
> Is this what my life is to be like?
> Better to head for the grave.
> A messenger comes, the grief courier, and the message is
> That the woman you love is in her house alone, and wants you
> To come now while it is night.
> Clouds unbroken, rain all night, all night.
> I don't understand these wild impulses,
> What is happening to me?
> A lightening flash is followed by deeper melancholy.
> I stumble around inside looking for the path
> the night wants me to take.
> Light, where is the light?
> Don't let your whole life go by in the dark.
>
> Rabidronath Tagore[4]

A ritual start to the day is primarily to create a transition, much like a night of trans- continental travel did for my solo pilgrimage. The simple Native American ritual of smudging the room as well as each individual with sacred smoke, is calming and it slows things down. Smell, the sound of the ringing bell, visual centering in the lighting of the central candle as well as seasonal flowers, some holy water all contribute to a sense of entering another time or space. Rituals sanctify the circle of people, the intention of this journey, the objects which have been carefully placed in the center.

Later in the day we created an outdoor fire ritual to honor the sacrament of *confession*. Bundled in layers of warm winter clothing people gathered at a nearby fire circle, with a wonderful roaring fire, thanks to the men of the group who kindled it. In circular movement around the fire each person released to the flames a *letter*, a naming of the sources within Self which were responsible for bondage or dis- empowerment. These could be images of persons, context, quality, phrase, concept. This particular ritual was an enactment of, "cutting off the power head," then watching it quickly turn to ashes. As people courageously made their statements of relinquishment there was a unified intensity of flame, smoke, intention, witness, which had its own power. It did indeed set the symbolic stage for starting or restarting the flame of authentic life.

.... *On my birthday I chose to write a full account of my parents, why I chose them and the learning I did and did not get from them. At the burning ceremony I was able to let go of my parents, as parent power, and it seemed to move me forward. I no longer was carrying resentment. After that I felt more at ease in my interactions with them.*

.... *Toward the end of the month I quite unexpectedly found myself in the company of one of the persons I allow to dis-empower me. I instantly remembered the fire ritual and once again heard my inner voice say, "I am not going to give my power away to this person." It was a challenging evening for me, but felt very rewarding after.*

Insight during the fire ritual is to understand a perennial truth of pilgrimage, that one must courageously risk the territory to 'get it on one's own pulse.' A central theme in a number of myths is about 'false self,' conviction of limitation or imprisonment. Here is one version from the *Sufi* tradition, the story of "*The Golden Eagle.*"

A man found an eagle's egg and put it in the nest of a backyard hen. The eaglet hatched with the brood of chicks and grew up with them. All his life the eagle did what the backyard chicks did, thinking he was a backyard chicken. He scratched the earth for worms and insects. He clucked and cackled. And he would thrash his wings and fly a few feet in the air. Years passed and the eagle grew very old. One day he saw a magnificent bird far above him in the cloudless sky. It glided in graceful majesty among the powerful wind currents, with scarcely a beat of its strong golden wings. The old eagle looked up in awe."Who's that?" he asked. "That's the eagle, the king of the birds," said his neighbor. " He belongs to the sky. We belong to the earth—we're chickens."

So the eagle lived and died a chicken, for that's what he thought he was.

Anthony de Mello[5]

Indoors, the second part of the empowerment ritual was to make and witness affirmations of Self empowerment. This was also an honoring of the meaning of the third *chakra*, the *Manipura chakra*, which means, "*filled with jewels.*" Just as gem stones are forged from the fires of the inner earth, so we become all that we can be through conscious transformation at the center of the personality. This is the equivalent of an alchemical process, of turning the lead of our lives into gold and/or jewels through the action of fire. In our simple ceremony each person announced, with confidence, their own valuable and significant attributes as their '*precious jewels*'.

How do *rituals* such as these which we celebrate on Sundays parallel outward journeying? On an outward journey such as the one which I had taken there is always a sense of the unknown, the mystery, "What will happen next?" One need perform nothing, except to be there in the world in an unusual circumstance. By dint of dislocation or depersonalization, as on a silent meditation retreat, the familiar has been released and the new will enter unbidden with its own synchronous timing. On the *Innerscape* journey we make a little more effort to bring the world, by means of symbol, to psyche. Hence the use of *myth, ritual, poetry, chant, guided meditation* and the pictorial images of *tarot* and *animal cards*. What is quite astounding is that *these chosen symbols* are often confirmed during the following month *in the outside world*. For example, during the watery month, one woman managed to have a flood in her home. Hawaii, beckoned strongly to another during the fire month. A past participant, after drawing a card relating to fear of failure, began horse back riding again and actually bought a horse during the (horse) power month of March. One woman, suffering from overeating and depression, unexpectedly went during the 'fire' month, on a hike (she had not climbed up anything in years) to the summit of a mountain where the sun blazed down. The breathtaking panorama of the world from this vantage point set fire to her drooping will and spirit.

Many of us appreciate, if indirectly, an empowerment when the sun shines on us. Indeed, there is an opportunistic tourist industry which has a captive audience from northern climates during winter months, those who wish to be hauled off to any land, will pay any price to be where the sun shines. This is the vacation solution to a dis-empowered or inauthentic life, a short lived, (although temporarily effective), hit of heat.

> "Time out" or "Time off" is not the same as returning home. Calmness is not the same as solitude. Vacation is not the same as refuge.
>
> Clarissa Pinkola Estes [6]

It seems necessary for us to, literally or metaphorically, burn away deeply held, restrictive beliefs. This yearning is amplified as the heat is turned up in "The English Patient," an award winning novel by Michael Ondaatje.[7] The story, (also film) transports us into a world of an unrelenting desert sun and flaming bombs of destruction during war time. After any war things change, for dissolution is an archetypal *necessity when a dusty status quo has set in* after a prolonged absence of authentic creative juices. These are absolutely necessary to sustain a vital culture.

> God's presence is there in front of us,
> A fire on the left
> A lovely stream on the right.....
> Whoever walks into the fire
> Appears suddenly in the cool stream,
> Any head that goes under water,
> That head pokes out of the fire.
> Most people guard against going into the fire,
> And end up in it...
>
> Rumi[8]

Jumping into the fire of life, taking action and its ensuing suffering and learning, is the sun filled theme made especially obvious in the movie version of *The English Patient*. The heroine, Catherine, is a true heroine, in that she readily enters the men's world of excitement and adventure. Mostly dressed in white (see Ch. 5) she is an archetypal, cool, open presence, self assured and unafraid even when warned by her future lover that, "the desert for women is very tough." Everyone in this story is dislocated to a world far removed from the British grey and moderate climate. *Santa Claus* in the desert is paraded dutifully at Xmas time, to reassure the determined. This has an illusory farcical quality about it especially as we have just been shown how the "red winds of the desert rain blood," as does the passion of the heart, the organ of fire.

Deep in a cave are found ancient mysterious pictures of people swimming; "if you walk into fire you end up in a cool stream." In this case the "water" is that of baptism *and* death. The lover accepts her fate, preferring to have the tides of fortune and passion etched on her body, rather than the "two dimensional cartography of powerful men, whose aim is to control the earth (and her-self)."

In the novel's war zone climate of heat, death, disillusionment and dislocation the status quo is quickly, perhaps too quickly, stripped away such that the awesome reality of context, inner *and* outer, is revealed. The cuckolded husband, for example, refuses to see the truth of his stereotypical marriage and the passionate nature of his wife. When forced to face the inevitable he is momentously disillusioned. To this he reacts and fatally so, although disillusionment if it can be suffered does have the possibility of awakening us to understanding that some of our deepest convictions are shallow, inadequate and wrong. After a first feeling of disillusionment with everything, new and unsettling truths gradually emerge. Another hallmark of pilgrimage, (as well as in this film's context), is the effect of dislocation. Dwelling in a different and unfamiliar context provokes a novel perception, revealing a hidden interior landscape. *What we see depends entirely upon the standpoint from which we look.*

The movie version, drawing on the subplot of the book, smoulders with short-lived, fiery passion and tension, in keeping with the excavation for yet unexploded bombs. It's an action packed story, inspired and dangerous. Fire burns and tragedy hovers. Individuation demands quite literally, *burning choices*, which carry consequences.

Any step in individuation is experienced as as a crime against the collective because it challenges the individual's identification with the collective, whether family, party, church or nation. At the same time each step, since it is truly an act of inflation, is not only accompanied by guilt but also runs the very real risk that one will get caught (in the inflation, the flagrant action) and that carries the consequence of a fall.

E. Edinger[9]

The first part of the *Innerscape* journey of restoration is about growing up into the fullness of our 'acorn' possibility but *individuation does not stop there.* It must be redeemed by growing not only taller but broader. Extending outward to include conditions and context, both inner and outer. Herein lies the path of wisdom. At the apex of desire and peril in our film example, is a floating world of awe, mystery, beauty. It transcends time and place, culminating in the final and moving scene, when heroine *Catherine*, (like *Icarus* in the Greek legend who flew so high that he melted the wax on his wings) perishes for her daring. Like all hero/heroines, she reconciles with death as inevitable and asks that her body be carried out into the palace of winds.

Death at the end of the story is triggered by repressed hatred, pride and possession. These are not unfamiliar antecedents to impulsive reaction. We may call it the counter-action of a hurting and deluded ego (over or under inflated) and again followed by a 'fall,' in this case an 'accidental' suicide.

When we suffer the cycle of inflation and deflation, we learn that it is one of the great engines of the human journey, one of the great mentors of the human spirit.........the fall gives us gifts of doubt, ambiguity, alienation, which feel less like gifts and more like struggles...but, we have a chance to find the Self that remains hidden ....and that Self is one of the greatest gifts we have.   Parker Palmer[10]

It is one thing to feel lost and insecure in the watery descent of uncertainty but perhaps preferable to the risk of taking action. Action *is* risky! No one really wants to expose themselves to the scrutiny of the world, or worse, oneself. Declaring personal places of dis -empowerment in our fire ritual is to take this risk with courage. It needs fire in the belly. "The English Patient," was such a great piece of literature because it allowed us a direct experience of this - that *living one's truth transcends even the fear of death*. Much of 'normal' human action is instrumental action that is taken as a means to an end, it is governed by a logic of success and failure. It discourages risk taking because success is valued over learning and failure is unacceptable. *Palmer* and *Ondaatje* both conclude that:

Truth is always preferable to illusion, no matter how closely the illusion conforms to our notion of the good-or how far the truth diverges from it.[11]

Palmer's thesis is that action and contemplation should be like yin and yang, a perfect *coniunctio* (yin/yang) of life and living.

The active life seems to have run amok in the twentieth century West. Our desire to conquer and dominate everything in sight means that there is less and less health in us. Action, not contemplation becomes the pathway to personal virtue, to social status and even to "salvation' for many modern men and women.[12]

"*What is right action?*" is to ask, "*What will lead to an experience of being fully alive?* "*What is my truth, what is meaningful for me at present?*" To be engaged is to be met by the gifts which life intrinsically offers and to be satisfied. Much action however derives from the "*emperor's clothes,*" an anxiously driven agenda of what others expect of us and how the world has come to habitually define us. Much of the ensuing action is then re-action, more like cogs in a machine than anything which has the hallmark of Self sustaining identity.

> I am not a mechanism, an assembly of various sections.
> And it is not because the mechanism is working wrongly, that I am ill.
> I am ill because of wounds to the soul, to the deep emotional self
> And the wounds to the soul take a long time,
> Only time and patience and a certain difficult repentance,
> Realization of life's mistake,
> And the freeing of oneself
> From the endless repetition of the mistake
> Which mankind at large has chosen to sanctify.
>
> D.H Lawrence[13]

"*Making it,*" is currently the norm of our society. This externally driven command permeates every area of life from making money to making friends, making a deal, making a living, making meaning, making war, making love, making a cloned human being, we even attempt soul-making. Since the Industrial revolution, *manufacturing has become our number one identity,* as we attempt to assemble from component parts a self produced Self! Why would we assume that we can 'make ourselves,' for what or whom and why would we want to? This is a breathless, frantic version of living the active life which constantly brings us to the brink of despair as we *make products of everything except meaning.* To accept the gifts and teachings which are intrinsic to authentic living is to become a grateful *recipient,* one who has time to hear the birds sing, to appreciate sun on face, to move with nature's vital and creative power in a balanced and receptive manner.

The 'fall' of the human being has been referred to by many wisdom teachers from East and West. *The Tao* expresses it as, *"our subjectivity is a mirrored, spiked casket."* One of the Buddha's most famous sermons, the *Fire Sermon*, addresses the delusion inherent in action- living.

Everything is burning. The eye is burning and visible sights are burning. The ears and sounds are burning, the nose, the tongue, the body, the mind. With what fires are they burning? With the fires of greed, hatred and ignorance; burning with anxiety, jealousy, loss, decay and grief. Considering this suffering one may become weary of these fires which fuel grasping. Being weary one may divest oneself of this grasping and in its absence become free...[14]

James Hollis, as a modern voice of wisdom, reflects this teaching as,

The great angst of spiritual dislocation is the central fact of our time. Awash as we are in material abundance yet we are more lost than any who have gone before.

James Hollis[15]

How to move in the direction of right action? We have already investigated earlier on this journey the re-active and depressive power of fear and guilt which lead to mechanization of living. It is important to look now at the third inner complex, a summation of guilty acts which eventually 'pins' life affirming energy. This is *shame.*

We are living out of complexes when we are dominated by historically charged ideas which lead to strong feelings about who we are or, in the case of *shame, who we are not.* Having these strongly charged implicit notions of self, derived in part from our (often early) biographies does not make us neurotic but avoiding knowing about them does. Facing in to the delusion of our supposedly well controlled actions brings us to *suffering the conflict, rather than reacting against it.* This process involves waiting until *it* moves. This is a most aggravating, difficult approach for Westerners, with our 'get on with it,' mentality. The alternative, however, pretending that there is no uncertainty or question, leaves us in the ever burning bush. C. G. Jung, in referring to *"The Garden of Eden,"* the myth of the Western psyche about the *fall* of man, speaks to a central issue of this part of our quest.

Man's whole history consists from the very beginning of a conflict between a feeling of inferiority and his arrogance. [16]

Shame, more than any other feeling, elicits a burrowing response. We may even feel ashamed about having shame! Children are frequently controlled by being told, "You ought to be ashamed of yourself" This is often heard as, lazy, stupid, ugly, crazy, for behaviors that were actually age appropriate when they occurred. However, parents who carry shame themselves inevitably pass that on to their offspring, if for no other reason than that they are potentially ashamed of themselves as parents. Indeed anyone brought up in the first part of the 20th century was likely to have been brought up with a guilty conscience, that feeling of being watched all the time by someone who was very hard to please. For many, this was none less than The Almighty Father, who had appointed one's own parents as his second in command. This sounds to adult ears quite ridiculous, but the legacy of personal and often crippling, *shame*, is the familiar starting point of the client/therapist relationship.

To be alienated though supposed wrongdoing, (mythically represented as original sin) is felt as alienation of ego from Self, that Self which is the ground and the totality of our being. In all psychological problems of *shame and guilt* the fundamental problem is one of a felt loss of connection in Self. In other words the ego- Self axis is broken. The part has been separated from the whole, therefore we feel to be, are indeed less than whole. We experience a lack of self acceptance, or low self esteem, a feeling of not being worthy to exist. Most people are surprised by experiences of unconditional acceptance, which, if convincing, can repair the ego-embedded- in- Self identity, and convey renewed strength for living fully and creatively. If we are to speak of personal autonomy and empowerment then we must ask serious questions about *guilt* and its full fledged sibling, *shame*. Otherwise our doomed lives are spent as though in a race, or as escape.

We are inclined to a sense of *guilt* due to a perceived sense of lack. In other words we are guilty by *omission*, not from the outcome of *commission*. There is something missing in us which our parents imply should have been there but for them and us it was simply missing. Perhaps we should admit now that we all have a basic psychological *"fault,"* where the word fault means, as in geography, a *gap*. We cannot remember what or who we are supposed to be! The only inkling that we have comes not from our remembering apparatus, the brain, but from that which is more closely linked to conscience, our feelings.

When I face my guilt, when I see that I have sinned-either by a doing or a not doing-and this makes me suffer not from a loss of face but from a lack of being, my conscience is awake and begins to function in a uniquely creative way.

Dorothea Matthews[17]

Shame collapses the central core of the body with a resulting misalignment of the posture and a severance of the integrity of the spine and the head. Readjusting the posture through hatha yoga, for example mountain pose and the warrior poses, gradually corrects the structural imbalance, returning feeling to the body. It reminds us *to stand as a warrior in our life.* Dignity returns to the physique with a corresponding integrative effect on psyche.

Shame cuts the sensing of Self, located as body/mind, in two. The result is that one's repose in life and posture in action is not seen as worthy of reflection and alteration. "Who I am," is seen as fatally flawed. The downward spiral of a diminished life is predictable as outcome. What is normally avoided is the direct apprehension of the cause of the omission. This is due to a lack of any compassionate feeling toward oneself and others. The solution lies in getting rid of the false guilty conscience which invites either penance, obsession or an insincere but appeasing apology, followed by a quick escape. (For example, the obligatory bunch of flowers which is offered following a marital argument—does one receive this appeasing gesture with gratitude, or recycle it to a worthier cause?) Here is one version of what it means to feel guilty.

.... *It's a cop out by which you give yourself a cheap punishment in order to get out of doing what you are responsible for.*

This brings us to the truth of the matter. Shame can be a useful, honest and *possible* feeling if it leads to real questioning. Its positive operative principle, *remorse,* is painful, costly but potentially purifying. There is an implicit idea of self responsibility in being able to look cleanly, clearly, at that which I may have omitted thereby willing a greater degree of mindfulness in future interactions. *Shame,* when properly encountered can lead us to a direct experience of both the body's instincts as well as psyche's feeling-conscience. Redemption, through realignment, is then possible. At this stage we may we stop blaming God, our parents or any one else for our own life and its consequences.

We have to *feel* shame, but we need sorrow as well; shame by itself can be completely selfish, a sort of reverse vanity. But real sorrow (not self pity) has in it something of another feeling, which could be called 'love'. We need forgiveness if we are to survive as men and women; and to be forgiven, we must forgive and that requires taking back upon ourselves the blame that we try to put upon others.

Dorothea Matthews[18]

Authentic inner work involves a gradual *shifting of the center of gravity of the personality from the ego to the Self.* The aim of all inner journeying is honest encounter at depth The result of such willingness is to be called a *hero* or a *heroine*, one who lives an active, personally directed life.

Empowered men and women frequently live unusual lives enriching ours with stimulating biographies. The world is richer because of the authenticity of their living. This has been a most dramatic accomplishment for Western women during this past century. When *Virginia Wolf* was asked to give a lecture on women writers in 1928 she was only able to find three! Now we have hundreds, thousands of women writing with their own voice from their own perceptions. Not only writing but also exploring the world.

At the turn of the century, a few determined post Victorian women, became part of the gold rush in *Western Canada*, they became hotel keepers, ran trap lines, lived in the wilderness and married as often as they wished, or not at all. A far cry from the expectations of a proper Edwardian woman.

One of the most famous artists and writers from that period is *Emily Carr*, (see also Ch. 9) who traveled extensively up and down the tiny communities of the *Northern Pacific* coast, writing and painting what she saw and felt, continuing despite lack of acknowledgment, hardship and poverty. *Carr*, since her death in 1945 has grown in reputation as an artist. She is now honored as one of Canada's national *heroines*. Less famous but no less worthy is water diviner, *Evelyn Penrose*, who lived and learned from the Native Americans. She wrote, *"I haven't just existed, I've really lived."* *Lillian Alling*, an unknown heroine who lived in New York and hated it simply walked out, deciding to walk back to Russia via British Columbia, Alaska and Siberia! Nothing, not exhaustion, not hunger, not a jail term would deter her. Hers was indeed a warrior spirit.

Eileen Caddy gained attention as a sort of mystical heroine during the sixties when, at a forbidding site in the east of *Scotland*, she and a few others, were growing enormous vegetables, cabbages, weighing fifty pounds or more. Scientists visiting the site at *Findhorn Bay* found that the soil of this previously barren land had turned into ideal earth for nourishing vegetables. They were baffled as to an explanation for what was going on. Eileen's story was very typical of the classical form of the hero's path, a vision or call, making an immense mistake, (in this case marrying the wrong person) living the wrong kind of life, then meeting the right person, (an odd quirky, spiritual man) and ending up in a highly unlikely circumstance. In her nightly meditations she had visions of a center to which hundreds of people would come, creating a spiritual community to surround the remarkable garden. Eileen herself thought this was nonsense but she persisted in following the inner guidance to create, what is still, a magnificent garden, built on sand and gravel through inner faith. She describes the early stages of her inner journey toward the amazing outcome of *Findhorn* in a useful gardening metaphor:

I have sometimes likened myself to a pot bound plant. Here was I with my roots coming out of the bottom of the pot and out of the top! I was very secure in that little pot and I didn't want to move out of it But if I went on like that I would simply die. So what do you do with a pot bound plant? You put it into a bigger pot. And how do you do that? You try to tap it out and if it won't come you have to break the pot and then you have to sort out all the roots. That's exactly what happened to me. The pot had to be broken, the roots sorted out. It was very painful and very uncomfortable. Then I had to be put into a bigger pot and when I outgrew that pot then I had to be put outside.

Quoted from Ann Bancroft[19]

"The Hours,"[20] is the title of a novel within a novel, which explores the life and death of Virginia Woolf. In it we relate to three persons, one male and two female, who are struggling like *Ivan*, in a kind of personal wasteland, living between two worlds. The old one of conditioned values-these are especially obvious at the turn of the 20th century when Woolf was living and writing. The new, heralding reinterpretation of gender roles, suggested by hero/heroines of the time. Initially, heroines such as these are alone with their radical perceptions, for they possess a valency for truth telling that is missing from culture at large. The novel/movie traces the outcome of this difficult passage for all three who find redemption in death, in this case the death of assumptions about living.

"*Miss Garnett's Angel,*"[21] a recent novel, similarly focuses on death/epiphany and the possibilities of a resurrected life. The story begins with death, the death of a life partner, which changes the main character's old 'self' assumptions thereby opening her up to the possibility for risk and re- visioning of her world. In this case a stay in Venice begins a whole new train of possibilities for living and adventuring.

Death is outside life but it alters it; it leaves a hole in the fabric of things which those who are left behind try to repair.......When in ancient stories heroes die, the first thing their comrades do, having made due observance to the gods, is sit and eat. Then they travel on, challenging with their frail vitality, the large enigma of non being. Miss Garnet, uncharacteristically decided to spend six months abroad. For Miss Garnet who had lost the only person she ever ate with (physical/ mental/ spiritual, food), the decision to travel was unprecedented.[22]

Having been through both a watery Venetian epiphany, a religious awakening, a thwarted romance and a resurrection of her true life path and place, the heroine symbolically images her journey like that of the archetypal wise hero's, the magi attending the birth of their savior.

Despite the hazards the Magi trusted their vision and followed it, even to a strange land (and a stranger god!) The Magi had followed the star where it took them and in the persons of Nico and friends she had followed them...... Long ago she had decided that history does not repeat itself; but perhaps when a thing was true it went on returning in different likeness, borrowing from what went before, finding new ways to declare itself....... [23]

Sally Vickers makes an archetypal conclusion about the journey of her heroine with, "*when a thing is true it keeps on returning in different likeness.*" What life asks of us, is that we *follow the threads.* For myself, a journey led to an expanded more authentic vision of my work in the world, as well as leading to a new 'home,' one more conducive to the maturing need for artistic and spiritual growth.

At first you go within to seek the patterns, stories, forgotten magic and knowing of earlier phases of ones existence.........to discover the structures within the self that remain unfulfilled and unfinished. These are often seen as hidden potential......if only a portion of that lost totality could be dredged up in the light of day, we should experience a marvelous expansion of our powers, a vivid renewal of life; we should tower in stature.......   Joseph Campbell[24]

Any phase of waiting and wondering prior to 're-membering' (meaning literally to get it in the body), is symbolically well represented by the shape of the *cross*, more specifically the *Celtic cross*. Unfortunately these days many associate the cross specifically with the Christian symbol of crucifixion, often negatively so, which serves to limit proper understanding of what is a powerful Western symbol for individuation.

The *cross* symbol by no means belongs only to the Christian myth for it has been found in many cultures. In Guatemala there stands a Mayan Temple known as the *"Temple of the Cross."* The cross here is for honoring a savior figure, the *Aztec, Quetzalcoatl*. That name translates as *"Feathered Serpent"* suggesting the uniting of opposite principles of the earth -bound serpent and the flight of a bird. On top of this cross is a bird, the quetzal bird and at the base a kind of death mask. In some artistic depictions of the western cross it is shown growing out of a skull, as a tree grows from a seed. In the *German* version an eagle sits at the top of Odin's tree with a dragon or worm gnawing at the base. Further, there is a squirrel, named *Ratatosk* (Swift tusked), who is continually running up and down the trunk, reporting to both the eagle and the dragon. Perhaps he is, in pictorial form, depicting the necessity of communication between all levels of being during a waiting period.

C.G. *Jung* attributed four psychological functions to the four limbs of the cross; sensation/ intuition on one axis and feeling/ thinking on the other. We all tend toward one of each pair so that to be released from this limitation we must dwell at the center, opening up to a circulation of "light" or awareness of the wholesomeness of four balanced attributes. This is how we may become '*unbound*' or touched by grace, which involves an opening of the heart, our topic for the next chapter.

We have examined how our lives become restricted through habitual conditioned patterns of behaving, as well as idiosyncratic defenses against the pain and struggle of choosing to be free. Wanting freedom is by no means synonymous with achieving freedom. We have seen that conditioned habits have replaced some of our more refined capacities and possibilities, such as attending to what *is* present within and without. We have, like the *Sleeping Beauty*, been asleep for a mythical one hundred years, asleep to the vast potential of life without knowing it. Awakening involves first waiting, then decisive action. Firstly, getting rid of that which leeches personal empowerment, secondly, taking steps toward the life we may dare to have. What this is, is often an old truth, even an ancestral truth but in a new form. It can enter best when we are open, attentive and patient.

All the fruit is ripe, plunged in the fire, cooked.
And they have passed their test on earth; one law is this;
That everything curls inward, like snakes,
Prophetic, dreaming on
The hills of heaven. And many things
Have to stay on the shoulders.
Steadiness is essential.
Forwards, however, or backwards we will
Not look. Let us learn to live swaying
As in a rocking boat on the sea.

Fredrich Holderin [25]

7

Where is love?

You are me, and I am you.
Isn't it obvious that we "inter-are"?
You cultivate the flower in yourself,
so that I will be beautiful.
I transform the garbage in myself,
so that you will not have to suffer.
I support you, you support me.
I am in this world to offer you peace;
you are in this world to bring me joy.

Thich Nhat Hahn[1]

It is Sunday. A Sunday for loving-kindness.
        A first hint of green spotting dreary brown prairies awakens the senses after a ghostly drive through a daylight savings Sunday morning, through a not yet risen city. Early light is a come hither for browned and patient edges, now frayed from winter enclosure, from descent. A flock of wild geese flying two by two, honking and proclaiming restoration, escort us beyond the city limits. Their hawk sisters hunt lazily across the foothills, breakfast already complete, easy eating now that burrows are open.
        This is the month that nature performs miracles, formless to form, early gifts for cleansing the doors of perception. One friend who knows about these things becomes *Dionysian* in April, brewing potions and tonics from nettles and dandelions, from sage and early grasses, restoring the body, redeeming the accumulated toxins. Yesterday hiking on the prairies, my blood felt quickened like sap by the carpet of purple crocuses with boldly opened yellow centers daring life again, sun to sun. I wanted to see the world from crocus's view so lay down, back to earth, vaguely thinking of soup for lunch and noting how the sky asked to be seen.

115

Love is for vanishing into the sky. The mind,
for learning what men have done and tried to do.
Mysteries are not to be solved.
The eye goes blind when it only wants to see *why*.
An eye is meant to see things
The soul is here for its own joy.   Rumi [2]

Lost in looking and listening, I became dimly aware of a soup smell an onion kind of smell, the ingredient I had forgotten to bring to the cottage right there under my nostrils, wild chives, growing in lively and pungent profusion. The necessary spring additive, the just-what-we-need for completeness gathered into my pocket gratefully. Later, along the game trail, fresh sage too and a blue bird, brilliant blue, as well as some fit and healthy deer. All this accompanied by the knock, knock-wake-up call of the brilliantly plumed, obviously busy, Pileated woodpecker. My rather depressed mood was by now transformed through participation. The blocked energy of too much head-thought had disappeared, gone to earth. *The heart of the matter had been revealed.* These gifts of earth-love, I thought, are symbols of her heart's longing for connection, for continuation. As always poetry, the language of the heart, says it best.

you only will create
(who are so perfectly alive) my shame;
lady through whose profound and fragile lips
the sweet small clumsy feet of April came
into the ragged meadows of my soul.
                                        e.e.cummings[3]

A centering ritual and the sharing of heart poems began the gathering on this April Sunday. If love *is* the *mystery of life*, and poetry its language, then poets we must now become. I have a wonderful collection of poems written by previous *Innerscape participants* as inspiration for the current pilgrim poets. For those whose muse has lain dormant this poet role may, at first, seem daunting yet as with the earlier 'art-mandala' project, once begun all succeed. There are no failures of inspiration and there is never any shortage of material.

A poet should think of all things as being given him, even misfortune. Misfortune, defeat, humiliation, failure, those are our tools—we are given mistakes, we are given nightmares and our task is to turn them into poetry. And were I truly a poet, I would feel that every moment

of my life is poetic, every moment of my life is a kind of clay I have to mold, I have to shape,
to lick into poetry   Helen Luke[4]

In a wonderful article entitled, "The Long Bag we Drag behind Us,"[5]
Robert Bly draws attention to our special gifts which have been hidden in
the bag along with all the things we were not supposed to feel, do, be or
say. In the past few months of this inner journey we have been hauling
things out of the bag! Bly suggests that we get out our own creativity and
start writing our own poems with our own voice. One past participant wrote
a wonderful soup love poem, now inspiring my prairie chive-sage soup,

> Someone you know and love dies,
> And you make soup,
> From Scratch.
> Slow and warm and soothing
> Patient Act of Love.
> Mozart rests at the root of my neck
> As I chop, sever, stir, sniff
> A sacred score
> Sacred soup
> Soup matters!
> I think it is the fragrance
> Fragrance seeping into pores
> Reaching our bones
> Skin to Skin.
> Onion and garlic
> Breath elemental into sterile air
> The kitchen blooming releases love,
> Let it simmer
>
> Judith Maxwell

Soup making, my spring walk, are examples of coming upon love
without seeking it. The flower is for everybody *and* for the one who takes
trouble to breathe it deeply and look at it with delight.

You come upon love not as the result of any particular effort or experience. Such a love, you
will find, is not of time; such a love is both personal and impersonal, is both the one and the
many.   J. Krishnamurti [6]

Good Friday and *Easter Sunday* this year fell in April, the month of
our inquiry into love. The *Christian* sacrament of death and resurrection,

parallels nature as the fragile beauty of new life magically appearing from barrenness, just as, the resurrected spiritual body transcends the material body. For us, as pilgrims, what is being transcended is the 'I/me' of our previous questioning, the one which, capable and operative still, is able to both recognize and yield to the 'Not-I.' This is a quantum leap, just as spring green leaps from earth. It takes the experience of love. A great love poet of this century, e.e. cummings, reveals to us the acorn of 'being love.'

Love is the deeper season than reason; my sweet one, and april's where we're.[7]

This seemingly innocuous little phrase carries huge archetypal meaning for it seems that spring invites the fire of union, the burn of the heart as *Rumi* described it, the burn which is everything. What is being referred to is the potency of the mixing and melting required in relationships of love that makes the experience of loving, the heat of it, a primary human vehicle of individuation.

As a chickpea must boil to become edible, as a grape must be stripped of its skin to become wine, as a seed must crack open to become a tree, so the seekers individuality (which is the sole cause of his pain) must be sacrificed in the fire of love for him to reach perfection.
Rumi [8]

Any symbolic image which is personally meaningful has the capacity to instantaneously open the heart. The *Christian* image of this most holy month, the cross of the crucifixion, is for many a potent image both personal and collective. Not many years ago I had an unexpected and memorable direct experience of Christian ritual and symbol which for all of my many years of study, (when I was searching for the fact and concept of it) I had not been able to encounter. It happened to be a very wet and bedraggled day which was also Good Friday as I passed through the city of Exeter on my way to a *Buddhist* retreat center in England. En route, I happened upon a Good Friday vigil, a procession , a ritual carrying of the cross *the sacred symbol*, through the streets to the cathedral grounds. Parking the car I got out and quite instantly had a profound and moving inner connection to the simple images of cloaked monks standing in the pouring rain, at-one with the plain, heavy, wooden cross. That moment "sizzled."

Strong intuition led me into the cathedral itself, where I attended the service, then the vigil, and did not emerge for four hours! The normally glamorous but now disrobed clergy, humble before altar and barren cross, the music of lamentation and purity, the vigil atmosphere, the prayers as personal inquiry, all blended into an outpouring and cleansing for me, quite unprecedented in my forty or so years of church going. A religious ceremony, yes, but also a timely spring rite -of- passage, to cleanse the doors of perception, to move from complexity to simplicity, to be awakened in time, to be extended, stretched, beyond the asleep 'I/me' preoccupation. That year it happened by way of an old tradition yet as a new experience for me. This year it happened through a timely connection to earth and sky, and by way of the crocus.

A previous group member also perceived the crocus, long before her heart's calling became specific, as a guide to awakening. For my own reasons and resonance I recalled her beautiful poem which was a request, a prayer for redemption, a calling to life and growth and blooming.

Crocus teaches me
as it seeks out the sun
to penetrate and soften.
A gentle touch on shoulder,
a turtle, going into my shell, shoulder.
This spirit touch brings me back,
Tough, growing low to ground crocus,
Furry practicality, now bold, unafraid
It shows a soft yellow heart-center,
petals open, declaring itself.
But I'm still tugged and tangled,
the sharpness of the bare, weaving branches.
All winter it's them I've been drawn to
Chaos, losing my grasp.
Mouth waters for it, belly aches for it.
But now the crocus, the soft uncomplicated crocus
Shows me another way,
through the tangle, past the tangle
crocus showing me the way.

Karen Wylie

This poem, poems in general, love poetry in particular, love, are all characterized by optimism. Like faith.

In traditional *Eastern* symbolism the heart *chakra* symbol, the *Anahata chakra* has a little subsidiary mandala or foyer which is the wish-fulfilling tree. As the energies which transform and their symbols which redeem 'I' break through, then we have the feeling that our wishes will be realized and they may well be. When the heart is opened and happy that happiness is for sharing. It does not wish to be owned. In the opening of the heart center we glimpse the possibility of 'spiritual' life, which is not a new life but the same life that we already have, now experienced as a happy life. A life free of 'me first' preoccupation.

Through truth, beauty, love and silence, the psychological tangle and physical constriction which we have previously focused on through the descent, has the possibility of being seen through, understood and transcended. Crocus-poet intuited this. At the conclusion of the Christian crucifixion it is given as a *sacred promise*.

"Peace I leave with you, my peace I give unto you not as the world giveth, give I unto you.⁹

The *"Anahata" yantra* is depicted as a six pointed star, the upward pointing triangle representing aspiration for spiritual freedom, the lower triangle representing physical inertia and psychological neuroses, our stuck places. *Crocus* has six petals, two triangles, perfectly balanced and in the center is the radiant sun. On the balcony at my friends' cottage is a wonderful stone *Celtic cross* with the same sense of center, in the heart of the circle. All of these symbolic images, from nature or cultural tradition, teach directly through an experience in the beholding. The experience is one of transcendence. ('I/me' into Self). Something in me quickens to see in these three symbols from very differing contexts, the same visual message. Spelled out in word symbols it is this: *human transformation, the place of balance of heaven and earth, the fulfillment of our quest, is found through the way of the heart and our capacity for love.*

In Chinese philosophy, the two sides of human nature are represented by heaven, *expansiveness* and earth, *solid ground*. We learn, from *hatha yoga* the importance of grounding in the lower body. Now its fruition is more obvious, that a grounded firm base allows the soft vulnerable front of the body to open. It is here that we let the world and others in when we extend our arms openly in trust and embrace. Supported yoga practices encourage maximum opening in the chest, rib cage, lungs and heart cavity.

Redemption of the constricted self through love, is contained in the story of the archetypal characters of our myth. The mythological hero *Ivan* has now had the experience of confronting both his own lack of awareness (going to sleep) as well the shadowy, frightening places in psyche. He has been asked the question of the deep by the death giving Goddess, the *Hierophant,* the *Holy Teacher,* the *Baba Yaga,* not once but three times; *"Do you come by your own free will, or do you come by compulsion?"* In other words, is this inner chaos/confusion/adversity of your own doing or did someone else make you do it? Do you take full responsibility or does your context, your history, your family, drive you to it? If we say, *" I decide,"* clearly we have still a limited view of 'I,' yet if we say, *"They made me do it,"* we dwell in ignorance. The wise ones will say, *" I don't know, I just don't know why I ask these questions. I don't know why I fell asleep, I don't know why I fell in love with the wrong person; I don't know why we humans keep crucifying each other; I don't know why my husband and I, my daughter and I fight all the time; I don't know any definitive answer as to why. I don't even know any more who this subject 'I' is."* This is to dwell in the imbetween world, to know it as the uncertainty of truth.

At this point, having honestly faced the 'baba yaga,' we are vulnerable enough to be penetrated by truth, love, beauty and forgiveness. We can lick the sores of the ugly hag, (our own and our loved ones' worst aspects), we can forgive and be forgiven. In the realization of our folly we are saved. As Woodman reminds us, *"Truly encountering 'her'(the Hierophant or inner teacher) burns away our infant baggage."* Out of darkness comes the daylight saving hour, the crocus, the promise.

It would be wonderful if that was the end of it and we all lived happily ever after but we seem to be blessed with poor memory for these wonderful and awe-filled moments. The symbol for the *heart chakra* is a *fleeing gazelle,* a puzzling symbol. Recently, walking in a valley, I watched deer totally alert to human presence, ready to flee. When they go, they go fast, a glimpse of white rump leaping. So with love, and with awakening, here now, then gone again, then back we go to the *Baba Yaga,* the holy teacher, for another offering of her (our) unappetizing food.

A number of years ago, when I undertook a long and serious psychoanalysis, my analyst generally said irritatingly little, yet occasionally enough to keep me hungry for more. Like all true teachers I didn't necessarily like what he fed me, but our agreement for this kind of feeding (of the unconscious with symbol) could not be broken. A couple of years ago, after I had lost touch, I sadly learned that he had died. I also heard, by reason of a rather unusual coincidence what he had said before he died. This was a learned man, much published and respected. He knew a lot about people, about the psyche. So what did he say at the end? He said, "Love is everything." That is all, *Love is everything.*

A wise elder, this man when dying posed for us the greatest question of humanity. *If love is indeed everything, then what exactly is love and how do we learn to really love?* Why is there so much preaching and writing about love since we are all in it in some form or other? If love is our essence then why do we have so many troubles which are love troubles? Why do we protect ourselves from love's wounds with distance and secrecy and coolness? Myths tell us that love comes from the arrow of *Eros* but it also tells us about a jealous *Aphrodite.* James Hillman warns us about love in the human dimension, as any encounter between two which asks for union and the birthing of new life (whether literal or symbolic) and that we would do well to keep in mind the following phrase before we fall into it.

" I adjure you that ye stir not up or awaken love until it please."[10]

"*Love does not please until we can somehow cope with it, and we cannot cope with it as long as it is an affective 'I-Me wanting' and not a state of being.*"[11] For it to be a state of being, as we know from our explorations, I must have learned to honor and love Self, I must have done substantial inner work, to have lessened attachment to 'I,' for Self is permanently awake to other. There are many who appear to outwardly love unstintingly but if the connection to the ground of being within Self is not yet formed then a love will have been stirred up which cannot please.

Slowly, on this inner journey, we are revisiting the inner conditions which prevent us from 'being love.' It is a circuitous route, by way of encounter with loving and with defense against the pain of loss of 'being loved.' Each of us can supply personal stories along this rocky road, testimonies of falling in and out of love, the struggles and expectations of living out an archetypal and cultural dream, whereby we are all supposed to live happily in love yet seem to fail and fail again. In the English language there are so many interpretations of this one little word.

One *Sanskrit* word for love is *bhakti* which stems form the verbal root *bhaj* meaning '*to participate.*' Love is the most profound participation of which we are capable, to be in touch with the essence of others, of all living things, is to dwell in a loving state of being. Thus, two people or sentient beings may be in the same contextual soul space without demonstratively sharing. Communion is not only, or sometimes even obviously, communication. To be in participation is the contact two can have from within, from below. In this sense each is connected to the present moment just now and *as it* is. The ground of being at depth is not personal ground but the universal support of each, which is beheld only through inner connection at depth.

Common language usage complicates our differential understanding of love. This word is used to mean infatuation, lust, pleasure, affection, charity, friendship, duty, religious feeling, national identity and a host of other assumptions. We are accustomed to using the word 'love' interchangeably with 'liking,'or 'wanting,' to describe any pleasurable affect and in just about any situation. It is often closely linked to a personal desire. Rarely, do we mean anything which approximates to bhakti or *being-love.*

Joseph Campbell, says that we have three possible states when we speak of love. One is *lust,* which he defines as the zeal of the organs for each other, the second, *agape,* a spiritual love. The third, coming from Europe in the Middle Ages as an approximated version of courtly love is what we would call *romance,* a love which is most definitely personal and which few manage to avoid.

The eyes go forth to find an image to recommend to the heart."[12]

These are seductive words and an observation explored by *Shakespeare* in more than one of his plays which to some extent have, along with the legacy of the Romantic age, shaped our ideas of love. The varieties of passionate love between the sexes were always Shakespeare's concern.

Romeo and Juliet, has likely been the most persuasive celebration of romantic love in western literature. For many, it has been unmatched as a vision of uncompromising mutual love that perishes in it's own fire of idealism and intensity. For its author there were only two possibilities, that love dies or else the lovers die. In all of the passionate entanglements in plays such as, *"As You Like It," "Loves' Labors Lost," "Much Ado About*

Nothing," "*Anthony and Cleopatra,*" no character went on to lengthy marital bliss, as if for Shakespeare the two situations, romantic love and marriage, were quite separate. From Juliet's lips we hear perhaps the best known declaration of romantic love ever written.

> And yet I wish but for the thing I have.
> My bounty is as boundless as the sea,
> My love as deep. The more I give to thee
> The more I have for both are infinite.
>
> Act 2 sc 2 131-35[13]

Falling in love, like *Romeo and Juliet,* is an innocent passion, full of youth and idealism but nevertheless true and pure. Campbell reminds us that the truly romantic heart is not a heart of lust but a heart that responds to the whole person-image. When the heart is completely taken by this image of love then nothing else counts.

> There is a place where love begins and a place where love ends.
> There is a touch of two hands that foils all dictionaries.
> There is a pair of shoes love wears and the coming is a mystery.
> There is a warning love sends and the cost of it is never written till long afterwards.
>
> Carl Sandburg[14]

We know a great deal about the initial flourishing of romantic love from the songs and stories of the troubadours of the twelfth century. It was then called courtly love, the symbol of which was the brave knight. He worshiped a fair lady as his inspiration. She was, for him, the symbol of *all beauty and perfection*. This ideal moved him to be noble, spiritual, refined and high minded. What kept everything in check, because most often the chosen one was married, was the cultivation of chivalry and honor. The ultimate sacrifice for this noble heart was honor for love. The suitor was severely tested, often by the lady herself, who had to be assured that her suitor had a gentle heart and was not just lusty! So there was a tradition of delay, test and trial, with an outcome of either rejection or the granting of *merci*, which may be a correctly placed kiss once a year or considerably more! *Campbell's* favorite trial of the whole of the Middle Ages (which he studied in great detail, including learning the language of Provencal) was the "*Trial of the Perilous Bed,*" one which just may hold some resonance for couples today.

The knight on trial, let's call him Lancelot, was brought in full armor into a room which was completely empty, except for a bed in the middle, which was on rollers. So, wearing sword, shield, spear, lots of heavy stuff he was to get into the bed, which immediately sheared away to one side. So then he would try again and the bed would go the other way. Lancelot finally thinks, "I've got to jump." So, with his full gear he then jumps into the bed, and as soon as he hits the bed it starts bucking like a bronco, all over the room, banging against the walls, until it finally stops. He was then told, "It's not finished yet. Keep your armor on and your shield over yourself." And then arrows and crossbow colts pummel him-bang, bang, bang. Then a lion appears and attacks the knight, but he cuts off the lions feet, and the two of them end up lying together, done for, in a pool of blood. The ladies of the castle, which had to be disenchanted by this great event come in and see the knight lying as if dead. One of them takes a bit of fur from her garment and holds it in front of his nose, which moves ever so slightly-he's alive! So, they nurse him back to health, and the castle is disenchanted. [15]

What was the meaning of a trial of this kind? *Campbell* and his colleague *Henry Zimmer* came to see it as the masculine experience of the feminine temperament wherein nothing really makes sense to the man but that's the way it is. Perhaps it was an old fashioned version of, *"Men are from Mars and Women Are From Venus."*[16] Another similarly instructive mythical trial was called the *Sword Bridge* where Lancelot, with bare hands and feet, had to cross a raging torrent along a bridge made of a sword. This is a motif from the *Upanishads* of the East, whereby any trip along the path of love, as destiny, is a razor's edge. It is quite likely, when following one's passion of the moment, to tip over, fall into a torrent and be swept away!

There are many stories, old and new, to instruct in the trials of the path of romantic love. One of the first recorded was written around the end of the twelfth century by an unnamed French poet, then developed by other writers especially those from the Celtic world of *Brittany* and *Cornwall* in *Southern England*. It is a story which has enduring reflections in great literature, opera, drama and film classics such as *"Cassablanca."* The perennial theme is that the *shadow of death makes eros, the archetype of the erotic, the partner of tragedy.* It is about the split between the world of obligation and duty, contrasted with the bliss of love which beckons to another world, a world of the timeless. One recalls, for example, the profound agony and ecstasy of a dying *Catherine* lost to her beloved *Heathcliffe*, in the nineteenth century *Bronte* novel, *"Wuthering Heights."*

A similar yet much older tale explored by Robert Johnson,[17] is the story of *Tristan and Iseult*, in which Tristan is a great and chivalrous knight of the kingdom of *Cornwall*, and Iseult, a princess and sorceress of power in the *Celtic* kingdom of *Ireland*. The two kingdoms are feuding. *Tristan and Iseult* fall in love through inadvertently drinking a magic potion intended for Iseult's husband and Tristan's king. Previously Tristan had drunk a poisonous potion prepared by the Queen, Iseult's mother. He was saved only by the skill of her daughter. So, in this story, both potions are for cure of the pain of love, the sickness until death which no doctor can cure. The message is that *in drinking the 'in-love' potion you have drunk your death.* The symbol of a potion tells us that this is not ordinary love between two which comes by knowing each other as communion but a mysterious, alchemical situation which is involuntary. They are possessed. As we say it today, *"they are in love with love."*

This archetypal situation is felt every bit as much in the present day by all who have drunk the love potion and consummated their union in the sacrament of love, sexual intercourse, in an illicit context. In this, and countless stories, the situation of romantic love is one of love against marriage, lovers against family wishes, counterculture against culture, the ecstatic against the profane. What is sought by the lovers is not human love, or relationship alone but a religious experience, a world which is outside of the mind of ego. Its concern is spiritual aspiration through the lens of romantic love.

When the beloved has the power to give "light to our lives" or extinguish that light, then we have adopted the lover as the symbol and image of God.

Joseph Campbell[18]

Robert Johnson explores the fallacy of romantic love as a basis for marriage. He speaks of our preoccupation with it as the single greatest energy system in the Western psyche, having supplanted religion as the arena in which men and women seek meaning. We cannot assume that the experience of love is necessarily the same for men and women. Indeed, the meeting of male and female is *the* meeting of differences for it contains the 'holy mystery.' Without mystery there can be no initiation.

Romantic love is one of those truly overwhelming psychological phenomena to have appeared in western history. It has overwhelmed our collective psyche and permanently altered our view of the world. As a society we have not yet learned to handle the tremendous power of romantic love. We turn it into tragedy and alienation more often than enduring human relationships. [19]

Johnson views falling in love as a veritable trial by fire, the equivalent of the *Zen* teaching of a " red hot coal stuck in the throat which we can't swallow and we can't cough up." This 'hot coal,' that feels to be out of control may alert us to a tremendous evolutionary potential which is trying to manifest. *"The beginning of wisdom is a firm grasp of the obvious,"* and maturity would bring us to see what is obvious, that it is quite unreasonable to expect   another fallible human to carry for us our happiness, wholeness, meaning, intensity, and ecstasy.

The power that forces you into consciousness and that sustains you in your conscious world proves to be the worst enemy when you come to the next center, for there you are going out of this world and everything that makes you cling to it is your worst enemy. The greatest blessing in one world is the greatest curse in the next.   C.G Jung [20]

The *Lovers* card in the tarot deck is instructive as symbolic image and teaching on the union of the opposites. The *Devil* card, which is an associated card, makes the problem of 'shadow' more explicit. We are now a little more accustomed to looking into the *"long bag of shadow"* and slowly come to see that the sacrament of marriage may only be truly taken when the projected shadow material, the stuff that makes us both fall in love and fall out again, is owned *a drama going on inside of us.* We are, more often than not, reluctant to train the binoculars on the inner landscape and its dramas.

Berowne, the male protagonist in the *Shakespearian* play, *"Loves Labors Lost,"* spends much of the play looking for himself in the eyes of a woman. When he meets *Rosaline*, a witty, capable and 'enchantingly negative,' feminist woman who does not accept his narcissistic projections, he has met his catastrophe, hence an opportunity - the Devil card! *Shakespeare's* observation is that men fall in love largely through visual stimulation, women fall in love more comprehensively, and subtly. *Berowne* and his four friends unsuccessfully pursue their objects of desire, demonstrating for us the folly of acting love and talking love without being-love.

Why, all his behaviors did make their retire
To the court of his eye peeping through desire:
His heart like an agate with your print impressed,
Proud with his form in his eye pride expressed
His tongue all impatient to speak and not see,

His tongue all impatient to speak and not see,
Did stumble in haste in his eyesight to be.
All senses to that sense did make their repair,
To fell only looking on fairest of fair.

    Shakespeare's brilliance differentiates relationships based on lust and those based on participation and honorable intentions. However, life is not always either noble or tragic. Lust and comedy have their place in all of our histories. Shakespeare's best loved example is perhaps in *'Much Ado about Nothing,'* made into a delightful film with *Emma Thompson* as a provocative *Beatrice*, who both knows and loves herself, indeed she is aware and awake to *Self* which lifts the feeling tone of this fated attraction to one of lightness even joy. She maintains a dance of folly with frustrating distance, playing at the game of love, acting love until she is out played, outwitted or offers *merci!* This is a joyful play one of wit, fun and folly. It is one of the very few plays which culminates in marriage although we must assume that in the union of Benedict and Beatrice, that this marriage is the beginning of a slow and simmering, not always tasty, soup pot!

    Who of us without patience and endurance can possibly unravel the complexities of independence *and* union? Berowne does learn about himself the painful way, through rejection.

Learning is but an adjunct to oneself
And where we are, our learning likewise is;
Then when ourselves we see in ladies
Do we not likewise see our learning there?
O! We have made a vow to study lords,
And in that vow have foreswom our books;
For when would you, my liege, or you or you,
In leaden contemplation have found out
Such fiery numbers as the prompting eyes
Of beauty's tutors have enriched you with. [21]

    The lovers card instructs on learning (often through awareness of self-projections) to balance the inner masculine and feminine elements, the aspects of soul, anima and animus. If we have not fully embraced these opposites then they fall into shadow, as elements being looked for in the beloved. Having found what we most want and possessing it in marriage, (a recent and western consequence of romantic love) then later do we reject those very attributes, as fantasy love turns to fantasy hatred. Only one strategy is left which is to *own those denied aspects as ourselves*.

Disparate parts of psyche seem like countries of the world, at permanent odds and constantly bickering with each other. Whether owned internally or projected onto our ex-beloved this is the archetype of war.It involves not only the hero, me, but also the other,as scapegoat, so that I in my rightness may be vindicated and justified. This plays out in our bedrooms, on school playgrounds and between the terrorists of the world stage. Blame always adheres to the other, since we live under the illusion that we know ourselves and have adequately dealt with our own negative intent. To the extent that I have to be right and good, *he, she,* or *they* become the carriers of *what I fail to apprehend in myself.* The people who are in the best position to help us see our shadow elements are those who know us well. Paradoxically they are the very ones who we are least likely to heed! But we can rest assured that any time our response to another person involves excessive emotion or overreaction, that something *in us* has been stirred. The unwelcome negative shadow qualities are in glaring contrast to the ego's ideals and wishful efforts. There are also times when our golden shadow is projected as admiration for those who, in thought word or deed, express the very gifts which lay dormant in ourselves.

Owning all of this is to sail into rough waters for it is the shock to discover shadow and one's moral obligation to truth. It takes courage not to flinch from what one sees as other, namely one's inferior self. Not only discrimination but self discipline is required, an effort of will. Our tendency is toward irresponsible repression which appears to be less painful and is anyway a habitual reflex. In a state of repression we simply look the other way, *outward.* It is important to understand that we are never irresponsible in the way we *are* or feel but growing up means to be responsible for the way we *act.* Growing into the beingness of love requires us to act, at times, *contrary to the way we feel.* This the real task which love prepares us for, *the* confrontation of adulthood. Nowhere is this more obvious than in the lengthy and enduring love and self surrender required in the adequate parenting of children.

Where love rules there is no will to power, and where power predominates there love is lacking. The one is the shadow of the other.   CG Jung[22]

This is the tough spade work part of *Innerscape* which was quoted in an earlier chapter. The ruler must rule, the king or queen, the noble ones must preside, that means our highest self and the practices which sustain 'her/him' are needed to hold us steady. Especially are they needed now in confronting love's battles, in this heart redeeming, cleansing- the- doors- of- perception, invitation of Spring.

Love grows in depth by virtue of lovers enduring encounters with each other, conflict and growth over a period of time. These cannot be omitted from any lasting and viable experience of love. They involve choice and will under whatever name you use. The love which is separated from will is characterized by a passivity which does not grow with its own passion; such love tends, therefore, towards dissociation. It ends in something which is not fully personal because it does not fully discriminate.   Rollo May[23]

The outcome of this patient and difficult inner work/outer intimacy is to balance *anima and animus*, as a harmonious oneness in Self. The sacramental ritual for this part of the quest is *marriage*. This marriage is within, a coming into harmony with oneself, living in a state of being-love. Because the work of *Innerscape* is primarily inner work it is not appropriate for group members to develop intimate relationships with each other. Those are to be found in living. A group of individuals on a journey are to some extent in a limbo space, a space out of life. The correct relationship is one of trust, kindliness and friendliness. Today, conditions were arranged so that small groups could be together all day, sharing, inquiring into love and compassion, meeting in a meditative connectedness. One activity was to take this cultivated care out into the community of the village to practice random acts of loving-kindness. An interesting exercise which saw group members playing with children, carrying a baby, picking up garbage, buying a startled boy an ice cream and giving a young person, five dollars. .... *I decided to continue this exercise, practicing random acts of kindness every day during the month. It was not as easy as I thought. Not everyone wanted to receive a flower from a stranger. I found it difficult to be creative with what I gave, also how my own lack of energy impacted on my ability to perform tasks with any genuine sense of love. But my perception of people changed. I really looked at them. I payed attention rather than moving along with my own inner dramas.*

Another heart 'gift' was to give hand massages since touch is the expression of connection and communion. For many the simplicity of this activity belied its profundity. More than one commented, "*I must go home and do this with my partner."* It is so often our closest that are neglected in gestures of friendliness and care.

> The ache of marriage
> thigh and tongue, beloved,
> are heavy with it,
> it throbs in the teeth
> We look for communion
> and are turned away, beloved,
> each and each
> it is Levithian and we
> in its belly
> looking for joy, some joy
> not to be known outside it
> two by two in the ark of
> the ache of it.
>   Denise Levertov[24]

"What is love and how do we sustain it in marital relationships?" As we have looked at the perils of projecting out our own shadow side onto the other and the shock of that revelation, we can see why commitment during the time of engagement and disentanglement is crucial, if we are ever to know what love is. As *Johnson* warns, our commitment to passion, (due to our misplaced belief in romantic love) is not a substitute for commitment to a human being. If we are immersed in the poetry and the play, as though it were all, then we are confused in thinking that this 'in love' archetype is applicable to human necessity. This is the key point in *Johnson's* differentiation of romantic love as an affect, which, if correctly understood and worked through, may lead to a spiritual and transcendental love. Another archetype, the one of loyalty or devotion (the servant as well as the warrior) is also required as a crucible for human relationship.

Almost everyone is looking for a committed relationship. Most people sense that this is what they need, and before they begin they assume that the single ingredient for relationship, the one that we can't do without, is romance. In fact the essential ingredients for relationship are affection and commitment.   Robert Johnson[25]

Tristan possesses two 'tools' which accompany him on this perilous journey, namely his *sword* and his *harp*. The one is either a tool of discrimination or a weapon of endings, the other an instrument of softness, gentleness of the feminine or the soul. It is the harp which saves Tristan's life, (although he needs both) just as it is the inner feminine value which hero *Ivan* pursues through various trials.

The sword cannot build relationships; it can't settle anything, it can't bind together. It can only rip apart. If you want to heal your relationship, then you must learn to use the language of the harp. You must affirm the other person, express your love and devotion. The harp heals and binds together, the sword (poorly handled) wounds and cuts asunder.

Robert Johnson [26]

In speaking of love we have attended to *communion* but in speaking of enduring relationship we inevitably arrive at the difficulty of *communication*. Every marital therapist has seen many a love bond be broken due to the incapacity to 'play the harp' through well chosen words. Many have difficulty in finding words to bridge and heal the sword's inevitable thrusts, the aggressive slings and arrows of self protected wounds. Words arising from the being-of-love, words of loving kindness are indeed the harp's music and almost instantly restore harmony and balance. Strange how we are still provoked into sword language!

For one human being to love another human being; that is perhaps the most difficult task that has been entrusted to us, the ultimate task the final test and proof, the work for which all other work is merely preparation.

Rainer Maria Rilke [27]

Intimate relationship is indeed a dizzying dance of polarities, a dance of coming together and apart, yielding and taking the lead, giving of ourselves and maintaining integrity. It is not an easy dance to learn, and many lose the rhythm, to end up in deadlocked positions, with swords out, not knowing whether to attack or withdraw. How do we learn the art of this dance, the grace and power of it? *John Wellwood,*[28] suggests that a meditation practice is most effective in learning to face the difficulties which *arise in relating to intimate others. The qualities we bring to our meditation* practice, of openness, trust and steadfastness are the very qualities we need to *remain in the present moment with just what is,* in the dance of intimacy. This is a balance place, one of remaining in a simple and direct relationship with things as they are and not as we would like them to be, or as we fantasize they should be.

Tony Packer, a post- modern Zen teacher, when asked about this dance of intimacy had only two succinct responses.

Leave each other alone (all one.)
Forgive each other everything right from the outset.

We have seen the difficulty in differentiating exactly what is going on in oneself and what is happening with the other. Many couples find themselves in a marriage of opposites. What were seen as wonderful and complementary traits initially, later become the awful things that one wishes one had noticed in time! What were initially benign or even endearing qualities later can become quite unendurable if we see them as being 'not-like-me.' For 'not-like-me' forces me to grow into acceptance, self appraisal and a confrontation with the righteousness and autonomous claims of the personal ego. In other words the work of loving

For-give is a word worth looking at carefully. For-to-give. The word gift lives in the word. This is an active not a passive word. To give-forwards involves an act of handing something to another so that from now on it belongs to them. It is an exchange of faith, in that what has been done can be undone and transcended by inclusion, not exclusion through forgetting. This is commitment, the promise to continue transcending through forgiveness.

Anyone afraid of breaking, within and without, is in the wrong marriage. Let it all go. Let the winds blow. Let's see what's left in the morning. That is the solace of marriage; the discovery of what is unbreakable among all that's been broken. The discovery that people must share not only what they do not know about each other but also what they do not know about themselves.   Michael Ventura[29]

Here is a remarkable, if ironic, case for separating relationship from marriage. The same differentiation that the church has been solidly holding on to for centuries, the famous, 'till death do us part,' line, the one which keeps the fainthearted from even setting out on this perilous, "anima/animus, bee-bopping, see- saw." Ventura, in very unchurch like language warns of the perils of pairing.

The archetypal pairings (my homeless waif to your loving mother; your tough street kid to my honky-tonk angel; your lost father, to my doting daughter; my Goddess to your worshiper; your client to my analyst; my intensity to your ground; your professor to my student, etc.) hold with attraction whilst they behave, but on the day when the little boy in him is looking for the mummy in her, and finds instead, on this occasion, a sharp toothed analyst dissecting his guts or, when the little girl in her is looking for daddy and finds a pagan worshiper who wants a goddess to lay with, which induces her to play -act a goddess to please daddy who's really a lecherous worshiper and,....... little girls can't come. Similarly, when a man's sexuality is in service to a guilty interior little boy it's not surprising that in the sexual encounter he is really still masturbating, and the woman who happens to be an adjunct, never feels seen or known. [30]

All of this goes on in marriage, as we are painfully aware, but the difference is that instead of disappearing, we marry this process in the other, we take it on, which encourages us to be actively engaged in mirroring the other through a willingness to tell it as it feels. To hold up a mirror for the other, which, when frequently repeated becomes rather obviously asking to be seen.

Perhaps all the dragons of our lives
are princesses who are only waiting to
see us once, beautiful and brave.
Perhaps everything terrible is in its deepest being
Something that needs our love.

Rainer Maria Rilke[31]

One of the most moving accounts of the transformation of an 'in love' relationship through the tempering fires of terminal illness, is told in *"Grace and Grit"* by *Ken and Treya Kilam Wilber.* Through the inevitable strain of care giving, seeking cures, loss of hope and finally death, this couple transcended to a truly enlightened experience of 'being- love.'In the book, both of them speak frankly about the testing of the crucible of marriage. As things worsen towards the end, *Ken* found insight then peace with the demanding requirements of continual and loving care giving.

.....within the realm of your own doing you have to affirm the choices you have made. That is you have to stand behind those choices which have molded your own fate; as the existentialists say, " We are our choices." Failing to affirm our choices is ' bad faith,' and is said to lead to inauthentic being. So, each day I reaffirm my choice. Each day I choose once again.

Ken Wilber[32]

The account of the death of *Treya* and the union of these two in 'one heart, one mind' is an exquisitely moving piece of writing-of-heart. A triumph of love and will, grace and grit. When *Treya* departed the body, what *Ken* was left with, were these words.

"Practice the wound of love." Real love hurts; real love makes you totally vulnerable and open; real love will take you far beyond yourself; and therefore real love will devastate you. I kept thinking, "If love does not shatter you, you don't know love." We had both been practicing the wound of love. Looking back on it in that simple and direct moment I think we both died.[33]

When personal love ends, as end it must, as *Thanatos* overcomes *Eros*, then we experience grief. None escapes it, by the time we reach middle age, there have already been encounters with loss and grief.

> Who then devised the torment?
> Love is the unfamiliar Name
> Behind the hands that wove
> The intolerable shirt of flame
> Which human power cannot remove.
> We only live, only suspire
> Consumed by either fire or fire.   T.S Eliot[34]

It is this emotion which more than any other renders us vulnerable to closing down by way of numbness and distance. There is a common defensive pattern of choosing to love less, feel less and be safe from the impact of loss. Such a decision, if not apprehended, leads to a profound wound, also *death of soul*. *When grief is properly expressed, then it leads to a revelation of the vast capacity of the heart to love, to be loved, and to go on loving.* The heart of compassion is born out of the deepest suffering, indeed the root of the word *passion* is the word *suffering*. It is a natural movement of an open heart and cannot be contrived. If it is then it is then shadow of resentment and exhaustion will surface. From wise and willing encounter with the sorrow and joys of loving we slowly reconstruct the always-so treasure.

> Again, again even if we know the countryside of love,
> and the tiny churchyard with its names mourning,
> and the chasm, more and more silent, terrifying into which the others
> dropped: we walk out together anyway
> beneath the ancient trees, we lie down again,
> again, among the flowers, and face the sky.
>
>   Rainer Maria Rilke[35]

8

What is true?

I do not know much about gods; but I think that the river
is a strong brown god -sullen, untamed and intractable,
Patient to some degree, at first recognized as a frontier;
Useful, untrustworthy as a conveyer of commerce;
Then only a problem confronting the builder of bridges.
The problem once solved, the brown god is almost forgotten
By the dwellers in cities -ever, however, implacable,
Keeping his seasons and rages, destroyer, reminder
Of what men chose to forget. Unhonoured, unproipitiated
By worshipers of the machine, but waiting
Watching and waiting.

                                                    T.S. Eliot[1]

It is Sunday. A Sunday for truth
The Goddess of Spring has been sullen at the start of May. Far from the image of May poles encircled by garlanded maidens dancing the fertility rites of *Beltane*, the land has become whitened with a late snowfall, crocuses and early blooms hidden, the river gushing with rising snow melt and in the shallows, intricate designs of crystals on driftwood. Chattering birds remind us of Spring, whatever the weather, eager toward their nests. Light flakes of snow fragile and transparent, disappear against the clouds some settling noiselessly, not enough to cover the ground. Traveling early the flat white of the sky gradually brightens to reveal a pale sun, the snow like white ash floating in the air. It is quite amazing to consider that every tiny snowflake is a perfect *mandala*. A corner of clear blue sky reveals dazzling mountains, silent witnesses to the charging river of life.

No matter the weather, this season is one of rapid change with sap rising and a populace on the move, motivated toward change. Change of clothing, houses, locales, adventures, get-away holiday plans. Similarly, in our most recent reading of the myth, *Ivan* has symbolically mounted the fire bird, having recovered a more mature, independent, confident Self. As for my own Spring change I have journeyed on the annual Spring pilgrimage across the Great Divide to the Pacific Ocean. Another ferry crossing, (no cars this time) to a small Gulf Island concludes the journey/ pilgrimage from a world of *speaking* to a world of *listening* and the question between which is one of *truth*.

Relationship with other is predominantly a function of seeing as our eye's perceptions extend us to the *outside*. Now we examine *listening*, as a more inward faculty, bringing the world inside as it were, to be apprehended, digested and subjectively reinterpreted. The outcome of this process is expressed through *language*. Language is always associated with the speaking body. It is idiosyncratic to history, time, place and culture. Our ears and eyes are drawn together by phenomena within the landscape, a natural and necessary trait for a hunter/gatherer people. We do not point our ears at things like cats and dogs do, we don't need to turn to hear things. Looking at things tells us where to go, what is around us but listening is done in one place, announcing where we stand in the scheme of things. *Eyes* actively draw us out into participation, *ears* are expectant and patiently receptive when directed towards, for example, person, tree, bird, rock, or dwelling. It is through our listening faculty that we await truth.

...ears.......are more inward organs; they emerge from the depths of my skull like blossoms or funnels, and their participation tells me less about the outward surface than the interior substance of things   David Abram[2]

A moment ago a robin sang its familiar melody outside an open window. This sound penetrated my concentration, linking my interiority with context, a reminder of the larger whole into which I am always connected. Listening encourages me to glance, then pause and *really* look, eyes responding to ears. Fully aware now. *Awareness* expands to take in the receding tide, an open expanse of flat water and now *smell* adds the soft-moist characteristic of ocean air. There is an occasional gull call, eagle call, the float plane engine, the dog snoring. Arbutus trees gracefully bend toward the seashore, pine branches swish on the roof, lime green tips of the young spruce dazzle like tree lights. Such a vivid green cannot help but invite. If I take up that come hither, and cross the lawn to taste one, I find that they taste as good as they look! A spring vitamin C, a tonic. This whole experience-in-the-moment, nature's calling card, her language, is just what I needed to return to a concentrated task with renewed vigor!

> A community of trees
> Thousands of bodies
> With a human body among them.
> Branches and leaves are waving
> Then the call of a creek
> And my eyes open to the sky of great mind,
> A smile is then seen on every leaf.
> The forest is here because the city is over there,
> But mind is gone with the tree
> And put on a new green dress.
> The sunshine is the leaves
> The leaves are the sunshine
> AllI other forms and sounds are of the same nature

> Thich Nhat Hahn[3]

Without thought this is the world complete and I, as silent sensory participant, a part of this whole. Such a context, invites a lessening of the I/me boundary, the separateness known only to man. That is why I came here as a synchronous finale to my personal quest, spent all of my savings against all sensible, rational advice to find a home, a dwelling which invited Self-in-context. Led by intuition, I stumbled upon the pearl beyond price, the old (out of) fashioned! Such a life, we may call it *aboriginal*, is determined by wind and weather, by seasonal necessity, by growth and blooming, always in touch with the miracle of life. There is nowhere to drive to, nowhere to go shopping, nowhere to be entertained, yet each day slips by from sun to moon, in a rhythm all of its own, asking only to be accommodated as the body/mind's needs are made known. What strikes me most, similar to meditation retreats, is the steady pace of being/doing, the sense of working in the here and now without a particular goal driven activity, just the process as part of the changing seasonal context and necessity. There is a correct time and tide for sowing, planting, reaping and harvesting, resting. Because of this order there is a calmness which accompanies the day's unfolding. All is punctuated by quietness. I cannot help but notice that *it is here in the listening that truth, the truth of no - separation, reveals itself.*

For the famous *Socratic 'Phaedrus Dialogue,' Plato and Socrates* went outside of the city walls into the countryside to *"test their citified knowledge against the older knowledge embedded in the land."* Plato was putting philosophy to the test, by exposing it to nonhuman powers, which for the entire history of mankind, had compelled awe, reverence and attention. In this dialogue, *Socrates* reminds *Phaedrus* that, *" the first prophetic utterances came from an oak tree."* He speculated about the watching *chickadees* in the tree tops, wondering if they were perhaps interceding on their behalf with the muses. Later, he tells a myth of how chickadees were once musicians, teaching people how to sing. In oral traditions, including our *Native American* one, there are always substantive stories alluding to the special communication capacities of animals, both with people and "the other world." One may dismiss these as primitive explanations or as acknowledgment of the heart of nature's essence, in this case the propinquity for song. Perhaps chickadees have the truth of song, singing the day, life, into existence in the emergent now?

The thesis of a *language of nature as the utterance of truth*, therefore the foundation of all original spoken languages, is explored at depth by *David Abram* in, *"The Spell of the Sensuous."* The same thesis is implicit in the writings of *Sir Laurens van der Post*, who, in referring to his native African landscape said,

...there.....I had an intimacy with man's remotest beginnings through the animals, plants skies, winds, the clouds, the seasons which even in their most severe or generous moments, gathered me from all ends of my being into the universe, as if into the heart of a family singularly my own.[4]

Sir Laurens van der Post's convocation address to the *University of Calgary in 1995* was a particularly memorable event. He wrapped his speech around the *context* in which he found himself, on this occasion, at "the place of earth meeting mountains." These foothills are, he said, symbolically implicit in everyone's mind, as an understanding that the heights of knowledge can only rest upon Mother earth, the feminine energies and values. He warned, if we did not maintain a deep respect for the earth, along with knowledge, that the heart of our life would crumble to devastating effect. He invited participants to a synchronous existence with and in our sensual context.

Recalling this injunction causes me to pause in writing *now* and notice a strong ocean wind blowing into the bay, waking up the senses, energizing the trees, the gulls, this body. *David Abram* recounts the import of the wind to the *Navajo* people. I look again, *what exactly is this wind saying*, from whence does it originate, over what territory has it recently past, carrying what voices, in what language?

According to native legend the wind of noon is the blue wind, called *Horizontal Blue Girl* and comes from the south; *Horizontal Yellow Boy* is from the west, *Dawn White Woman* from the east, and *Darkness Man* from the north. So which holy wind of the sacred four directions is my wind today? After a promenade along the deck, with a chiffon scarf I return invigorated, excited, creative, and filled with the South West wind/sun, sparkling off turbulent water, just right for the mid-afternoon Yellow Boy. I had no intention of writing about wind when I began, but here is the context informing the words blown through finger tips as weather and language, synchronous and true. Interestingly, the four *winds* are referred to in *Navajo* wisdom teaching as the four *words*, linked to the sacred breath, of the four cardinal directions and the sacred mountains of the world. From here the *Holy Wind* is said to approach and enter into the various natural phenomena of the world and so to provide the means of life, thought, movement and speech to plants, animals and all other Earth surface people.

Wandering upon the Saskatchewan prairies in personal exploration of the particularities of her husband's land, *Sharon Butala* declared that, "This land makes Crees of us all." Here she refers to the local indigenous people, who had the same sacred relationship with this natural environment as did the Navajo with theirs. She went on to say that they developed the culture they developed because it was the best fit between themselves and the land.

........it was the *land* that taught them that. They adapted to the land and not the other way around as the Europeans so stupidly did...........in our human arrogance we assume that we can affect the land but it can't affect us, but Nature is affecting us without our being aware of it. .... I am suggesting that the ways in which such a closeness affects us, from dreams to more subtle phenomena, (such as the invisible energy of history apprehended by different parts of the body) are real, and that we should stop thinking with our inflated egos that all the influence is the other way round.......... I am coming to believe that our alienation from the natural world is at root of much that has gone so wrong in the modern world, and that If Nature has anything to teach us at all, her first lesson is humility

Sharon Butala[5]

.... *I have had eight days on a sail boat and have quite amazingly had nights of vivid dreams, since I haven't had any for a long time, is it sleeping on the ocean that is giving me these dreams?*

David Abram suggests that the source of stress in modern culture lies in the paucity of relationship *between* the human community and the natural landscape. He describes perception as a concerted activity of *all* the body's senses, an I-thou participation. According to Native perception, although invisible, Holy Wind affects our bodies and can be recognized by the swirling and spiraling traces that it leaves in the visible world.

There are whorls at the tips of our fingers. Winds stick out here.................it is the same on our toes, and where our soft spots are at the top of our heads. Some children have two spirals, some have only one....those with two live by means of two winds. The winds sticking out of the whorls at the tips of our toes hold us to the Earth. Those at our fingertips hold us to the Sky. Because of these we do not fall when we move about.

James Kale McNeley[6]

Standing barefoot upon the windswept beach I plant my toes in the earth, fingers reaching to sky, toward a deeper appreciation of the context-container of 'my' life. I/me is so small here, so insignificant, so transparent, to be blown through, or swept away by the tide. I must confess that after a lengthy spell in the city I was starting to wobble....Are there any possible wind-words, accurate enough for this inner knowing?

We fall down and down, until we touch the ground, until we relate with the basic sanity of the earth. We become the lowest of the low, the smallest of the small, a grain of sand perfectly simple, no expectations......... If you are a grain of sand, the rest of the universe all the space, all the room is yours, because you obstruct nothing, overcrowd nothing. Here is tremendous openness. You are the emperor of the universe because you are a grain of sand.

Chogyam Trungpa Rinpoche[7]

.... *This month I deliberately planned for time in nature in order to listen. It was amazing, on the beach feeling the ocean kiss my body, in the forest hiking alongside a waterfall and a magical walk in a city park where a swan invited me to sit at a bench. I felt no gap between all that is and isn't. I sang out and the wind blew harder in approval.*

Air is the element traditionally associated with the *chakra* energies between heart and head. It's symbol is the *antelope*, representing "Lord of the Wind," which is *the breath*. It is through this wind/word/breath that the gross physical body of matter is purged, opened up to the subtle body of the spirit, the expanded Self. The name for the fifth *chakra*, or energy center of *breath exchange*, located physically at the throat, is *'Visshudi'* which means 'to purge. Every breath reminds us of the totality of Self-in- context. What you breathe out I take in, what I release out I give to you. Air/ether is, in the Eastern system the agent of *'lightness of being.'*

The equivalent of, 'en-lightening,' in our Western myth, is *Ivan's* mounting of the firebird and *his symbolic movement in air and upon air.* *Baba Yaga's* severed heads which decorate her fence must be negotiated by *Ivan* prior to liberation on the firebird. Skulls are symbolic of cutting off the body/ego's dominance, much like the necklace of skulls worn by *Baba Yaga's* sister, the Indian goddess *Kali.* The flower of new life comes from having killed off the old one or having seen through its limitations. In order to really breathe the 'breath of God' *we must pull up this etheric energy, against ourselves as it were, we must be willing and available to be blown through by this wind.* For the *Navajo* wind exists all around *and* within the individual, entering and departing through respiratory organs and whorls on the body surfaces.

Just as we are nourished and influenced by the air at large, so do our actions and thoughts affect wind, word, and world. We are not passive with regard to this *Holy Wind* but rather participate *in* it as one of its organs. Personal intention could be thought of as an interior wind which participates in the Holy invisible wind around us, thus it engages and subtly influences events in our surroundings. Hence the emphasis among many native people upon *concentrated thought and prayer in order to influence and aid earthly occurrences from the un-manifest to the manifest,* carried on the wind.

Pilgrimage involves a retraining of our capacity to *truly listen.* What was once a well honed faculty in us, as with all animals, has rapidly atrophied in the technological world, where our contextually-mindful focus has narrowed to one of concentrated, goal-driven, attention, usually future oriented. *We look without listening, and speak without looking,* let alone hear what we are saying, nor do we notice the wind's words or the river's song as reply.

Wind, as breath, enables us to speak. We have already translated the Greek word for *psyche* as breath but it translates literally as, *'gust of wind.'* Numerous ancient languages have identical words for wind, spirit, soul and breath. In *Hebrew* they are all one word, *ruach.* In modern languages vowels are the sounds made by unhindered breath, the 'unstruck sound' which we referred to in the previous chapter as the sound of the universe,"Om," more accurately phonetically sounded as, "A-u-i-e-o-mmmm." These are the central sounds of words with consonants accompanying or 'sounding with' the vowel. It would be true to say that a meditative life naturally has more vowels and fewer consonants. In most chants it is the vowels which are sounded, lending a sense of floating in space and proceeding to endings which are unhurried and graceful. Vowel sounds are the ones which nourish, not wound, as do some of the sounds which escape from loud stereo driven automobiles. Nature herself has a chant which is tonal in context, therefore consonant with soul life if we are able, at least occasionally, to escape the incessant and inescapable consonant noise of modern life!

Today, as an exercise in awareness of speech, group members will tell their stories of the month with a tape recorder recording as they do so. This is a little artificial in a way but sometimes quite illuminating to hear ourselves speaking. This exercise also has the effect of slowing down speech, such that the sounded breath of vowels and awareness of the spoken consonants, is encouraged. Not only what we say, the words, the phrases we habitually use but also how we speak, what we convey, are an invisible aspect of our idiosyncratic use of language, and of self perception. .... *For most of the month I was paralyzed at the idea of listening to the tape and I waited until the last week. I actually enjoyed listening to it and found the group very supportive. I know the confusion in the speech is also in my head. I find it hard to follow the rhythm of a conversation and be part of it, it's like I'm either too silent or want to say too much and interrupt people. I do feel like a child when it comes to language....a silent child embarrassed by lack of speech and the numbness that takes hold when someone talks to her.*

Mans word
is the daughter of death
We talk because we are
mortal; words
are not signs, they are years.
Saying what they say,
the names we speak
say time: they say us,
we are the names of time.
To talk is human.   Octavia Pay[8]

Words are not mere sounds for clucking at each other, although they may all too frequently, in cadence, content and rhythm, mimic exactly that. Often we do not think what we say or say what we think. There is an Ancient Chinese saying from *Lao Tzu*,

He who knows does not speak; he who speaks does not know.[9]

This month's quest is questioning language, *"How well do I listen to others? What is the tonal quality of my voice and what does it convey? Do I speak my truth? What repetitive words do I use which direct my experience and influence my relationships? What do I know of myself when I am silent?"*

.... *When I did the affirmation, "People listen to me and value me for who I am," it struck a cord. I couldn't hear it enough, I had an insatiable need to be listened to.*

The word is not just a sound or written symbol but a force whose power literally creates life events.

.... *I grew up where children were to be seen and not heard. Speaking my truth has come later, but I am keenly aware of the limitations I still place on myself in this regard.*

No other animal can speak although they certainly possess idiosyncratic language but for us *speech is the most powerful tool we have.* This is a two edged sword, it can create a good wind or an ill wind. It can further love and connection or insult and separation.

One sentence crosses the empty space between us. It settles on his lips.
I fill my glass again. I drink. The veils drop between us.
I am admitted to the warmth and privacy of another soul.   Wolf [10]

..........*This month I have realized how negative, hurtful, gossipy words flow more easily than loving comforting words. My words can be extremely negative and judgmental. Especially with my family I need to say the positive words not just think them. I assume that they know how I feel, but if they are just listening to my words, maybe not. When my kids get off the school bus they don't know that I've been watching the window waiting for them to come and that I'm so happy they're home. They hear " Why aren't you wearing your coat," or, "Where's your backpack?" Maybe I'll try telling them how happy I am first.*

Impeccability of one's word is defined as one of the four great agreements of human discourse by *Don Miguel Ruiz*, where *impeccability* means, *"without sin,"* that is anything which goes against the Self and the Self is the totality. *Being impeccable in speech is the correct use of human energy which implies being in harmony with the whole.*

If you make an agreement with yourself to be impeccable with your word, just with that intention, the truth will manifest through you and clean all the emotional poison that exists within you. But making this agreement is difficult because we have learned to do precisely the opposite. We have learned to lie as a habit of our communication with others and more importantly with ourselves. We are not impeccable with the Word.

Don Miguel Ruiz[11]

Discrimination of the word, our word, is becoming more and more urgent in this age of instant communication, where *Internet chat* lines employ a kind of *psuedo speech* to convey as little as possible, as quickly as possible to the greatest number of virtual reality people. There is little consideration of the false impressions spread by instant verbiage which fails to take into account much of its own cloned context. It is not a medium which encourages responsible thought and expression yet it is increasingly the choice method of communication, one which fails to allow for the necessity of contextual mutuality in real relating. Further, it emulates frenzied publicity over private, careful and caring discourse.

> There's something dangerous
> In being with good talkers.
> The fly's stories of his ancestors
> Don't mean much to the frog.
> I can't be the noisy person I am
> if you don't stop talking.
> Some people talk so brilliantly
> that we get small and vanish.
> The shadows near the Dutch woman
> Tell you that Rembrandt is a good listener

Robert Bly [12]

The kind of words which we utter, and in this we differ, are differentiated as language, and language discriminates us as belonging to a particular culture, geography or location. Even the boundaries of language are now disappearing, to be replaced with a kind of modern rather meaningless and impoverished vernacular, one which conveys everything and nothing to everyone and no one. Original languages such as *Hebrew, Sanskrit, Chinese* and various aboriginal oral traditions all derived from their context. *David Abram* has explored the origins and meaning of natural language. For example, the word for a certain bird is the sound of that bird, a written *Hebrew* letter is actually a symbolic image of what it depicts. *Joseph Campbell* makes the point that in older languages such as *Latin*, the noun and verb were together. For example in Latin, 'amo' is one word meaning what in *English* is two words 'I love.' In modern languages the emphasis is on the individual, separated from action and connection.

Human language arose as a means of attunement between persons, but also between the *animate landscape*...... *By denying that birds and other animals have their own styles of speech, by insisting that the river has no real voice and that the ground itself is mute, we stifle our direct experience. We cut ourselves off from the deep meanings in many of our words, severing our language from that which supports and sustains it. We then wonder why we are often unable to communicate even among ourselves.*

David Abram[13]

.... *I started the month stumped. Stumped over my words. I wonder, question now, whether these words that have flowed from me so easily are connected to any truth, if they are honest.*

As soon as we acquire a sensitivity for environment for the quality of experience, the wind and weather of it, you realize that its not that solid, for the weather is always changing. *There is always something happening which cannot be pinned down with words and thoughts.* It's like the first day of Spring, or a Sunday in May when it snows, there is a special quality about it all which cannot be fully worded, especially in our enfeebled syntax. It is what it is, an envelope of 'I-It,' ever changing, faster and more completely than any of our cliched weather talk. This is also true of the inner landscape which is, perhaps, even more elusive to accurate representation. Emotion compacted into words, images, colors, scenes, phrases, voices, finer and finer attempts at precision, conveyed perhaps better in writing than speaking.

.... *When I speak I throw away my words, my voice fades, I know I won't be heard, I don't believe I will be understood. My words do not communicate who I am, so I don't make much effort to present myself.*

Writing in my journal is very helpful. It truly gives me a voice and a space to be heard.

Words expressing the song of the soul need the wind to run through them. In this book I have endeavored to let the world speak through the poetic. For it is in the word pictures of poetry and the space between the words that the closest approximation to the real is found.

> Words even if they come from the soul, as fog
> rising off the sea covers the sea
> It's noble work to build coherent
> philosophical discourses, but
> they block out the sun of truth.
> See God's qualities as an ocean,
> this world as foam on the purity
> of that. Brush away and look
> through the alphabet
> as you do the hair covering your
> beloved's eyes. Here's the mystery,
> this intricate astonishing world
> is proof of God's presence even as
> it covers the beauty.
>
> Rumi[14]

Writing is a leap of faith, every word- page a testing of truth and the accuracy of chosen language. Sometimes in authoring 'truth' I am uncertain where to go next, at times, like the tide, I empty out and need sustenance or inspiration. What works for me and has now become an *afternoon habit is to go to the garden and to wander about a bit, in and out of the greenhouse and just let it speak to me.* "I need water," or, "I could use a new planting" or," this would look lovely there," or, "how about some weeding, to give me space?" Two hours or so of digging in the earth, and I am centered, reconnected, more trusting of what the whorls on my fingertips are creating in their intimate dance with my *Dell. Sharon Butala* describes a similar process when she wanders the land for inspiration:

I knew, as I've always known with each book, that the best parts aren't pieces that I imagine myself, at least that's not how I conceive of them. They seem instead to come in a splitsecon of insight, as if the inside of my body were, at such times, a darkened theater into which a shaft of wisdom, some visionary light suddenly is thrust........[15]

Today it is tomatoes that are asking for attention, and they shall have it. This is how *Findhorn* came into being. This is what the hummingbirds are teaching, to fly here or there, to that flower or this, taking a little from over there putting it over here. This is how nature does it, this is how the soul speaks. When I return to writing, to emptying myself so that the right words have room to form, it feels as though I am still weeding as though the leaves and stems, the breeze and clouds are still within. Tomatoes, lovingly planted, are encouraging for there will be juicy red fruit at the end......the tides flow and shape themselves thus:

The recovery of spiritual authority in our time obliges resumption of personal access to the Gods. We may know that we are in the presence of transformative energies, when we experience resonance, depth and enlargement through encounter with the numinous. The principle of resonance suggests that 'like summons like.'... The resonance within us cannot be willed, it happens...... it is the surest guide to finding our own right path............
J Hollis[16]

A word tree provides a visual and attentional tool in order to reflect on familiar usage of words. Just exactly what do I mean when I say that? Leaves are filled in one word at a time on this personal, *"tree of saying."* .... *The tree of saying was immensely healing and constructive for me, adding leaves when negative talk marched along my tongue My words are bold now, they stand out.*

On this May -Sunday the sacrament is to go to the river to make a confession, a private and personal taking stock of the 'will-full I/me' and the ways in which, identified with that illusory self, we have ceased to listen and behold. Taking time, on this grey and moist afternoon, each in private communion with rock and wave, we ritually set afloat delusions, on a self created or found 'boat,' then await the river's response, as the language of silence and truth. Silence is not an absence of anything but a shifting of attention toward a subtle language which speaks directly to soul. .... *Throwing that boat into the water was so empowering for me. I began letting go, with forgiveness, that moment. Mistakes I've made have taught me lessons, to be who I am today. I've thrown a lot of twigs into the river this month. It's a powerful way for me to let go. Bye-bye masks, illusions, people pleaser, chatter box, leech, judgement, fear, drama and co-dependence! Now I'm swimming with the flow of the current instead of upstream.*

Launching the 'boats of baggage' was to be a deeply moving

experience for many including myself. I found myself engaged in the shallow side pools reflecting the sky which, just as I was leaving, yielded up a treasure, a beautiful knotted and gnarled root. Ice crystals dangled from it sparkling, like an exquisite Japanese sculpture. It spoke visually and directly to me of the need to be simple and still in order to rescue the treasure. It now continues to speak in beauty from a Japanese vase in my meditation space. To directly perceive any object is to enter into relationship with it *as thou*, to feel oneself in a living interaction with another being. *To define 'it' as inert is to turn off the senses.* That would be to view the root removed from the world whereas, at the river of our meeting and now, in the daily meditations, we are co-contextual participants.

Today, at this particular moment in May, it is the sea which speaks, steel gray to the rain filled sky reflecting light and ripple, dancing with the wind and hugging the rocks with a full tide. Yesterday the wind spoke as a blowing and knowing, today, in a very different mood, calm waters lazily reflect the sky. The nearness of the sea seems to invite an intense awareness of an unusual nearness of earth, sky and life in which I experience a profound sense of at-onement as well as gratitude.

> Sssh the sea says
> Sssh the small waves at the shore say, ssh
> Not so violent, not
> So haughty, not
> So remarkable
> Sssh
> Say the tips of the waves
> Crowding around the headland's
> Surf. Sssh
> they say to people
> This is our earth,
> Our eternity
>
> Rolf Jacobsen [17]

It is difficult to convey, in written word, the magnitude of this awareness or sense of presence of the river, ocean, or full moon which is so immediate. It reassures. Tide goes out as the world comes in. Moon waxes, moon wanes, tide time, river time, moon time are all our time. On this Sunday afternoon we had difficulty in reclaiming one woman from the river, for she, like *Siddhartha*[18] who gained enlightenment beside a river, had entered river time. Moira and the river were flowing at their own speed and even our calling to her was drowned out by the sound of the passage of water, so we sang and awaited her release.

.... After the experience at the river, this month I decided to focus on listening, both listening to myself and observing listening in others. I found that we all, myself included, interrupt fairly consistently. I practiced just listening, without getting ahead to my own response.

For one woman the river did not speak but sang.

.... I have had a sore throat on and off for a long time, but since that day I have started singing and my throat has cleared, it feels now like its doing what it's supposed to do.

At the time of working out *Innerscape* ideas, I felt prompted to create a visual representation of each monthly topic of inquiry as a *mandala*. Often, the shape of it was triggered by time in nature, or a dream, much as the writing is now, five years later. I still look at and ponder these very unique shapes and symbols and through every *innerscape* passage learn a little more about them. The fifth drawing corresponds to our May investigation into language, speech, listening and silence. The symbol in this *mandala* is a blue/silver tree, half of which is in shadow. On each side of the tree sits a bird. One bird is singing, the other watching, one in shadow, one in the light. For many years I had been fascinated with the *Celtic* design of, "two birds on one tree." As a child I remember seeing it on a brass plate in a village church in England. I did not understand for many years what it symbolically represented, although I knew that it was found in many traditions. It is mentioned in the *Upanishads*,(the great wisdom poems from around 500 B.C.E.)

Like two golden birds perched on the self same tree,
Intimate friends the ego and the Self
Dwell in the same body. The former eats
The sweet and sour fruits of the tree of life
While the latter looks on in detachment.
Mundaka Upnishad III-1

Through meditation I have come to know the two birds of my own nature. The one, the I/me who speaks to others, and the other the background 'me,' better described perhaps as an I-Thou who is 'aware-ing' or witnessing, listening-in-context. When we examine a little more closely, that is take seriously the owl's question of "Who?" then who indeed is speaking and who is listening? Wherein lies truth? Which bird am I, *'the speaking one,'* or the *'aware -of -speaking one,'* both of which I think of as me? Do I ever truly articulate what I think/perceive and how would I know? Who is it who decides the flow of words which exit my lips toward another? Is that flow more a demand than anything, that the other attends to me and believes me as me? Am I, as listener, doing that for the other? In the meantime of our discourse, how are the background 'myself' and 'yourself' interacting? What does the rain, the blackbird, the stereo music contribute to our dialogue?

The rain surrounded the cabin........with a whole world of meaning and secrecy, of rumor. Think of it: all that speech pouring down, selling nothing, judging nobody, drenching the thick mulch of dead leaves, soaking the trees, filling the gullies and crannies of wood with water, washing out the places where men have stripped the hillside. Nobody started it, nobody is going to stop it. It will talk as long as it wants, the rain. As long as it talks I am going to listen.   Thomas Merton[19]

Much of this 'language' remains hidden from view behind a rather dusty pattern of words. When we look carefully at this pattern, we find that we are, so often, habituated to speaking 'dead' words of conditioned responses, reactions and cliches. *Jacques Lacan*, a French philosopher, linguist and psychoanalyst, devoted a lifetime of serious professional inquiry into the illusive structure of our primary communicative process.

The true me is the speaking and not the spoken about 'I'. In fact the main factor that creates the gap between the speaking 'I' and the spoken about 'I' is the presence of the other, i.e. the listener. The presence of the listener- real or imaginary-influences the desire behind speaking in a manner that puts the true desire of the speaker in a questionable position. [20]

Lacan, gets to the core of this double sense of I/me, more accurately expressed as, *"I who speaks to myself, as other."* This is our most common form of inner discourse which goes on unceasingly as a normal state of affairs. It assumes that another with whom I engage is the same as *myself that is, carries my projected self identifications.* There is a huge claim being made here, by *Lacan*, his followers, and, by the *Eastern* wisdom and meditation teachers, that *this is all a delusion!* In our neurotic and ego-defensive condition, it is felt to be such a necessary delusion, that it is the normal state of perception, unwittingly, leaving us in never-never land, from which some day, like *Sleeping Beauty* we will awaken. We would be wise to consider, what is it that the prince of this myth awakens the sleeping maiden from? When the 'I' is not aware of its own separateness it falls into the fake belief that it is everything, the spoken about 'I' *and* the true thing.

Pema Chodron reminds us to regard all that you believe in all describable phenomena, as a dream.[21] The witnessing bird on the tree is the same as the one who, through practice, comes to watch and listen to this illusory reality. The one who, not caught in the subject/ predicate word trap, just listens and listens broadly, inside and outside - all one. This is why I think there is sanity in listening *with* nature, of training in being. This 'just being' is to heal the ego-illusive split. When we do, we feel renewed, refreshed, at ease, at one. Listening in being, in silence, is to feel a burden lifted.

It is easier to see the 'splitting' aspect of language in writing than in speaking. We have all had the experience of reflecting on a conversation, wondering "Why on earth did I say that?"or, "I should have said...." Do we ever say what we mean to say? What was actually said at the time, what is being reflected on as having been said, what should have been said, are all part of the delusion, the long bag we drag behind us, of mis-takes. The further it is removed from direct experience the less true anything is. Freud devoted an early volume of writing to dreams as truthful language, as well as slips of the tongue, forgetting and jokes, in their relation to the unconscious (we are suggesting that this is the witnessing one). Body language, artistic symbolic expression are also closer to 'the moon' than speech, which is like a "finger pointing at the moon."

I am astonished as I draw the veil off things with words, how much, how infinitely more than I can say, I have observed.

Virginia Woolf[22]

One woman participant, had an extraordinary dream which returned her to childhood, to a garden she had grown up in, and showed the extent of her 'forgotten' observations.

.... *The dream began in a corner of the backyard in the house I grew up in, I lay down on the ground on a still cloudless day in early summer. Normally the grass would have been dried a crisp brown, by this stage of summer, but on this day, in the dream, it was moist, green and damp as well as particularly soft. As I lay there I could hear everything, the sparrows as they spoke to each other, the summer buzz of locusts. Before long, I became small, like Alice in Wonderland. I could see the tiniest detail of all that was around me. I could see with absolute complexity and precision the smallest forms of life. I peered under a leaf and saw a large bug, a beetle maybe. On its soft underbelly rested a brown long legged spider. It seemed as though they were in an embrace, though it could have been one of death, I didn't stay long enough to find out. I could venture into the vortex of a flower and I explored the delicate veined cone of the white petalled flowers which grew there, the ones my mother called a weed but to me were crown jewels of the wild flowers. I remarked on the stillness of a bumble bee as he rested on a flower's edge and I could sense the life of the great oak trees lodged at the corner of the house.*

Who I think I am as a person describing the inner journey is not the inner journey, so its possibilities in discourse and prose are endless. To the extent that I am currently a participant in *and* witness to the inner journey as it unfolds in myself and context, then I may come closer to an accurate representation in symbol. The more complete the language of symbolization the closer my approximations may be, as in poetry. By examining our speech, through feedback about what has been heard,(so often different from what one thought one had said), by a willingness to sit quietly and notice the words inside, rather than engaging with them, we may more courageously approach truth.

The person who speaks and is satisfied with what he says, is not simply misguided he is wrong. Every statement that does not provoke change and strangeness within itself is wrong. Spoken Truth which seeks to remove itself as certainty from the contradictory process of language becomes falsehood there and then.

Jaques Lacan[23]

Is what I am about to utter, a demand and desire of my imaged self, or is it one of connection, mutuality and shared meaning? The attempts of *dialogue groups* are along these lines of learning *to speak carefully together.* An attempt is being made to find a way through words and false images, toward a truth of humanness. The aim is to establish a community of conscious and aware co-*habitants in the world of truth.* In a true listening community of many egos, through careful listening to what is being said, we are in a position to realize the truth of the Self. We have the opportunity to directly encounter our-self as it really is, a Self-in -context.

This is challenging work of the moment, to both speak and witness speech. It requires both a training in listening and a training in silence which was referred to earlier. This is precisely why all meditation teaching trains the mind slowly with much practice, to go against the normal drive, the torrent of words and thoughts and remain still, centered and watching. The practice itself has been suggested throughout the *Innerscape* journey but now becomes essential if we are to go any further beyond the psychological preoccupation of the 'I/Me' life to an *open ended awareness of an' I-Thou' life*. We shall look at this more closely through the last stages of our inquiry.

Reading, especially some of the great writers of the past century, is a joy of discovery of observation and an articulation of the difficulty of spoken language. *Virginia Wolf* is one such example of an authentic discoverer of the inner world. She wrote as an artist, mystic and seer. She was highly perceptive of the problems inherent in speech, speaking often in favor of 'the treasure of silence.' What depression showed her and is asking of us, is more listening in silence.

My book, stuffed with phrases, has dropped to the floor. It lies under the table, to be swept up by the charwoman when she comes wearily at dawn looking for scraps of paper, old tram tickets, and here and there a note screwed into a ball and left with the litter to be swept up. What is the phrase for the moon? And the phrase for love? By what name are we to call death? I do not know. I need a little language such as lovers use, words of one syllable such as children speak when they come into the room and find their mother sewing and pick up some scrap of bright wool, a feather or a shred of chintz. I need a howl; or a cry. When the storm crosses the marsh and sweeps over me where I lie in the ditch disregarded I need no words. Nothing neat. Nothing that comes down with all its feet on the floor. None of those resonances and lovely echoes that break and chime from nerve to nerve in our breasts, making wild music, false phrases. I have done with phrases. How much better is silence: the coffee cup, the table. How much better to sit by myself like the solitary sea bird that opens its wings on the stake. Let me sit here forever with bare things, this coffee cup, this knife, this fork, things in themselves, myself being my Self. [24]

9

What is an intelligent life ?

The poem is not the world.
It isn't even the first page of the world.
But the poem wants to flower, like a flower.
It knows that much.
It wants to open itself,
like the door of a little temple,
so that you might step inside and be cooled and refreshed,
and less yourself than part of everything.

Mary Oliver[1]

It is Sunday: A Sunday for Understanding.

To encounter the world as being part of everything, as *Mary Oliver* must have done, is to be astonished, for it is a moment of deep significance far removed from our normal subject-object view. The condition for this to happen is one of silent waiting, looking, listening. It is akin to what *Wordsworth* described as, "emotion recollected in tranquility," of sensations "felt in the blood and felt along the heart and passing even into the purer mind." As *Siddhartha* listened, so *Oliver* looked, she looked and saw, especially into the temple of the flower and other growing things. Similarly, *Sharon Butala*[2] saw her way into the life of stones upon the so-called desolate prairies. In looking we perceive 'just a flower' or 'only a stone,' but in 'seeing' we encounter the whole.

Recently on my morning walk when rounding a familiar corner, I looked, then *saw*, the first foxglove. From a few yards away it looked like a feathered thing, a flower-swan, long necked and graceful, silky plumage. From close range each flower possessed a most cooling, startling long deep well, a temple. In another week or so toward the end of June, there will be hundreds, pink, purple, dazzling dancers but this one, the first, called attention to itself, alone, white, a *visual poem*.

Such a moment of intuitively 'seeing' into the heart of a flower is in intensity, much like *Emily Carr's* trees or *Georgia O'Keefe's* flowers. Both of these artists were passionate creators of soul-images of West coast flora.

As artist's they insisted on looking into the thing itself, deepening the hue of canvas and color until it speaks through form to formless, not the detail of flower or tree, forest or ocean but its life as mystery, as symbolic suggestion. As participant/viewer one is drawn into the sensuality of stamen, feast of colored petal, a curtain of hanging foliage, a swirling spiral of evergreens. *Carr, O'Keefe, Oliver* and *Butala,* are all recent 'seers' in their capacity to look and listen, to hear and see. Through skillful means of expression each has succeeded, as artist, in communicating their moment of understanding. This is how Carr expressed the human vestigial capacity for clairvoyance (clear seeing).

Sketching in the big woods is wonderful. You go find a space wide enough to sit in and clear enough so that the undergrowth is not drowning you. Then, being elderly, you spread your campstool; and sit and look around. "Don't see much here." Wait.....Everything is waiting and still. Slowly things begin to move, to slip into their places. Groups and masses and lines tie themselves together. Colors you had not noticed come out, timidly or boldly. In and out, in and out your eye passes. Nothing is crowded, there is a living space for all. Air moves between each leaf. Sunlight plays and dances. Nothing is still now. Life is sweeping through the spaces. Everything is alive. The air is alive. The silence is full of sound. The green is full of color. Light and dark chase each other. Here is a picture, a complete thought, and there another. There are themes everywhere, something sublime, something ridiculous, or joyous or calm or mysterious. Tender youthfulness laughing at gnarled oldness. Moss and ferns and leaves and twigs, light and air, depth and color chattering...........you must be still in order to hear and see.[3]

Emily Carr's art 'took off,' from her cloistered impressionistic early work belonging to the niceties and charm of Victorian life, when she began to travel to and later live in coastal wild places. There, she was able to identify with the primal energies which she encountered as the spiritual connection that she had been seeking. As well, she found in the Indians' carvings the same perception of communion with the environment which she developed in her own work, as poetry in word and painting.

What is poetic imagination? *Jaques Maritain* has defined it as "*the intercommunion between the inner being of things and the inner being of the human self.*"[4] Carr's creations were in response to her relationship with 'the infinite' which was able to 'cast out the personality' such that the soul could be filled with the spirit which informs nature. Poetic communion was, for her, a true religion, as *genuine art springs from a profound experience of the self in the world and the world in the self.*

God got so stuffy squeezed into a church. Only out in the open was there room for him. He was like a great breathing among the trees. In church he was static, a bearded image in petticoats. In the open he had no form; he just was, and filled all the universe.[5]

Awesome in its capacity to awaken the language of soul, Carr's art has had great impact. In her powerful portrayals of lost and hidden totem poles she provides us, as viewers, with an awareness an *understanding* of what the soul may already know. Of Indian carvers she says:

He wanted some way of showing people things that were in his mind, things about the creatures and about himself and their relation to each other. He cut forms to fit the thoughts that birds and animals and fish suggested to him, and to these he added something of himself. When they were all linked together they made very strong talk for the people. He grafted this new language onto the great cedar trunks and called them totem poles and stuck them up in the villages with great ceremony. Then the cedar and the creatures and the man all talked together through the totem poles to the people....When you looked at a man's pole you knew who he was.[6]

Foxglove of the morning, a flower poem, any poem by Oliver, viewing an Emily Carr rendering of totem such as *"Big Raven,"* a freshly cut rosebud in an old English stone bottle on my desk, *Great Blue Heron* stalking the bay on a grey blustery evening, a grand symphony, a solo violin all do one thing. *They take your breath away.* For the first second or two of the inward gasp, one is wide open to a newness, a freshness of 'seeing' and an immediate knowing that one may be changed by this.

Art, has been historically associated in both East and West, with profound spiritual transformation for, when we look at any beautiful object or symbol, we suspend all other thought and activity, at that moment we are simply *aware.* We are contemplating from *inside* the object. At such a moment of contemplative awareness we *suspend* continuous mental activity, that of wanting, not wanting, planning, fantasizing, etc. This is what totem poles did, what village church bells did, what the 'hunting-horn' did, what real art and music does, what nature does, *rivet attention. In such a moment we rest in the way the world is,* as it is, not as we would wish to have it be.

Great art grabs you, against your will, and then suspends your will. You are ushered into a quiet clearing, free of desire, free of grasping, free of ego, free of self contraction. And through that opening or clearing in your own awareness may come flashing higher truths, subtler revelations, profound connections. For a moment you might even touch eternity;
Ken Wilber[7]

Hearing and seeing in nature or, in its spiritually rendered symbolic form, art, poem, music, reminds us to be fully present now. In the moment of communion there is an indigenous experience of faith and myth. Great painters and composers speak to us thus of what was most significant to themselves, because all quality art arises from the depths of the artist's personal perception of spirit. It is faithful to the archetypes of life, death, beauty, truth, and their shadows. Modern art and composition is especially significant in its capacity to unbalance by confronting us with an unusual viewpoint. Such an experience releases us from our habitual view. When the breath is taken away I/me disappears, time disappears, all gone, in an awestruck moment of astonishment, of immense questioning or clear seeing.

To understand is, quite literally, to 'stand under' in admiration, or perhaps skepticism. It is really an existential attitude, whereby 'we stand under the power of the risky attitude of knowing. Raimon Panikar[8]

The Upanishads in the East and Thomas Aquinas in the West were explicit in their definition of "knowing." Independently their thinking represented a continuity of perception which was separated by a span of seventeen centuries. Interestingly, this was identical with that implicit in Carr's and the native carver's hand-work, namely, to be one with the thing known.

Thich Nhat Hanh translates the Buddhist term, prajnaparamita as, understanding through the unfiltered expression of open ear, open eye, open mind that is found in every living being. This is intelligence, a state which is open questioning and unbiased. Nowadays due to the shift in the meaning of knowledge, 'to understand' has been reduced to concepts such as calculate, to search the web, to supply with facts and to foresee. In modernity understanding has become 'over-standing,' which is to apply predetermined categories to identify an object, therefore to no longer understand the thing as itself in context. This modality of 'over' implies a superiority, which is a far cry from Carr's encounters in the wilderness where humility accompanied the first and last brush strokes.

Besides the sheer joy of true encounter, of standing under something as an innocent, there is a further possibility which is to intuit the nature of this ego, the I/me self, as an insubstantial and fleeting entity like everything else. It can literally be blown away by the truth inherent in a moment of pure perception! Perhaps superior 'I' is after all rather empty, stuffed up with dead things, perhaps it is not so worthy of all our time and preoccupation, perhaps 'I' am not so worth worrying about!

> Why are you unhappy?
> because 99% of everything you think
> And everything you do,
> is for yourself,
> And there isn't one.   Wei Wu Wei[9]

What direct and unadulterated perception/participation shows us is that another dimension of 'knowing' is possible. In immediacy we may see, as did *Blake*, "*eternity in a grain of sand*," or in my current example, the temple in the foxglove. When attention becomes more focused then coherent knowledge is gained through insight, not intellect alone. The happenings which transform us, are, as we pilgrims have noted this year, uncannily synchronous with a slightly less than conscious 'need'. Some would call this the *voice of soul* which is only heard when given assent. This is the requirement of journeying, *to give participatory assent to soul.*

One *Innerscape* participant, when making a big decision this month about profession, found that when leaning one way, (towards his heart's wish but financial deficit) he 'saw' a hawk circling overhead, a heron walking towards him and an unmistakable smell of tobacco when walking through previous Indian territory. These phenomena halted the anxious, yet logical, preoccupations of "for and against." They demanded, look here, look now, pay attention. How could he not view this as intelligent?

Blowing of the horns followed by sighting of the firebird, in 'The Maiden King,' was portraying through myth symbol the same mind-stopping phenomena which we have been apprehending in flower, nature, art and 'happenings.' Indeed, even in the psychodrama spontaneously acted out by *Bly* and *Woodman* on the video series, they 'got it' on their own pulse. There was a shock value when the bird appeared. In many myths the appearance of a bird heralds a moment of transforming insight and movement. The swan-maiden appeared to *Ivan* as potential at the start of the tale and now reappears in 'ordinary' reality at the end. The final scene of the story takes place at this feast and birthday celebration of union, of masculine and feminine.

The happy ending of the fairy tale, the myth,.....is to be read, not as a contradicton, but as a transcendence of the universal tragedy of man. The objective world remains what it was, but, because of a shift of emphasis within, the subject is beheld as though transformed.
                                                                            Joseph Campbell[10]

What is eaten is an egg, symbolizing a fully awakened intelligence. This must be sought *through attention to the inside of things*. As in many fairy stories the treasure, the egg, is well hidden behind the veils of obscured perception, enveloped in coverings. In this case buried in a box, under an oak, in a duck which is in a hare. Somewhere, deep inside these protective layers of the familiar, clinging to the known, experimenting, sacrificing, learning to fly and fall, we arrive at the hero's redemption, as true Self. Learning through defeat, test and trial to pay attention, to stay awake, he (and we) solve the mystery of birth. In eating the golden egg we are reborn, made whole again, as an "awakened" human being.

Around the time of late Spring this year, I was lucky enough to catch sight of *trumpeter swans* as they migrated through the foothills on their way north. Hundreds of them, for a day or two, gathered on a body of water, not far from my city home. One fellow watcher shared with me his disbelief that after traveling all over North America looking for swans he had come across them here, in a city no less, and close to home. In itself that was the archetypal story of his hero's journey, but here it serves to emphasize our fascination with *swans* as representations of grace, beauty, other-worldliness. They are all body and little head, glide effortlessly on water, look both strong and soft, in short, perfect images of balance with two huge white wings elegantly folded. If the center of instinctual life and intelligence is the belly, then a swan is all belly and fullness, with a low center of gravity. In its beauty we sense a harmonious proportion of body to head, an enviable capacity to walk, swim, and fly, a defiance of gravity in flight, a stability of pairing, (swans mate for life) and a call which sounds like a death song. The ballet *"Swan Lake,"* when sensitively danced, can still, after a dozen or so performances, 'take my breath away.' Such must have been *Ivan's* experience when the thirty swans flew in to greet him. *Rilke* was one of a number of poets to address the captivation of the swan as archetypal symbol,

> ... to die, which is a letting go of the ground we cling to every day,
> is like the swan when she nervously lets herself down
> *Into the water which receives her gaily*
> *and which flows joyfully under*
> and after her, wave after wave,
> while the swan unmoving and marvelously calm,
> is pleased to be carried, each minute more
> like a queen, composed, farther and farther on. [11]

Traditionally, the Eastern symbol for the sixth *chakra* energy center is, interestingly, *the swan*. One who lives out of this center embodies these attributes of what without exaggeration we may term, 'amazing grace.' To live like a swan is to love enduringly, to live in balance and harmony and to die as a song of letting go. In eastern terminology, this would be a state of enlightenment, free from subject-object alienation. In the Zen, "ox-herding pictures," which pictorially depict the journey to enlightenment in ten stages, the ox (our own true nature) gradually transforms from black to white, as the doors of perception are cleansed. In the eastern chakra system the sixth *chakra* energy center at the point between the eyebrows is white."*The lotus named Ajna is like the moon, beautifully white.*"[12] White can be startling especially when directly illuminated. My own previous encounter with white (see Ch.5) had been quietening, reminding me to be a watcher not a doer, to enter rather than act upon. In ancient oriental wisdom teaching *Lao-tse* linked this witnessing presence to stillness and to destiny.

> Push far enough towards the void,
> Hold fast enough to quietness,
> And of the ten thousand things
> none but can be known by you.
> I have beheld them wither they go back.
> See, all things howsoever they flourish
> Return to the root from which they grew.
> This return to the root is called quietness;
> Quietness is called submission to fate;
> What has submitted to fate has

become part of the always-so.
To know the always so
is to be illumined.........[13]

Free will and fate is of central interest in most spiritual and esoteric traditions and has woven itself as one of the 'white' questions throughout this inner journey. We have taken the view of 'fate' as a particular quality of each life and destiny as representing the individuation path for a particular individual, leading to evolution of consciousness into maturity.

As the moon influences the tides, the sun, the seasons and plant growth, so the planets as archetypal principles affect our interior solar system or psyche. Warren Kenton, a *Kabbalistic* scholar, describes the astrological influence on each of us as coming from a particular part of the Divine world, with a special function for each. The key is to be aware enough to develop a capacity to observe the psyche closely in order to identify its patterns, strengths, weaknesses and tendencies. In this way, *the way of the inner quest one learns to become attentive to the path of destiny and not to be subject to it. " How?"*

Qu: If there is a particular reason a person exists in this life how can someone come to know that in himself or herself?
Ans: The key is to identify your type and your talent, and in finding these you then discover your calling.
Qu: With some people you get a sense that they missed their moment, that somehow they had a chance to connect with their destiny and just didn't do it. Do you think it's possible to miss your moment in life?
Ans: I've seen it happen many times with many people. It comes from the delusion they want to be something they're not, so they miss their moment, people get another chance but through vanity, laziness, stupidity they blow the next opportunity and so on until they learn the hard way.
Qu: You might think that the door is always open for a person, but it does seem to close. It has to close...... As life unfolds, are there opportunities that are unrepeatable?
Ans: You have to recognize and seize the moment. That crucial window may be a day or an hour, when you are shown quite clearly what you're supposed to be doing. What works against it is if you are interested in something else at the time, which diverts your attention..........many people remember the moment, either when they missed their opportunity or they took it.

Richard Smoley with Z'ev ben Shimon Halevi[14]

At this time group participants will look again with a sharpened perspective, at their own unique path of destiny recalled from *Seeds* time, and now 'seen again' through a more refined capacity to look *and* see. We are much like a *Russian* doll, a *babushka*, possessing a number of 'selves' each fitting neatly into the next, so that at first glance they *look like* one. During the past nine months we have metaphorically separated the bodies of babushka, peeled away the layers of archetypal patterns, looking carefully at habits of mind, each of which support the next, for better or worse, for awakening or sleeping. We have followed along with *Ivan* through his slumber, deception, lostness and reconciliation, as both a separated man and an individual. At this the sixth stage of our inquiry into Self, the pieces of psyche are more balanced and whole. As discriminating individuals, we possess the possibility for clearer view and choice. Simultaneously, we honor the personal 'flowering' of the *Tree of Life*, which, when wholesome, is matched in the flourish of the summer season as well as in the present place on the path.

Come, dear, with your innocent eyes
And look at the clear blue ocean of life,
And look at the green color'
The manifestation of suchness.

Even if the world was shattered,
Your smile will never vanish,
What did we possess yesterday
And what will we lose today?

Come dear. Look right into existence,
Adorned by illusion.
Since the sunflower is already there,
All flowers turn towards it and contemplate

Thich Nhat Hanh[15]

The flavor of this Sunday is like a celebration, as is *Ivan's* symbolic reunion with his beloved. Also, because it is the season for blossoming, because we have come through six intensive months of personal confrontation. As we intuit the lightening of psyche's burden there is very real delight in the freedom gained. Such a time requires a symbol as a flourish, as a personal extension of power and peace.

Hermes, an all too human trickster of a God, was also the initiate of the *wand* or rod. It is this symbol on our medical prescriptions, which represents health and vitality. An ancient hymn addresses *Hermes* as wielder of the dreaded yet respected tool of *speech*. It also reminds us that *Hermes* held in his hands the *"blameless tool of peace."* This was his wand which, as the story goes, had been placed by *Hermes* between two warring serpents who, in response to his magical words, coiled around the rod in union, in perfect balance and harmony. This little story is not quite so charming or innocuous as it appears, for we may well be the serpents in our warring struggle for power and survival, man/woman; east/west; north/south, anywhere there are artificially created boundaries and borders without a unifying principle. The staff of *Hermes* is exactly that, *a symbol for a unifying center* around which the opposites can focus and unite.

The counterpart for the wand within the human body is the spine. This body 'wand' localizes a center of operation for the muscular system, hence the emphasis on *ground, breath and spine* in *hatha yoga* practices. The chaotic serpents can be thought of as aspects of the conditioned I/me which find harmony, when focused, on a center *outside of themselves*. Any *axis-as-center* (see Ch. 3) is the human balancing place, one that links the opposites of heaven and earth, lower and upper, left and right, front and back, the conscious and unconscious. As such, it is rightly considered a *place of magic, power creativity and truth*. In a number of cultures there have been mountains, real or mythical, said to be at the center of the world. Temples are designed to be symbols of 'cosmic mountains.'

A builder of a church or temple firstly erects a pillar at the sacred center. The 'Tor' at sacred *Glastonbury* in Somerset, England is on the highest mound created by humans. There, it is surrounded by a huge Zodiac carved into the countryside. *Stonehenge* was built so that, at the equinoxes, the sun and all the heavens confirm the site as being at the center of the world. Lourdes, and other pilgrim sites are *centers*. It is because of this (as unifying principal) that they have the power to cure and heal.

In Greek myth and ritual as well as more currently in the novel, *"Harry Potter,"*[16] the rod or wand, was widely used as a central focus of personal power. It was an honored magical instrument which because of its power could make dreams come true, as well as stranger things. Watch what happens as Harry selects his wand! Consider why everyone, young and old have been drawn to the power of this young boy's wand. Harry is a moral tale therefore a tale of two centers, the symbolic and the real.

We have the capacity to live at the place of 'me' as center, from where I view and judge the world, or, as an object in the world (the foxglove, the painting, the wand, the temple) is present as center thus moving our small self to the periphery.(See Ch. 2) From this broader perspective arises the capacity for love, truth, beauty, union and moral action.

The *Ajna* energy chakra, as our awareness center, is the eye of the mind. The eye sees, the mind's eye knows, for '*ajna*' means both '*to know*' and '*to command.*' The knowledge referred to has an immediacy and directness, like the art/flower encounter that transcends the logical thought processes. Where rational thinking requires deduction before conclusion, *direct knowing is not a conclusion but a realization.* The symbol for this in the eastern system, is two wings or petals on either side of a stem, much like the caduceus, the wand and the swan. The image evokes a sense of wholeness of activity of the two hemispheres of the brain, a balance which does not prefer one over the other. To date, in order to recreate balance, we have particularly focused our inquiry toward relational, connective, intuitive perceptions and activities, those which have atrophied in our current left brain culture of facts, conclusions and solutions. The right brain contribution is more one of holding the question and awaiting realization, something which has been perennially understood by the artist and the seer.

.... *I have a beautiful story about my wand making. I felt strongly that I wanted an eagle feather for my wand. I knew where there was a nest and thought I would find one under the tree there, but never did. Later in the summer I was mountain biking with the family to the 'lost' lakes, and in the meadow in front of the lake there were eagle feathers strewn all around. I can still see us in slow motion, in our glory, gathering feathers. I was truly given a gift that day!*

.... *My wand experience was an extremely challenging, rewarding and above all a valuable lesson. I learned that when I am stubborn I am not on my soul's path, and am blocked. I was quite sure about where I would and would not find my wand. I wandered to the likely spots but just couldn't see it. Then one day, looking at a mound of driftwood right outside my cottage, a pile which was 'junk' for removal, I found just the right piece the right length. It had been staring at me all summer long. So many experiences around this wand have been reminding me to stay open and have faith.*

Well into the journey of inquiry, the June gathering marks a transition. At this stage of my own pilgrimage, after intensive questing and journeying, I needed digestion time, inner solitary time, as well as chance to anchor the practices of looking and listening. For the next three months group members are on their own in order to feel their way into what is theirs. They are encouraged to seek out contexts in which the mind can be quiet, free and unoccupied, in order to listen inwardly, to participate with soul in this journey. It is a chance to exercise imagination and creativity. There is a focused practice of daily loving kindness meditation and remembering, to remain linked one to another, as spiritual friends in companionship, during the absence.

Simone Weil[17] suggested that real education is in awakening and training the faculty of *attention*, so that we are able to attend to the voice of the living God. This voice *Innerscape* translates as the voice of Self, that is 'self-in-context.' To take an attentive walk as an embodied communion practice is one simple way of encountering space, time, gravity, energy, attending carefully to points of exchange with the environment. Breathing in, as the trees breath out, moving the air the body presses against, connecting to soil beneath the feet, enjoying silence with stones, letting sunlight warm the skin, trading breath, moisture, heat nourishment and awareness with the pulsing contiguous world.

> Not a tree, but the tree
> we saw, it will never exist, split by the wind
> and bending down like that again.
> What will push out of the earth
> later, making it summer, will not be,
> grass, leaves, repetition, there will
> have to be other words. When my
> eyes open language vanishes
>
> Margaret Atwood[18]

To pay attention is to be interested in the life of things, not only things of beauty but the ordinary tools of every day. In our life long impatience we miss much. C.G. Jung used to greet his saucepans in the morning upon arising, which sounds odd until one is given a chance for the mind to quiet, as on a week long meditation retreat, finding, in silence, the outstanding form and aliveness of every object, shining with its own presence. In every day life it is very easy to miss the small symbols. In attending properly, and waiting, as *Emily Carr* was prepared to do, the intersection of the two worlds breaks through, and a recognition (not a seeking of) meaning is possible. As *Margaret Vanier* [19] commented, *"there is an intelligibility in the universe: if any facts astound us that one should!"*

Loss of meaning and increase of depressive symptoms in a culture which is a slave of, 'too much and too many,' means that we cannot remain mindful because we have no time, no silence and no freedom from interruption. Much of what we have aspired to in the course of this year of self tending/Self attending is a counterbalance to the dominance of doing, perceiving, acting and thinking. Throughout the year, daily meditation practice has been encouraged which is the arrangement of time and circumstance in which to sit, stand or walk alone (all one) in silence and pay *attention. Thomas Moore*[20] speculates that depression is an illness most like the heavy planet *Saturn.* Renaissance medical texts present *Saturn as the patron of silence.* Could it be that depression as an illness, is a symptom arising out of our neglect of silence, Saturn's treasure? Saturn enters as a kind of, "willed introversion," says Campbell, who sees the healing possibility as,

....a time of responding to nothing but the as yet unknown demand of some waiting void within, a kind of total strike....as a result of which some power of transformation carries the problem to a plane of new magnitude, where it is suddenly and finally resolved.[21]

The *Tao Te Ching* repetitively urges the virtues of simplicity and silence,

If you correct your mind, the rest of your life will fall into place.
This is true because the mind is the governing aspect of a human life.
If the river flows clearly and cleanly through the
proper channel, all will be well along its banks.
To correct your mind rely on not-doing.
Stop thinking and clinging to complications;
keep your mind detached and whole.
Eliminate mental muddiness and obscurity;
keep your mind crystal clear.
Avoid daydreaming and allow your pure original insight to emerge.
Quiet you emotions and abide in serenity.

Tao te Ching[22]

We have looked carefully at the hidden aspects of psyche which await retrieval through dream, myth and symbol. This has been a fruitful, illuminating and Western oriented *inquiry,* but it is to the East that we must turn for further instruction if we are to penetrate more deeply to the original ground of mind.

The intriguing thing about the mind is that you can't put your finger on it. The brain we can, it's physiological and we tend to think of it as a supercomputer, but the mind is another matter completely! The brain edits and transcribes the constant information flow, whilst the mind watches/witnesses. The only time we don't edit is when we are fully in the moment. Physics has now shown that the immediacy of perception/observation is a participatory moment. The described universe results, in part, from our observation of it. It is a co-creative event. I bear in mind, in my memory, in the deepest sense, the whole world.   Laurence Fisher[23]

'I' turns out to be a center of consciousness among other innumerable such centers, each reflecting and changing each. We must wholeheartedly agree with *Shakespeare* who, through *Hamlet*, remarked; "What a piece of work man is!"

The greatest art of living in today's world is through balanced intelligence, which involves raw intuition, imaginative response to self in world, and a rational intellectual capacity for clarity and differentiation of facts. The outcome of such a balance announces itself as insight. *Insight* involves an intuition of mind *and* heart that takes us beyond knowledge and towards wisdom. It has to do with deeply understanding the nature of things rather than knowing a lot about them. Not everyone wants insight but a pilgrim must agree even though truths can be unsettling. What is needed is a stronger capacity for both awareness and equanimity. This is usually cultivated through an *intentional*, committed meditation practice. As one past participant said;

.... *From my formal meditation times I carry more mindfulness into day to day life which brings more insight. I catch myself having repetitive thoughts, judging and resenting. I'm also more aware of my feelings and less likely to feel overwhelmed by them. And I get some distance, objectivity, perspective on issues.*

Insight meditation is a simple art of refining awareness so that direct insight and clarity of mind may arise. This state is perhaps the best definition of operative intelligence for the human being. *Eastern teaching* says to us not journey, investigate, seek, analyze, but *look straight into your own nature.* This is not easy, nor possible without opening the 'third eye,' the one that looks *and* sees. Unfortunately most things take place in our lives as though this third eye was permanently closed. Experience and inquiry has shown us that we cannot open it by effort, therefore any action towards cultivation must be one of relaxation.

Relaxation of mind consists in a certain kind of glance within. This inward glance is the one I make from the center of my whole being, when I reply to the question, *"How am I feeling at this moment from every point of view at the same time?"* This is often referred to as developing the inner witness. It is the 'wholesomeness' of being for which we have been looking for on the *Innerscape* journey. This mindful remembering of Self *reorients mental geography towards the intelligent.* In meditative awareness as much attention is paid to the *state* of mind as to its *contents. To develop mental clarity and watchfulness within is to invite insight,* therefore to become one's own therapist.

This *is* my conviction for the *Innerscape* journey, one of self responsible body/mind attentiveness which leads to Self recovery and healing. The outcome of this orientation to living is an intelligent, coherent, fulfilling and inclusive life.

> The perfect way knows no difficulties.
> Do not try to find the truth,
> Merely cease to cherish opinions,
> Gain and loss, right and wrong,
> Away with them once and for all!
> In not being two all is the same.
> All that exists is comprehended therein.
> It matters not how things are conditioned,
> Whether by being or by not being.
> That which is, is the same as that which is not,
> That which is not, is the same as that which is.
> If only this is realized
> You need not worry about not being perfect [24]

10

What is transcendence?

Listen! I will be honest with you,
I do not offer the old smooth prizes, but offer rough new prizes,
These are the days that must happen to you.
You shall not heap up what is called riches,
You shall scatter with lavish hand all that you earn or achieve,
What beckonings of love you receive you shall only
answer with kisses of parting
You shall not allow the hold of those who spread
their reached hands toward you.

Walt Whitman [1]

It is Sunday: A Sunday for Renunciation

Today's September sky is a particular shade of intense blue, a perfect complement to autumn shades of golden. A familiar 'V' formation of geese fly high in the clear blue, as they and we, head purposefully toward home. This year long cycle of inquiry returns both seasonally and in content to the starting point. *We have circled truth.* Whilst the noisy geese, honking their way south in this autumn sky, have an appealing beauty, their message goes even deeper reminding us that we too are part of the everlasting circle of coming and going. What is eternal is not the goose, nor this group, nor its members, but the cycle.

During the past cycle we have challenged cultural conditioning. Habitual responses when unquestioned serve neurotic gods, perpetuating a life of constriction and clinging. The root of words like anxiety and anger is *"angh"* which means "constriction." The constriction of self with too narrow a myth to live by restricts soul life. C.G. Jung speaks of neurotic living as, *"the suffering of a soul which has not discovered its meaning."* *Buddha,* in leaving his childhood home of a lavish palace with a parental protective mythology, went outside its narrow confines to find out about the rest of life. What he found in observing human conditions of ill health, poverty, meaninglessness and decay was that life, however carefully guarded, necessarily entails the pain and difficulty of loss. What follows is suffering when the small self (I/me) tries to cling to its narrow world view. *Buddha* discovered that the only way to overcome this suffering (of restriction) was to find out about the root cause. And the root cause, he said, was in *trying to cling to that which is impermanent.*

Participating as we must, in the great cycle of birth and death, we are reminded in this fall season of the brevity and fragility of green, new and begetting. Attachment to the eternal Spring or Summer of our lives *is* what creates suffering. Autumn leaves, like us, become first golden then dull, wet, mottled, torn and shredded. At this time we are invited by nature to properly consider ageing, perhaps to view it not only as the demise of the body but also as the harvest of soul. A rich soul-harvest lends strength and poise when the body gradually fails and becomes feeble.

Despite the natural slowing of autumn, twenty four hours of contrived illumination goads us into unnatural patterns of permanently accomplishing. There is, however, a dignity and mystery to the carpet of leaves, the darkening days and the geese heading south. The soul responds deeply to these symbols as a prelude to disappearance. Such is the transience of the season and transience is the force which makes a ghost of every experience. No act of will can heal our fear of non being but *being in harmony with the seasonal rhythm,* can. Then, *we are living a symbolic life,* a life of meaning which is consonant with the universe. According to all mythic systems living in accord with the gods is to be in harmony with the Tao. This *is* the secret to living well. In so doing we are aligned with a wisdom greater than our capacity to conceptualize, rhythms greater than our own contrived comings and goings.

The remaining pilgrim's question is one of loss, or more precisely *renunciation,* a willingness to let go, a relinquishing with ease and grace in the face of the inevitable. Ours is an age of acquisition if there ever was one in which questioning is largely reduced to, *"how much, how many, how often and how fast?"* We may recall, but briefly, that the important questions of democracy and religion have always been, *"who, why and how."* To thoughtfully negotiate, *"giving up and giving over,"* may well be the greatest challenge in the history of humanity. People are not joking in their attempt to purchase life after death, more time in this body glued together with spare parts, a personal R.R.S.P. treasury amassed beyond any reasonable need. It is not too difficult to see that the worship of the economic god, as acquisition of everything but time, is what has derailed us from the real joy. The secret wisdom of the opposite is *renunciation*. This journey has been about learning to look, listen and to ask the right questions and there is a *decisive turning point in pilgrimage when this, now obvious, counter-question is understood*. C.G. Jung puts to us the decisive question.

Is one related to something infinite or not? This is the telling question of life....If we understand and feel that here in this life we already have a link with the infinite, desires and attitudes change. In the final analysis we count for something only because of the essential we embody, and if we do not embody that, life is wasted.[2]

This essential, simple wisdom is that to receive something we must sacrifice something. It is a difficult lesson indeed in these days of "want, have, get," where we could be haunted by the imperative of Jesus, *"Whosoever seeks to gain his life will lose it: but whosoever loses his life will gain it."* The drama of the cycle of sacrifice has reverberated beneath all great stories throughout history. We are fascinated by this great archetypal mystery the eternal return. It both captivates and terrorizes us. On the one hand we cannot help but seek it out by opening to experiences of the sublime, on the other we tend to want to pretend that it does not exist and keep ourselves safe by closing down.

For the past three months the *Innerscape* group of inquirers have been without the support of planned group meetings. They have been asked to retreat alone, meanwhile to carry each other in their hearts. Our smaller size today signifies that for this particular group there has been a consequence to traveling solo. Possibly the implied constraint of renunciation was premature for some. One man is missing because, "he has a new job in a new kingdom," another woman has "fallen in love," (therefore, is also absented to a more immediately appealing, exciting kingdom), and one woman has simply fallen. Like Jack and Jill, she and her husband fell out, and down the rabbit hole of fear and anxiety she/they tumbled. All these are understandable human dilemmas, nonetheless they are indications of the perils of this risky journey. The disappearance of fellow travelers rocks the faith of the remaining ones. The spaces of absence in which a candle of remembrance was lit for each, are strikingly present.

```
Let it go-the
smashed word broken
open vow or
the oath cracked length
wise-let it go it                    was sworn to go
              let them go-the
truthful liars and
the false fair friends
and the boths and
neithers you must let them go
  they                               were born to go
              let all go-the
big small middling
tall bigger really the biggest and all things,
  let all go dear                    so comes love
```

e.e.cummings [3]

This poem stands our normal I/me view on its head. It is reminiscent of the 'Hanged Man' tarot card, which speaks to the unexpected, the way in which life has a habit of undoing the best laid plans, as I had found some years ago on the second part of my own pilgrimage. The presence of this archetype is a sure sign that the journey now has us. We are no longer in control.

Yoga poses for this month do likewise, that is, turn everything we have learned and practiced to date, upside down. The *head stand* has been called the king of all yoga poses, not because it is that difficult but because it demands complete presence in the moment. No before or after, no change in thinking, no unconsidered movement, no lack of mindfulness will it tolerate, for a few degrees from center and all simply comes tumbling down. There are a number of possibilities in yoga for letting go by changing the body's normal vantage point. All upside down poses require stillness and steadiness. In them, movement is restricted, and blood flow is reversed which has the effect of calming the mind. Balance is the outcome and perhaps a dawning emergence of the 'right question,' which has to do with letting go of what 'I' can accomplish.

The reader may recall from *Chapter 2* that the *Jewish kabbala* conception of the *'Tree of Life,'* is also upside down. This may seem puzzling but is resolved through direct understanding when in repose in any one of the inverted yoga poses. Whilst the body alignment and balance remain the same, the roots are changed. However deeply into matter we have grown habitual roots some day, one day, they must be ripped out. We can choose to practice releasing these attachments and find out that if we are balanced *the root is within and not without*. This possibility exists regardless of actual roots having been planted in actual matter.

Early on we learned the rooted *mountain pose* in order to re-gain *stability*; in tree pose, half of the roots are removed as we look for *balance*; in *inversions* we subtract all usual roots to discover *freedom*. All of these poses done at a simple or more complex level, bring about a sense of tranquility, a meditative state. Something as simple as laying upside down with the legs up a wall for five or ten minutes can settle a racing or conflicted mind state, by shifting mental activity from doing and trying to being and letting. Similarly, a hurried body accustomed to goals and 'deadlines,' will experience rest and renewal.

As the annual cycle returns group participants repeat a 'tree of life' drawing. What is most striking about the changes in general, is that many trees are now drawn with balanced roots and branches. Many trees can easily be turned upside down and still appear normal. The trees drawn earlier in the year were less balanced often with diminutive roots, branches or both. What has now been drawn is the *kabbala*, the spiritual tree. At some level beneath words, the understanding that life comes out of nothing and disappears into nothing has been embodied.

> Stop and listen to the heart,
> the wind outside,
> to one another,
> to the changing patterns of this mysterious life.
> It comes moment after moment
> out of nothing and disappears into nothing.
> Live with less grasping and
> more appreciation and caring.   Jack Kornfield[4]

In her diaries, *Helen Luke* mentions a friend, an eighty year old dying woman, whose last words were, *"I feel as though I were being turned inside out."* To this we may add, *"and upside down,"* for death makes us present to the counter-question of familiar life. The question which, like the effort of mindfulness practice goes against the flow. It was this which *Jung* was addressing when he said, *"We must accomplish our death."* *Rilke* faced the same challenge in his contemplative exploration of the meaning of life which culminated in an epiphany, expressed in the epic poem, the *Duino Elegies,*[5] which begins, *"If I cried out, who would hear me up there among the angelic orders,"*

This long poem addresses *the* question of how is it possible to live when the fundamentals of our life are so incomprehensible? When we are inadequate in love, wavering in our determination and impotent in the face of death, how is it possible to exist? *Mary Oliver asks,*

> Do you have a question that can't be answered?
> Do the stars frighten you by their endless number?
> Does it bother you, that mercy is so difficult to understand?
> *For some souls it's easy; they lie down on the sand*
> and are soon asleep.
> For others, the mind shivers in its galacial palace,
> and won't come.
> Yes, the mind takes a long time, is otherwise occupied
> than by happiness and deep breathing.[6]

Rilke wrote *'Duino Elegies'* shortly before the first world war. Now a century later, war continues to be omnipresent. The reality of conflict and wounding floats daily across the TV screen of nations. It is only by feeling the tragedy of this defense/attack pattern in our own lives that we see what it takes to turn it on its head. To get to this awareness is to shift from the externalized projection of self to *witnessing withinness.*

For those group members who are feeling compelled by the push or pull of external life demands, any commitment to movement away from that feels impossible. Such is the lure of sensual pleasure, perceived necessity, or the call of achievement. Once a commitment to the spiritual life is felt deeply then nothing can pull one away but it takes time and determination, a lived maturity, to confront the demons of distraction. Meanwhile, the rationalization of 'I' reigns supreme! As Hollis reminds us, *emotional maturity is the capacity to tolerate anxiety, ambiguity and ambivalence and to move, anyway.*

"Withinness," is a way of accessing a dimension that has no locality in time or space. To gain access to this world we cannot try but only receive in a kind of effortless attending. The *Taosits* call this attitude, "wei-wu-wei," which means "action no action." Father Thomas Keating says, *"the chief act of will is not effort but consent."* To try to accomplish things by force of will is to reinforce the false self, but as the will goes up the ladder of interior freedom its activity becomes increasingly one of consent to the inflow of the grace of spirit. A very lovely *Christian mantra* which can be repeated any time, anywhere, especially in willful moments, is *"Consent to the Presence of Spirit."* It is great to say it slowly with an emphasis on the word 'consent.'

The energy of this quality of existence, in Eastern terms, is the energy of the *Sahasara chakra*. This energy is conceived of as a wave of infinite speed allowing it to be everywhere at once, yet having no perceivable location. Such ultimate states of consciousness are described as being omnipresent, hence the notion that we carry the whole world inside of us. *Thoughts* are the forms by which this consciousness manifests into form through our bio-computer brains. The *chakra* energy center which draws most life energy will determine the kind of thoughts which 'seed' the flower of our actions. The content of body/ mind, far from being limited by the story of 'my' life, is potentially expansive beyond measure. It is not a container that gets filled up but can be experienced eternally as an open possibility. When *kundalini* rises, (as it does through the cultivation of awareness) we find ourselves reorganizing our lives to match the higher order,to a more evolved, graceful mode of thinking. We undergo the transformation from personally centered thinking to becoming a spacious channel. This is the *meaning of transcendence,* to grow larger than the small self such that, *"Human presence becomes a creative sacrament, a visible sign of invisible grace."*

> I arise today
> through the strength of heaven,
> Light of sun,
> Radiance of moon,
> Splendor of fire,
> Speed of lightening,
> Swiftness of wind,
> Depth of sea,
> Stability of earth.
> Firmness of rock.
>
> St. Patrick [7]

From an Eastern perspective the consciousness of Self, stabilized by the mind as witnessing presence, does not depart the body at death but rides with it in a very subtle, physical form known as *Prana*, or *Ch'i*, translated as breath, wind, air, subtle energy. In the West, the sense of nothingness which is conveyed when contemplating the impermanence of life (that is *death*), can be unnerving, with little perceptual consolation. The intent of this confrontation however, is not at all morbidity but rather to bring us into an acute perception of the *perfection of the present moment*. It may only be realized through personal insight, and cannot be taught.

C.G. *Jung* reminded us that, "*People who most feared life when they were young, suffer later just as much from the fear of death.*" It is this fear which is addressed in the depth of meditation practice and arose as a central theme in my own pilgrimage. *Joko Beck* a respected American Zen teacher speaks thus:

Intelligent (zazen, or meditation) practice always deals with just one thing; the fear at the base of human existence, the fear that *I am not*. And of course, I am not, but the last thing I want to know is that. I fear to see what I am which is an ever changing energy field. ..the only thing that matters is seeing with an impersonal searchlight: seeing things as they are. then,...we just live our lives. And when we die, we just die. No problem anywhere.[8]

Living with the realization of non-being, is to "*prize depth over abundance; wisdom over knowledge; humility over arrogance; experimentation over security; growth over comfort; meaning over peace of mind.*"[9] On a daily basis our capacity for love, goodness, truth and participation with beauty, invites us to fully live.

I talk directly to your soul. Listen to me. There is life without love. It is not worth a bent penny or a scuffed shoe. It is not worth the body of a dog nine days dead. When you hear, a mile away and still out of sight, the churn of the water as it begins to swirl and roil, fretting around the sharp rocks-when you hear that unmistakable pounding-when you feel the mist in your mouth and sense ahead the embattlement, the long falls plunging and steaming- then row, row for your life, towards it.

Mary Oliver[10]

Suggested activities for the summer pilgrims are designed to increase awareness and to enjoy a full participation in *this* moment of living. Besides encouragement to spend much time in nature, each participant drew, in late Spring, the name of another group member who would become, for the summer months, a 'secret' friend. To that person would be sent out a daily blessing or prayer, an act of care, of recognition of our mutuality in Self. In the *Celtic* tradition, this soul friend is called an *anam cara* which implies a true friendship, one that is invulnerable to distance because one is understood and loved. Love of this kind honors the sacredness of each person. The *'anam cara'* meditation serves both as a loving guardianship of the bonds of continuing group support, as well as encouraging the daily meditative practice for deepening awareness and presence. If consciousness is dulled then this prayerful communion grows faint. If strengthened through practice it benefits both self, other, and the group as a whole. It is also a teaching in compassion which is to give without thought of anything in return. Some found the daily practice an enlightening one as personal barriers fell away.

.... *When I drew the name of my secret pal I felt resistance, as she was the only person I have had trouble relating with! Well, I did think of her often and with warm regard so through the process I came to a non judgmental acceptance of this person. I feel really good about this.*

.... *It has become clear to me now how love itself can heal. It was always hard to say "I love you," now it is easier. I loved the practice all summer, and have felt the energy of my anam cara. I learned a lot about myself in this giving.*

Through the three months apart awareness of presence was seen as the greatest gift which could be offered to each other. As a symbolic gesture of this attitude of sending or give-away, each person spent time contemplating what talent, creation or possession they would be willing and able, to give away to their *anam cara* at the first meeting in September.

In the native American tradition the give-away animal is 'turkey,' At each Thanksgiving, *Turkey* gives its life for the nourishment of the people. This is a tradition which has succeeded into modern culture, although nowadays more with an emphasis on greedy eating than consideration of what exactly we are giving, able to give, and giving thanks for. Native people not only shared a well earned feast after the hard work of harvesting, but also considered it a great honor at this time to give away their most favored possessions. Renunciation of our 'stuff,' no longer comes easily in a culture where everything has a purchase price. Consideration of what *can* be given is a tough contemplation exercise, leading to close scrutiny of attitudes about *holding on* to *"my"* precious objects, money, time, energy, indeed all that holds us in bondage. The other side of 'gifting' is in *receiving*, both the anonymous daily blessing, as well as the symbolic 'gift.' It is odd to have no one other than the flow of deserving life, to thank. *It is not so easy to simply to receive!*

.... *The most amazing thing transpired through this gifting process. I looked everywhere for the perfect gift for a long time, then at the end 'saw' it in my jewellery bag, an opal spider necklace. On the day of gift giving I couldn't believe that my anam cara talked about how spiders had recently come into her dreams! It was so right to give her my necklace.*

.... *Choosing a turkey gift was an interesting experience. I saw my selfish nature rear its head. Originally I thought of giving away my favorite articles of clothing but only if I could find something new to replace it! What I did eventually choose to give was a very special object which had helped me to get back on the path. This I wanted to pass on. It has helped me look at other things, like an idea of a dream house, which I cling to.*

What matters in this unique form of giving is that the gift of energy embodied in the object is not personal or 'owned' by anyone but comes directly from the creative source, *as a blessing* to be passed on. Whatever is given is to be held in *'present presence'* until the river of life asks for its release to another. In this way the process is far more than our familiar gift giving. As symbol of the blessing of awareness and care it passes on the deepest part of being human, that is, the Self. It is equivalent to the kiss which awakens the sleeping *"Sleeping Beauty,"* after one hundred hidden years.

A few years ago I was personally gifted at the 'turkey' ceremony with a very tiny, unpretentious figurine of the *Indian Goddess Tara*. There are some interesting stories relating to Tara as a protectress. She carries the energy of a *boddhisattva of compassion*, who can be called upon in times of dire need or distress. When I received the gift I was grateful for the figurine but little realized just how potent a gift this was. (Do we ever recognize the divine walking into our lives?) I had placed little Tara on my meditation altar and had taken to chanting the, 'Om Tara' chant. A few months later due to an odd set of events, I found myself in the city with no home to live in and was shortly due to leave for the summer. I was staying with friends but feeling a bit desperate as nothing I looked at was available or seemed right. In this frame of mind one day I went for a short walk, letting my legs choose the direction, when I saw a small condo hidden away but with a 'For Sale' sign. I instantly knew this was right and, despite rather great odds, within twenty four hours it was mine, exactly what was needed. What I did not know until after I had signed the purchase agreement, was that I had just bought # 10 Tara Green! I found out then that the green form of Tara is said to be her most potent form of manifestation. Since that day I have treasured Tara and her/my home turned out to be a blessing, which, at the right time, has now passed to another deserving soul. *It is the nature of 'soul' gifts to be handed on.*

At times like these we see the amazing mystery of this dancing world and so we learn to love our life.

> When Death comes
> like the hungry bear in autumn;
> when death comes and takes all the bright coins from his purse
>
> to buy me, and snaps the purse shut.....
>
> I want to step through the door full of curiosity, wondering:
> what is it going to be like, that cottage of darkness?
>
> And therefore I look everything
> as a brotherhood and sisterhood...
>
> And, I think of each life as a flower, as common
> as a field daisy, and as singular...
>
> And each body, a lion of courage, and something
> precious to the earth.
>
> When its over, I want to say: all my life
> I was a bride married to amazement.
> I was the bridegroom, taking the world in my arms...
>
> Mary Oliver[11]

The sense of soul value, or consciousness, being carried by objects which are passed on through time beyond the history of one life span, is an ancient theme. Perhaps time has little to do with this energetic valency which is better thought of as an eternal field of 'soul' consciousness available here and there, now and always, to sensitive recipients. *Egyptians* buried many treasures with the dead expecting them to be valued in the hereafter. The new, and usually very young, Dalai Lama is selected on the basis of responding to personal objects from his previous incarnation. At times we all are startled by a perception of having been at a place before or knowing something or someone deeply yet newly. The same words, names, or numbers seem to show up repeatedly in personal addresses and locations. We tend to 'recognize' (see again) certain faces as though they were familiar.

A variation on this theme, has been recently explored in the novel *"The Girl in Hyacinth Blue."*[12] The mythic story traces the unintentional but meaningful lineage of 'owners' of a timeless Vermeer painting and how the painting has affected and connected the lives of those who loved it. Indeed it was not even the painting but the quality of perfect sky-blue achieved by the artist, as well as the mystery of the girl who watched and waited. Everyone who owned the painting was also waiting for something. Similarly in the story of *"The Red Violin,"* made into a film spanning centuries and countries. The special violin seemed to carry its owner's passionate energy and story, through the centuries of ownership. Whoever owned it acquired both ecstasy and loss as well as an obsession with its beauty. These two stories attempt to portray that soul objects, when created with great focus and care, appear to 'carry' their qualities with them. Such is the intention for the 'turkey' gifts.

This is not quite the same as ideas of reincarnation or rebirth, a pervasive theme for three or four millennia in India. One which is paralleled by the idea of an afterlife in the Western Christian/Judaic traditions. On these topics I choose an *agnostic* position, in acknowledging that *I simply do not know* about possible states of consciousness beyond the confines of this physical matter. Physics may now be suggesting that concurrent states of being are a reality but this is far from being understood. *Belief* can be reassuring, a defense against the terror of nothingness. Historically, it has been manipulatively used by religious organizations to control behavior of the masses. Belief is largely made up of projections of wish fulfillment, indoctrination and rationalization, which may be simply comforting or downright dangerous, as in the case of the current wave of young suicide bombers in the Middle East. It is a trap to link transcendence with a motive of rebirth whether in hell, heaven or another incarnation.

This journey of self's integration in Self is one of *being fully present here and now.* Of seeing the world as it is, in the fullness and richness of the possibilities of creation and manifestation, as well as in the sadness of disintegration and the ugliness and pain of human omniscience. To live with an open heart and wise decisions, to learn to let go of clinging, to be free to move with the changing energy flow is a worthy outcome of conscious living and has no need for further justification or projection. The business of dying may elicit more shadow material than any other human preoccupation, (as it carries the greatest fear) so it is one which requires careful attention.

The aim of meditation practice is not one of separating mind and body, transcending by negating. Meditation is not a disembodied process, or an escape from physical reality. Mindfulness actually reveals mind and body to be in constant communication, each responding and shaping the other. In concentrated one pointed states of mind, physical sensations of breath are associated directly with changes in mental state and subjective experience. It is possible to feel an emotion or an idea *before* it manifests as such.

When working in a concentrated manner, I find, quite often, that I am able to walk straight towards a book on my shelf, which will orient me to the present topic, encouraging the next idea into manifestation. This innate awareness which we have called 'withinness,' is a form of 'knowing,' of intelligence acting within which has the capacity to free us from any preconceived view that the mind and body, or the subject and the object, are separate. It appears to manifest simultaneously through 'me', a painting, a violin, a page in a book on the shelf, or a face in a crowd. In the moment of connection there is no duality, no self and other, no before and after, only Self encompassing all.

The fruition of this practice may be called *transcendence*, which represents one continuum of development from the bounded 'I' (bound to passing conditions), to an unbounded Self permanence, which is the experience of union, or to put it another way, *awareness of no-self*. The Self is now perceived as it is, *no longer symbiotically annexed to the ego*. As meditative development proceeds the ego-self (I/me) peels away from confinement at lower developmental levels, to identify with a higher order of energy vibration. It is always and increasingly, inter-connective. The self transcends the previous more restrictive structure, integrating it in the newly accessible, more expansive structure. It is even possible that this process may continue in this pattern of *transcend by inclusion* to levels beyond the existence of the physical or personal body. This, of course, remains speculative. The only well laid out schema of consciousness outside of the physical realm is the *Tibetan Buddhist* one, where this expansive movement evolves beyond death to pure consciousness, before re -involuting into matter. Most of us cannot verify this, either through deep meditative insight nor experience, but we do know when 'I/me' becomes transparent in *this* world. About this *Ken Wilber* says:

...the form of transcendence......traces a gentle curve from sub-consciousness through self consciousness to super consciousness, remembering more and more, integrating more and more, unifying more and more, until there is only that Unity which was already the case from the start, and which remained the alpha and the omega of the soul's journey through time.[13]

It is one thing to think about these things, to have glimpses in practice and daily life, especially under conducive retreat conditions, but it is another to return from pilgrimage and to *live* at that higher ordering of human potential. The center of gravity of the personality can and does sink back to where the action of I/me is currently located. This is likely what happened to our missing fellow travelers. There are times a plenty when we can talk the talk, but not necessarily walk the walk! As *Wilber* says, in order to live from a higher (more expanded) level, the self has to actually die, to release its attachment at a lower level, and *it is much easier to chat about the higher than to die to the lower...* However, the natural tendency of the psyche is to grow, ascending to Spirit, whilst the natural tendency of love is to descend to meet matter. The branches and the roots of the *Tree of Life*, grow and meet each other.

If the mind were clear
and if the mind were simple, you could take this mind
this particular state. And say
This is how I would live if I could choose:
this is what is possible.....
But the mind
of the woman imagining all this. The mind
that allows all this to be possible....
Does not so easily work free from remorse
does not so easily manage the miracle
for which the mind is famous.

Adriane Rich[14]

Growing up into consciousness, is firstly an *emptying*, hence our current emphasis on *releasing out, relaxing out, giving out, letting go*. Although the grip of the 'I/me' world feels quite natural whilst we are *in it*, it actually lies at the root of all suffering. Emptying is the way to release the defensive tension of the whole organism, such that what is there, awaiting illumination, may precipitate growth. The 'grip' is experienced as an obvious rigid tightening of muscles at times of anxiety, shame or embarrassment. (discussed in Chs 5 & 6.) *Emptying is a process, not a goal* and one which we cultivate in meditation practice. This is *not* adding something or believing something, but is found in experiencing each breath as an opportunity to release outward, dissolving the lump of I/me solidity. *It is this very process which frees us.*

> When the doors of perception are cleansed,
> One will see the world as it is, infinite.
> When man has closed himself down,
> He sees but blindly,
> Through the narrow chinks in the cavern.   William Blake[15]

The wise one, the one who has walked the walk, is one who has come to dwell in emptiness, who is not caught or held in fixed belief, who lives connected to all of life is a *bodhisattva*. This is one who hears the cries of the world and responds with deep compassion. As such he/she has died to the short term, limiting compensations of self gratification, has transcended the need for constricted clinging in the Great Connection of Being. It is thus through dying that we fully live.

> This is love: to fly towards a secret sky,
> to cause a hundred veils to fall each moment.
> First to let go of life.
> Finally, to take a step without feet.   Rumi [16]

11

Who Am I? Who Asks?

Walk as if you were kissing the earth with your feet,
Then the marks left by your feet will be like the marks
of the emperor's seal
calling for Now to go back to Here;
so that life will be present;
so that the blood will bring the color of love to your face;
so that the wonders of life will be manifested,
and all afflictions will be transformed into
peace and joy.

Thich Nhat Hanh [1]

Late in November, at the coast, the earth is still warmed by the afternoon sun. Within this context I have been inspired to plant bulbs, daffodils, tulips, crocus, garlic. This is a new venture for me, resonating with this earth friendly setting. Each afternoon for a few days, utterly absorbed, I have found the right spots for digging small earth caves in which to plant these luscious, juicy, rich containers of spring flowers. No one can undertake this late Fall ritual without awe, at the potential of the swollen root and the necessary incubation in darkness, the cold and wetness of winter's death like holding. Unlike seeds which need warmth and immediacy for their rapid life cycle, the bulb is full enough to wait, rich enough to endure, not one but many cycles, wholesome unto itself as tulip, daffodil, as ordinary magnificence. Far from being depleted by blooming, bulbs grow and expand over five or six years, then they are ready to be divided and multiply further. Apart from the sheer pleasure of this task, it is fairly obvious that coming into focus at this particular time, it is a symbolic action, for the ending of this cycle of writing and pilgrimage.

Pilgrims are present to each day, its weather, its tone, its unique call to action in time. They are alert to synchronous happenings which can change plans or surprise us into a new focus of attention. Similarly with dream images which do not disappear with morning light but ask for resonant creative expression. *Phil Cousineau* suggests that the art of pilgrimage is *'the craft of taking time seriously, elegantly.'* What every traveler sooner or later confronts, is that the way we spend each day of our travel is the way we spend our lives, for the meaning of the true life we long for is always found in the *here and now.*

.... *There are many things from the year which I hope to take with me but the most important one is to live in the present, enjoy the now and not worry about what maybe or what was*

In undertaking any kind of pilgrimage we are all living out of the hero/heroine *archetype.* This may be acted out in many ways, whether mapping the inner psyche, the back yard or like *Odysseus,* the universe. That is irrelevant, what does matter is the engagement of the human need to *expand the limits of the known and the possible,* to move from innocence to experience, from naivete to wisdom, from identification to individuation. Reading myths (or these days, watching movies) about these universal motifs inspires us to listen to the soul. It is this *listening* which is the way in to the inner landscape which we have encouraged repetitively through many modalities.

Any odyssey is incomplete without a final planting as symbol of the individual *participatory* life, as well as a gift of inspiration for the future. Towards the end of the famous Grecian myth of *Odysseus,* there is yet one more action which he must perform to complete the hero's journey. The final instruction is given to *Odysseus* by a *blind* seer, *Tiresias.* He is told that after arriving home he must undertake a final journey. He is to go, this time, on foot inland, carrying one of his great oars, and he is to travel to a country where no man has ever seen the sea; there he is to plant his oar and leave it for men to see, then quietly return home, make sacrifice to the gods, and live in peace until *"death shall come to him gently out of the sea."* The final act of an epic voyage, is to deliver a symbolic invitation to the people, then wait, as the winter bulbs, for the next cycle of blooming.

Faithfully supporting this symbolic activity, a recent and timely dream of mine was about the proper baking of garlic bulbs. In the dream, my mentor and I were preparing them in a very exact manner, so that when one set was finally 'baked' to perfection they could be set on one side, to be guarded and protected whilst awaiting the treasure which they represented. This was evidently an 'alchemical' dream, the main theme in alchemy being the transmutation of matter, that is, base matter into gold. The 'lead' of the personality was seen as being alchemically transformed through the fire of awakening to its golden possibility. This is the 'work' of redemption, (of psyche,) redeeming a supreme value from its bondage in base matter or *prima materia*. Psychologically, what is transmuted is the ego-self identity, which we have referred to as, I/me. The purpose of 'cooking' this composite mixture was to free the Self or archetypal psyche from contamination by ego dominance. The dream symbols are informing about bringing forward the gold of the spirit at the conclusion of this *Innerscape* journey.

The way of inner pilgrimage has been represented in part, through the window of depth psychology, with especial reference to the pioneering work of C. G Jung, and more recently those who have responded to his initiative of inquiry into psyche, as the Western spiritual perspective of the realization of self in Self. *Marie Louise von Franz*, summarizes the journey of individuation which we have traveled.

Whenever a human being genuinely turns to the inner world and tries to know himself/herself-not by ruminating about his thoughts and feelings, but by following the expressions of his own subjective nature, such as dreams and genuine fantasies-then sooner or later the Self emerges. The ego will then find an inner power that contains all the possibilities of renewal. [2]

Self is an archetype of natural wholeness, it is not at all mysterious but simply the one who is right now in front of us, *fully aware* whilst acting and being. As the Zen texts say, *"illuminatingly so."* The archetypal symbol for Self, the circular *mandala,* is one symbol along with the *tree of life,* which has provided a foundation for travel. As such we have explored these meta symbols of inner pilgrimage with careful attention. Once introduced to the empowerment of artistic creation and the healing possibilities of these images, many have been amazed at how the symbolic creations, begun early in the year long quest, continue to speak and speak powerfully. I, and others, once started, have found that the creation of *mandalas* has become a life habit for healing, or for joyful expression.
.... *I have meditated upon my mandala much in the last few months-remembering how its creation came slowly as I integrated my thoughts and visions. Many times I have been brought to tears looking at it. It's call to my true path is strong....and for healing.*

During late Fall I created a seasonal *mandala* as expression of that which had been most apparent on October walks, namely the amber colored leaves connected each to each along the forest path by a myriad of threads, woven by spiders. On sunlit mornings the sparkling display was quite brilliant and inviting of the artist within, for, as we have learned through experience, *by reverently participating in the landscape, one dwells in the holy land.* On this occasion it also invited proper attention to the amazing activities of *spiders,* which synchronously, in turn, led to a teaching.

In *Native American mythology Spider Woman* is the weaver of the earth, her peoples and their destinies, the idea being that both individual and collective fate is woven up through the course of our responsive or reactive living. The choice is ours and often depends on our capacity to pause, wait and listen. This was one of my own early 'discoveries' when journeying. It became a key principle throughout the inner pilgrimage.

"Have you ever seen a spider make a web? The thread comes out through little holes right above his ass. It is so thin you can hardly see it. He makes a trap for the bugs in the air. Before the web is made, before the bug is caught, the bug knows nothing of webs. It's as if the bug and the web didn't exist. The bug dies, he is eaten, he becomes material for a new web. The wind tears the old web down."
"The point then, is to hold still, to stay in one place?"
"Yes."
"To wait. Is one supposed to wait for.....what? Do you wait for something, for something to appear?"
" You wait for yourself."
"I'm already here."
"No. Not really.
"Oh..."
" You are stretched out like a string all over the place. The end of the string is here, the rest is there and there and there, back there on the mountains on the other side. You must reel in the string, you must roll yourself up in a ball and then unravel yourself out here where you have the room and the clear light to study the condition of the threads. Once you have the string all laid out, once you have repaired the worn pieces, you will establish certain points. Between these points you will line out the string until you have made a web, strong, very taut. The impact of a breeze on one edge will be felt on another. Sunlight will bounce when it hits, as though it were a trampoline. The sunlight will turn somersaults and you will know you have made the thing well. Then listen for the wind. The sound of the wind on the threads."

Barry Lopez[3]

.... *You cannot be on this journey without awakening something. Once the seeds are planted there is truly no turning back. I had my life packed away in neat storage for far too many years before I started this Innerscape journey.*

Imprisonment in a "packed away life," is a common experience for many and is the source of suffering, culminating in all kinds of symptoms and feelings of malaise, such that, *"we are locked in, and the key is turned on our uncertainty."* The question, which life poses from birth, is, how are we to overcome this suffering and imprisonment, which is caused by a perception of ' I/me' separateness?

Longing for union, within and without, leads to regression, to a state of no -anxiety, a state of no -awareness. This is what we have termed the *'going to sleep'* solution, which is widely promoted, as various avenues of pleasure seeking and addiction in our culture. This is quite understandable when we consider the enormity of standing before this chasm of uncertainty. there is no-one to save us, no parent, no one true god, no guru, no ideology, in the face of the incredible complexity and ambiguity of modern life. Here is an excerpt from the *Chinese Taoist* philosophy, a story about the attempt by one man, whose life is bound like ours, to seek an answer from the sage *Lao Tzu:*

Lao Tzu to the seeker

"When, a moment ago, I looked into your eyes
I saw you were hemmed in
By contradictions. Your words confirm this
You are scared to death like a child
who has lost Father and mother
You are trying to sound the middle of the ocean
With a six foot pole
You have got lost, and are trying
To find your way back to your own true self
You find nothing
But illegible sign posts pointing in all directions
I pity you."

Ten days later, after meditating on this, the desperate questioner returns hopeful after trying to cultivate more desirable qualities. *Lao Tzu* retorts:

" Miserable!"" All blocked up!
Tied in knots! Try to get untied!
If your obstructions are on the outside
Do not attempt to grasp them one by one

And thrust them away. Impossible!
Learn to ignore them
If they are within yourself.
You cannot destroy them piecemeal,
But you can refuse to let them take effect.
If they are both inside and outside,
Do not try to hold on to Tao—
Just hope that Tao
Will keep hold of you!"

in Thomas Merton[4]

This poor seeker has no choice now, but the application of two qualities, discovered by one of our group pilgrims,
.... *The gifts I gained the hard way during this Innerscape pilgrimage have been trust and awareness.*
The invitation here, if there really is no enduring escape from contradiction, is to ask the one question, which seers always provoke, that is, *how may I be fully born?* It is the answer to *this* question which the Sunday pilgrims sought as they garnered their courage and set out. Of this, *Tibetan seer, Sogyal Rinpoche* says,

Looking in will require of us great subtlety and courage-nothing less than a complete shift in our attitude to life and to the mind. We are so addicted to looking outside ourselves that we have lost access to our inner being almost completely.[5]

One year later we have found out that some semblance of an honest appraisal can only be found by first developing awareness, intuition, reason, the capacity to love, to such a point that our ego-centricity is transcended. It is no longer prioritized as the star performer. The gift is a sense of harmony, a oneness with the world. Moreover, to be fully born is not one act but a process. *To live is to be born every minute.* Having discovered these life enhancing qualities, still, we forget again, get kicked out of the Garden of Eden one more time and, like the quoted group participant pack our real life away in storage. *Innerscape is about unpacking.*

Well being is possible only to the degree to which one is open, sensitive, responsive, awake empty. It means to be fully born,to awaken from the half slumber of ordinary man, to become what one potentially is.
D.T Susuki [6]

190

Rilke, whom we have quoted for poetic inspiration, made the observation that we are not yet ready to live the answers but we who choose to delve in to the quest know hat we have little choice but to find and augment the *right questions*. If we do then we possibly have the option of *living our way into the answers*, the place where choice and destiny meet. C.G. *Jung's* comment, after decades of exposure to neurotic suffering, said that its cause was most frequently that people settled for the wrong answers to the questions of life. He said that many are confined within too limited a spiritual horizon, with a life insufficient in (soul) content, and therefore, meaning. The quest then, has been one of soul, of meaning, which is to have risked the experience of life at depth.

The initial question of my own and others' quest, besides how can I be rid of unpleasant symptoms is generally a version of, " Who Am I?" What part of me should I get to know so that I can say I have fully lived this life rather than just visited here? What symptom or symbol is now demanding my attention? What do I need to let go of? Where am I stuck? How do I discover my un-lived potential which has been in prison?

"What, or Who Am I," is *the* question which gives expression to perhaps the deepest search we have, the one underlying our whole life. A *Chinese Zen master* said that *this question calls for the concentration of "one's whole body, with its three hundred and sixty bones and joints and eighty four thousand pores."* Perhaps this is why all pilgrimages are depicted as arduous! Virginia Wolf, deeply pondered the implications of "Who am I?" which approximates the first half of our inquiry, but went further, as did we, towards the end, into, "Who is it that asks the question?"

And now I ask, " Who Am I?" I have been talking of Bernard, Neville, Susan, Rhoda, Louise. Am I all of them? Am I one and distinct? I do not know. We sat here together. But now Percival is dead, and Rhoda; we are divided; we are not here. Yet I cannot find any obstacle separating us.[7]

Wolf's speculation is about boundaries, therefore, in the face of death, she approaches the question of "Who am I" as, "Who am I not?" The answer, depending on where she or we draw the boundary of 'I,' will be anywhere from an all embracing inclusiveness of Self/ cosmos and all that is in it, to a narrower definition, including only things or images which belong to the category of 'mine.' *Pilgrimage encourages us to expand our boundaries along with our questions,* which is why *Ken Wilber* calls suffering, *" the first grace,"* for it is the one thing which ego cannot alter being now caught in its own conclusion. *Awareness of suffering, without exception, calls us to the path,* for it marks *birth,* birth of expanded vision and creative insight. We have discovered that our *boundary lines are also our battle lines* and it is here in our self/other conflicts that we have encountered shadow. Implicit in the drawing of boundaries is the manufacturing of *opposites.* Inside/outside, me/not me are the basic forms. Moreover, *a world of opposites is a world of conflict.* Shadowy places gather momentum around our boundaries requiring reinforcements of *fear, guilt, shame* and *blame* to keep it all in place.

Our attempt has been to shine a light of possibility, in the form of symbolic as well as physical expression, through appropriate yoga poses, into these knotty and stuck places. What exists in psyche has been found as stored tension in the body, sometimes initially more obvious, as physical sensation. Immediate attention to the body is *always* a guarantee of living in the *now,* in truth. Through an integrated perspective of body/mind organism, as well as through a steady daily practice, we have created opportunity to illuminate body parts as home to psyche and soul. Feeling attention to all of the body's surfaces, muscles, joints and organs over the course of a year, has revealed, quite obviously, areas of tightness or numbness as places of energy blockage. Having recognized this, release has been found through repetitive aware practice and exhalation of breath. Focused attention upon the simple act of breathing reveals much, not least of which is the realization that the body, the physical home is one of our blessings.

Bless the fingers,
for they are as darting as fire.
Bless the little hairs on the body,
for they are softer than grass.
Bless the lips
for they are cunning beyond all machinery.
Bless the mouth
for it is the describer.
Bless the tongue
for it is the maker of words.
Bless the eyes
for they are the gifts of angels,

for they tell the truth.
Bless the shoulders
for they are a strength and a shelter.
Bless the thumb
for when working it has godly grip.
Bless the feet
for their knuckles and their modesty.
Bless the spine
for it is the whole story.   Mary Oliver[8]

In becoming reacquainted with the uniqueness of our body, its beauty, foibles, folds and wrinkles, we have come face to face with our own soul uniqueness, as our lived story. For it is true, especially by the middle years, that *biography begets biology*. What is required, at any age, *is surrender of the ego and its acquired body-beautiful imaginings, to the request of the Self.* When the body is considered to be separate from the head, (I *am* my thoughts but I *own* a body) if not befriended it becomes an enemy and often a lifetime war of "working it out," or "getting it into shape," is waged. The comfortable realization of person-body-hood, with all of its perverse permutations is an act of praise.   Implied, is the overcoming of intimidation by fear, to be who we are meant even designed to be, rather than letting anxious, petty, preoccupations stand in our way. Whenever the 'ego-idea of self,' surrenders to *the Self* and agrees to serve the larger perspective then we move towards wholeness.

Wholesomeness has obliged us to account for opposites. Interaction as,' I-Thou,' has called for enlargement of 'my-self,'so as to contain the perceived 'not-I' (this could be, 'I and my body,' or 'I and another'). Enlargement of view has provoked growth. In examining our (love) relationships carefully, we have seen that *we cannot find any relationship which is more evolved than the level of development we bring to it.* Holding the tension of opposites has challenged discrimination of what we owe to ourselves and what we owe to the world. In every instance of questioning during pilgrimage we have found a constantly shifting being-with and no permanent answer.

The unrelated human being lacks wholeness, for he can achieve wholeness only through the soul and the soul cannot exist without its other side, which is always found in a "You.' Wholeness is a combination of "I and You." These show themselves to be parts of a *transcendent unity whose nature can only be grasped symbolically.*   CG Jung[9]

Tony Packer constantly challenges the notion of separation at boundary edges, encouraging us to see where subject/objects rather than dividing at their boundaries, *touch and unite with each other.* Nowhere is this more obvious than in the sense perception of *listening.* Where is the division between the sound and the hearing?

We have similarly explored no boundary by 'seeing' through the eye of open hearted, poetic and artistic sensibilities. As a result of direct observation we have found there to be *no boundaries in the natural world,* not even boundaries of speech or language, when these arise out of the world they are intended to represent. *"Present awareness brings the whole drama (of separation) to light instantly!"* This wise woman illuminates the problem of our woes in the simplest of observations:

So, what am I and what are you-what are we without images to hide our true being? Yet, there is the sound of the wind blowing, trees shaking, crows cawing, woodwork creaking, breath flowing without any need for divisive thoughts. Thoughts are grafted on top of what is going on right now. In that grafted world we happen to spend most of our time.

Tony Packer[10]

.... *I have come to know that each moment can only be lived one breath at a time. There is nowhere else for life to occur. I cannot make time pass other than it will. I can however live in that moment and no other.*

This pilgrim has made significant progress, for she has found a way into *the* answer to *the* question. It is in the simplest thing, the thing we have all been doing since birth, which is to be here, still and breathing. I *find it quite remarkable, despite such an insight, how frequently there is an urgency to do something,* or to make a future plan to do something. Often, I find, there is an initial sense of dread which accompanies just being, breathing and allowing an emptiness on the calender.

Ken Wilber has challenged us provocatively to honestly look at our attitude to living. He suggests that, *"we are not really searching for an answer because we are busy fleeing it, - every time we move away from present experience."* It is *this* and *this* and *this* experience which holds the alchemical key, the answer to the question. Pilgrimage has brought into view an inner landscape which is never definitive, such that it asks for a relaxed, open, undefended state of mind, prepared and ready for what is now. What we sought to know as, "I /Me" *is* God's presence, that is, a fully embraced Self-in-context. Travel teaches the necessity of dropping resistance to circumstance which is not easy, as many of the present moments are not particularly pleasant ones. But when we do we are healed, whole and fully living!

> I live my life in widening circles,
> remembering backwards a little
> and sometimes even forward
> *knowing, sensing where I am going*
> calling it, for now, Ithaca.
> I know for sure I will be blown of course by fearsome winds,
> transported to some moment I have never seen before,
> And find in it exactly
> where I need to be.
> I will meet, not make
> the dragons and monsters of my heart
> who want my care and understanding.
>
> Pat Clifford

Our attitude for journeying has been one of waiting on truth, expressed in the above pilgrim's poem of her journey. What we have looked for is the simple, whole and complete truth of each breath/moment. Freedom, we have found, is in *being-with*. Implicit in the willingness to release defenses, (those which are part of the control of I/me boundaries) there must be trust in a certain *goodness*, which wants the best for us, is wise and which will contain us. As pilgrims and communing members of a group of fellow travelers we have been cultivating faith in such, 'goodness,' for it is this which quiets the self centered ego, inviting trans-personal centeredness.

Hope in such intrinsic goodness, expressed as charitable and moral acts, is one remaining human possibility in a world run riot with programming, wiring, unbridled greed, ecological devastation, and short sighted violence.

> There is a goodness, a Wisdom that arises,....to save us if we'll let it, and it arises from within us, like the force that drives green shoots to break the winter ground, it will arise and drive us into a great blossoming....into that part of ourselves that can never be defiled, defeated or destroyed, but that comes back to life, time and time again, that lives always, that does not die.
>
> China Galland [11]

.... *I have spent much more time alone this year and silent. I now realize that I have enjoyed it or when I have not, it hasn't felt like the end of the earth. The big pit of want and need is gone. The realm of the possible has been entered.*

To have been a pilgrim is to have converted to living a *religious life*. Religious, not in the sense of expounding a creed or fanatically supporting a cause but as one who approaches life with care, with reverence; who examines everything as carefully as she can; who is not afraid of paradox, ambivalence, ambiguity, indecision.

Ken Wilber coined the phrase *"passionate equanimity,"* to sum up the right attitude in what were for him at that time, conditions of arduous pilgrimage. It implies a quality of deep caring but without particular attachment to outcome, ringed round with an understanding of waiting on the universe. The outcome of such an attitude is to be set down on the right road and pointed towards a firm and future footprint.

.... *I have waited long enough to now become clear on what I want to do with my life, the dream can come to fruition. Once I am clear in my vision and trusting of the universe, then things fall into their proper place.*

Virginia Wolf, attempted to capture the essence of here and now being in an experimental writing- feeling tempo, like walking on water. This same rhythm seems to have sounded throughout the inner journey. Like us, she tried to understand, in her case through writing, this vast uncertain, ever changing watery world. The water in my bay has tossed, blown, stormed and calmed as I have written and journeyed inward, alone, and with this group. Like the water of our planet, our lives are *both* the surface of things and the depths. Under blue sunny skies the bay water seems sparkly, calm and clear, but when night time comes the same vista looks dark, deep and foreign.

We have longed for, struggled at times, to find something firmly remembered, definite, a heavy vessel to cling to, a pacified Poseidon to control the waves, yet whose life has ever remained like that? This year, have we found anything solid which could be held on to? *To search for the truth of life, is to discover that it is never in any one place, it is never fixed.* Lao Tzu, the most ancient of our quoted wisdom teachers, taught only one thing, which is that *Truth is paradoxical.* It is to be found in any and every bucketful of water we draw from the well. We try to make order, but the order is only provisional. Like water walking, *pilgrimage teaches above all that we cannot afford too much certainty,* but the real soul food, that which is buried in the bulb, which endures through all seasons, is faith.

> You walking, your footprints are
> The road, and nothing else;
> There is no road, walker,
> You make the road by walking.
>
> Antonio Machado[12]

Looking for my footprints in this shared, watery, soul shaping context, I have been, in this very moment am and always will be, making the road. Along this road of faith, we are privileged with the mystery that life constantly and synchronously reveals, as more footprints, more road. We have learned patience, to await the depth and breadth of our lived soul story as it unfolds. We have cherished mutuality of meaning, caring and meeting of other at depth, as thou. We can say that, in facing into the cave of shadows, we have glimpsed the pearl beyond price which now grows slowly, simply, as a unique, authentic way of living, responding and being. The circle of Self has been, *is* protected, like the moon guarding the planet, with compassionate care.

Now,
> What can we do but keep on breathing in and out,
> modest and willing and in our places,

> *Listen, listen I'm forever saying.*   Mary Oliver[13]

Appendix

The Story of The Monster of The Deep.

A caravan of men and camels were crossing the desert and looking for water when they came to a deep hole dropping into the earth. Naturally, they lowered a bucket into the hole but with each repeated effort only the rope was returned. No bucket and no water. Having desperate thirst, and puzzled, they now lowered a man into the hole, but he too disappeared. Then another and another. Finally, the wisest and bravest man offered to go down to search out the mystery and to find water. When the wise man reached the bottom of the hole he found himself facing a horrible monster. He knew instantly that there would be no escaping the obvious fate of his predecessors, so he was brought to sharp awareness of everything before him. The monster said, "You may only go free if you answer my question correctly." The wise man had no choice in this matter but to listen carefully and answer thoughtfully.

"Where is the best place to be?" asked the monster. The wise man looked around seeing this deep dark, dank, and dreadful hole but did not wish to insult the monster by naming some other, more beautiful place. He said, "The best place to be is wherever you find yourself; wherever you feel yourself to be at home." The brave man was rewarded for his presence of mind, for the satisfied monster released both himself, the lost men and buckets full of water.

The Story of The African Necklace.

One day, a young woman with the most beautiful necklace, went down to the banks of the river to wash herself. There, waiting in ambush, were a group of other young women, led by the most envious one, who planned to humiliate this young woman of virtue who seemed different. None of them wore their necklaces (an unprecedented move) and they told her that they had decided to throw their necklaces into the river as an offering to the river god. The young woman had a generous heart and so instantly took off her own precious necklace also throwing it into the river, whereupon the others dug up their necklaces from the sand in which they were buried and thence ran off, laughing mercilessly at the devastated young woman who had been tricked. She, though well intentioned had allowed herself to be duped, and now wandered desolate along the river bank, praying to God to restore her necklace.

At last she heard a voice telling her to plunge into a deep pool nearby, which she did without hesitation, bidden as she was, by the gods. She landed on the river bed to find an old woman waiting. This old one was exceedingly ugly and repulsive, covered with open sores. "Lick my sores!" she commanded the girl. Because of her compassionate nature the girl began to do as she asked. Then the old woman said; "Because you have not flinched from doing as I asked, I will hide and protect you when the demon of the deep comes looking to devour your flesh." At that, they heard a roar, and the huge monster of the deep came calling that he smelled a human. The old woman, who had hidden the girl, put off the monster and he left cursing.

Then the old woman gave her a necklace even more beautiful than her previous one, and told her to go back to her village following her instructions. She said, "When you have gone a short way from the pool you will see a stone on the path, you must pick up this rock and throw it back into the pool. Hence continue onwards, without looking back, and take up your ordinary life in the village." This she did faithfully and shortly returned to her home.

The other girls could hardly believe their eyes when they saw her return with an even more beautiful necklace and wanted to know where she had found it. She replied quite honestly that it appeared at the bottom of the pool. Without hesitation the others raced back to the river and jumped into the pool. There they met the old woman who commanded them, "Lick my sores!" but these girls refused, telling her she was far too repulsive, and demanded necklaces. In the midst of this came the roar of the giant demon, who seized upon those girls one after the other and made a mighty meal of them.

The Story of The Maiden- King, or The Firebird.

Once upon a time in a certain kingdom, there was a merchant whose wife died, leaving him with one son, *Ivan*. A *tutor* was found for the son, and the merchant remarried. Since *Ivan* was now a young man, and very handsome the *stepmother* fell in love with Ivan.

One day *Ivan* went out fishing with his *tutor*, on a small raft when they suddenly saw thirty ships making their way towards them. On these ships sailed the beautiful and noble maiden *Princess*, with thirty other maidens who were her foster sisters. When the ships came close to the raft, they dropped anchor and invited Ivan and the tutor aboard the finest ship. The *Princess* told Ivan that she loved him and come from afar to see him. He was enchanted by her and so they were betrothed. The *Princess* told Ivan to return to the same place the next day and then she sailed away. Ivan went home and went to sleep. The *stepmother* invited the *tutor* into her room, plied him with alcohol and then questioned him as to what had happened when they were out at sea. The *tutor* told her everything. Upon hearing the story , she gave him a pin and told him that the next time the ships came into view that he should stick the pin into *Ivan's* tunic. The *tutor* agreed that he would do as she asked.

Next morning *Ivan* arose to go out to sea on the raft. When the *tutor* saw the ships in the distance he stuck the pin into the young man's tunic. Immediately Ivan felt very sleepy and said that he would take a nap and that the tutor should be sure to wake him when the ships approached. The ships came close and the princess sent for *Ivan* but he was sound asleep. The servants tried to wake him but all effort was in vain, they could not wake him, so the retinue of ships left. The *Princess* told the tutor to bring Ivan on the following day and he agreed. As soon as the ships had sailed away, the tutor pulled out the pin and Ivan awoke, realized that the ships had left and called to the princess to return. But she could not hear him. He went home sad and perplexed.

That night, the jealous step mother again took the tutor into her room, made him drunk, questioned him about everything that happened, and then told him to do likewise the next day. Again *Ivan* went fishing, the pin was stuck in his tunic and he slept through the *Princess's* visit. She left word one more time that he should come again.

On the third day he again went fishing with his *tutor*. They came to the same place and saw the ships sailing at a distance. Once again the *tutor* stuck in the pin, and *Ivan* fell asleep. The *Princess* dropped anchor and sent for *Ivan*. The servants tried every possible means to rouse him but to no avail. This time, the royal princess found out about the stepmother's deception and the tutor's treason. She wrote to *Ivan* and told him to "cut off the tutor's head," and that if he loved her he should come and find her "beyond thrice nine lands in the thrice tenth kingdom."When *Ivan* awoke, he was beside himself at the loss of the princess who had sailed away. The tutor unaware of the content, gave Ivan the princess's letter. With no hesitation Ivan read it, took out his sword and cut off the treacherous tutor's head. He sailed to shore, collected his belongings, said goodbye to his father, and set out to find the thrice tenth kingdom. He journeyed here and yon, searching, for a very long time, for "speedily a tale is told, but less speedily a deed is done."

Finally *Ivan* came to a little hut which stood in an open field, turning on chicken legs, and with human skulls decorating the fence. He entered and found an ugly old hag, the " *Baba Yaga*." Gleefully, she rubbed her hands at the sight of him, anticipating her next meal. " Fie, Fie," she said, " the smell of such a man was never heard of nor caught sight of here, but now it comes by itself."Young man, are you here of your own free will or are you hear by compulsion?" Ivan, nervously responded, " Largely of my own free will, but twice as much by compulsion, and for the rest, I don't know anymore. I have been seeking for a long time, the thrice tenth kingdom, do you know where that is?" *The Baba Yaga* looked him over thoughtfully, and then, apparently satisfied, said, " I do not know where it is, but........... my second sister might know."

Ivan thanked her and walked on for a long way, and a short or a long time, before he finally came to a second hut like the first and there too found another *Baba Yaga*. "Fie , fie, " she said, "The small of a man was never heard of nor caught sight of here, but now it comes by itself. Young man are you here of your own free will or do you come by compulsion?" Ivan responded, with some trepidation that he really didn't know how he got there, but that he was looking for the thrice ten kingdom. *Baba Yaga* said she did not know where it was but that her youngest sister may know. "She also gave Ivan a warning," If she wants to devour you, which she will, take three horns from her and ask here permission to blow them, blow the first one softly, the second one louder and the third, louder still." Ivan thanked the *Baba Yaga* and went on further.

He traveled long and far, eventually coming to another little hut, standing in an open field and turning on chicken legs, and with skulls decorating the fence. He entered and found another *Baba Yaga*. Upon seeing the handsome *Ivan*, the ugly old hag gleefully began to file her teeth for her intended feast,"the smell of such a man was never heard nor caught sight of here, but now it comes by itself." *Ivan* immediately demanded the three horns which she reluctantly delivered over to him. He blew the first one softly, the second louder and the third with all his might making a huge sound. Suddenly, birds of all description swarmed around him, and among them a large brilliantly plumed *Fire bird*. "Sit on me quickly," said the great bird, "and we shall fly wherever you wish, if you don't come with me the *Baba Yaga* will devour you."

Ivan had no sooner seated himself on the bird's back than the *Baba Yaga* rushed in, seized the fire bird by the tail, and plucked a handful of feathers from it, but the bird escaped capture, and flew for a long way with the merchant's son until it finally came to a sea, across which it told Ivan lay the thrice times ten kingdom which he sought. The bird could take him no further so *Ivan* was left to his own devices once more. Thanking the bird for saving his life, he set out.

He traveled for a long time and again came to a hut in a field which he entered. He was met by a kindly old woman who offered him food and drink, asking him where he was going and why he traveled so far. He explained that he was looking for his beloved, the *Maiden Princess*, to whom he was betrothed."Ah," said the old woman, "she no longer loves you, and if she gets hold of you she will tear you to shreds, her love is stored away in a remote place." "Then how will I find it?" "Well...... my daughter who lives with the princess is coming to visit me today, and she may be able to help us." Then the old woman turned Ivan into a pin and stuck the pin in the wall. At night her daughter flew in, and was asked where the princess hid her love. The daughter said she did not know but that she would try to find out.

The next day, she again visited her mother and told her, "On this side of the ocean stands an oak; in the oak there is a coffer, and in the coffer there is a hare, in the hare there is a duck, in the duck there is an egg, and in the egg lies the *Princess's* love." *Ivan* immediately set out for the place she had described. He found the oak and removed the coffer from it, then he removed the hare from the coffer, and the duck from the hare, and the egg from the duck. He returned with the egg to the old woman. A few days later came the old woman's birthday to which the princess and her thirty foster sisters were invited. She baked the egg, dressed *Ivan* in splendid royal garments, and hid him.

At midday, the princess and the thirty other maidens flew into the house, sat down at the table and dined. At the end of the meal the old woman served them each an egg, and to the princess she served the egg which Ivan had found. As soon as she bit into it she recovered a passionate love for the handsome young man, and began to speak about him. At that moment the old woman brought Ivan out of hiding and the princess was overjoyed. There was much celebration! The *Maiden Princess* then left with *Ivan* for her own kingdom where they married and began to live happily and prosper.

Notes

Introduction

1. Taken from a report in 'The National Post,' January 15th, 2004, p. A.14
2. James Hillman & Michael Ventura, *We've Had A Hundred Years of Psychotherapy And The World Is Getting Worse.*
3. James George, *Asking For the Earth*, p.23
4. Joseph Campbell, *The Hero with A thousand Faces*, p.97
5. Quoted by Robert Bly, in *The Soul I s Here For It's Own Joy.*
6. Jiddhu Krishnamurti. The statement made by K. on Aug 3rd 1929 as he resigned his position as head of the Theosophical Society began, "I maintain that truth is a pathless land and you cannot approach it by any path whatsoever, by any religion, by any sect. That is my point of view and I adhere to that absolutely and unconditionally. Truth can never be organized." Quoted in full in Pupul Jayakar's," *J.Krishnamurti, A Biography*, p.78
7. James Hollis, in "On This Journey We Call our Life."
8. Advice from C.G Jung.

Chapter 1.

1. Phil Cousineau, *The Art of Pilgrimage, The Seekers Guide to Making Travel Sacred*, p.9
2. Mary Oliver, *The Journey*, p.114
3. Robert Johnson, *Balancing heaven & earth*, p.48
4. E.L Doctorow, *City of God*, p.4
5. Thich Nhat Hanh, *call me by my true names*, p.141
6. C.G. Jung, *Memories, Dreams & Reflections.*

7. Thich Nhat Hanh, *Ibid*, p.189
8. Robert Johnson, *ibid*, *Prologue*, p xi-xii.
9. Vimala Thacker, *On An Eternal Voyage*, p.68
10. See Appendix, for full story of, "The Monster of The Deep,"quoted from Helen Luke, *The Way of Woman*, p.xv.
11. D.H. Lawrence, *Song of a man who has come through*, from *D.H. Lawrence Poems, Selected and Introduced by Keith Sagar*.p.72
12. Colin Fletcher, *The Man Who Walked Through Time*, p.54
13. James Hollis, *Creating An Individual Life*, p.69
14. D.H. Lawrence, *ibid, Song of A Man Who Is Not Loved*, p. 67
15. Helen Luke, *Such Stuff As Dreams Are made On, The Autobiography and Journals of Helen M. Luke*, p.161
16. John O' Donohue, *fluent, in, connamara blues*, p. 41
17. See appendix for full story of *The African Tale* as told by Helen Luke in, *the way of woman*, p.97
18. In James Hollis, *Swamplands of The Soul, New Life In Dismal places*, p.57 (from C.G. Jung, *The Collected Works*. Bollingen Series XX.)
19. From, Meister Ekhart, *The Book of Divine Consolation*, 1313-1322 in Dictionary of Philosophy, Ed. Robert Audi.

Chapter 2.
1. Norma Goodrich, *Priestesses*, in *The Great Goddess*, by Muten Burleigh (Ed) p.66
2. C. G Jung, *Modern Man in Search of A Soul*, p.74
3. Harish Johari, *Energy Centers of Transformation*, p.77
4. Caroline Myss, *Anatomy of The Spirit*, p.76 onwards.
5. C.G. Jung, see, thesis of, *Modern Man in Search of A Soul*.
6. James Hillman, *Insearch*, p.55
7. Roger Cook, *The Tree of Life*, p 9 and onwards. The illustrations in this book, speak a thousand words of understanding.
8. Lynne Baker(author), *Art Therapy with Emotionally Disturbed Children*, p7. and onward.
9. James Hillman, *ibid*, p232
10. Cited in Susan Fincher, *Creating Mandalas*.

11. *The Great Vision*, in, *Black Elk Speaks*, p.16
12. Albert Low, *the butterfly's dream*, p.90
13. Edward Edinger, *Ego & Archetype*, p176
14. C.G. Jung, *Man & His Symbols*, p. 213-217
15. Joseph Campbell, *Myths To Live By*. see chapter 2, "The Emergence of Mankind," p.19-42
16,17 & 18. Joseph Campbell, *ibid*, p.19-42
19. Rollo May, *The Cry for Myth*.
20. G. Highet, *The Classical Tradition*, p.540
21. C.G. Jung, *On The Nature of Psyche*, p.277.
22. Archibald MaCleish, *JB*. p.46
23. Robert Johnson, *He*, p.11
24. Katha Upanishad in Mircaea Eliade, *Yoga, Immortality & Freedom*, p.117
25. James Hillman, *We've Had one Hundred Years of Solitude*, p.50.
26. Rumi, *Like This*, p.35
27. Thich Nhat Hanh, *ibid*, *Froglessness*, p.180
28. Katha Upanishad, *ibid*. p 118
29. Vanda Scaravelli, *Awakening The Spine*, p.36

Chapter 3.
1. F. Scott Fitzgerald. *The Great Gatsby*.
2. Robert Johnson, *Balancing Heaven & Earth*, p.48
3. James Hollis, *Creating An Individual Life*, p.68
4. Rumi, *The Essential Rumi*, "Community of The Spirit," p.3
5. John O'Donahue, *Elemental*, in *Connamara Blues*, p.125
6. & 7, Sobonfu Some, *Welcoming Spirit Home*, p. 64-66, in Vol.25, #4 *Parabola* p.19
8. The Nomenology Project, *The Hidden Truth of Your Name*.
9. Gary Goldshneider and Joost Elfers, *The Secret Language of Destiny. A personology guide to finding your life purpose*.
10. Saffi Crawford & Geraldine Sullivan, *The Power of Birthdays, Stars and Number, The complete personology reference guide*.
11. Rider Waite, *Tarot Deck*.
12. Angeles Arrien, *The Tarot Handbook. A detailed guide for*

calculating and understanding the Life Soul Path.

13. Jamie Sams & David Carson, *Animal Medicine cards*.

Chapter 4.
1. Thich Nhat Hanh, *call me by my true names,* "The Sound of A Great Bird," p. 93
2. Poem by Felix, in We-Moon, annual calendar with inspirational feminine artists and poets, as well as moon/sun transit, information. 2003, p.51
3. Marion Woodman & Robert Bly, *The Maiden Tzar.* See appendix for story retold as, "The Maiden King."
4. Bly & Woodman, On Men & Women, A six part video series produced by Applewood, for CBC T.V.
5. Marie Louise von Franz, *The Cat, A feminine tale of redemption,* p.79
6. Pema Chodron, *The Places That Scare You,* p. 7
7. Naomi Ozaniec, *Chakras For Beginners,* p. 1
8. May Sarton, *Invocation To Kali,* in The Great Goddess, p.72.
9. William Stafford, *"A Ritual To Read To Each Other,"* in, "The Darkness Around us is Deep, Selected Poems of William Stafford, pp. 135f. quoted in James Hollis, "On This Journey We Call Our Life" p139
10. Marie Louise von Franz, *The Feminine in Fairy Tales.* p.211
11. Deng Ming-Dao, *365 Daily Meditations,* p.27
12. Nancy Wood, *Knowing The Earth,* in We- Moon, 1993,
13. From, C.G. Jung, quoted in, Stephen Cope, *Yoga and The Quest for the True Self,* p.173
14. Margaret Laurence, *A Jest of God,* p.120 & p.173
15. Pema Chodron, *ibid,* p.25
16. Marion Woodman, *ibid,* p.27
17. James Hollis, *Creating An Individual Life,* p.46 & 48
18. Edward Edinger, *Ego & Archetype,* p.68 and p.26
19. Yvonne Johnson & Rudy Wiebe, *Stolen Life.*
20. From, *20 poems of Kabir,* in The Soul Is Here For Its Own Joy, by Robert Bly, p.79-96

Chapter 5.
1. D.H. Lawrence, *Poems*, p.209
2. Thich Nhat Hanh,"the song of no coming and going," in, "call me by my true names," p. 86
3. Stephen Mitchell, transaltor of the "Tao Te Ching," reading #78.
4. Mary Oliver, *The Leaf & The Cloud* , p.5
5. Marion Woodman, in, *The Maiden King*, p.148
6. Joseph Campbell, *Transformation of Myth Through Time*, p.98
7. Clarissa Pinkola Estes, *Women Who Run with Wolves*, p.256
8. Mircae Eliade, In *Parabola*, Vol XX #1,p.52
9 Richard Wilhelm (trans), *The I Ching or Book of Changes,*
10 Richard Willhelm (trans), *ibid*, Reading, The Well p.185.
11. Joseph Campbell, *The Power of Myth*, p.58
12. Wilhelm/Baynes, *The I Ching, or Book of Changes.#48.* p.185,"The Well."
13. Juan Raimon Jiminez, *Oceans*, in Robert Bly, *ibid*, p.246
14. Joseph Campbell, *Thou Art That*, p.31
15. Henry David Thoreau, *Walden*, p.256
16. Robert Haydn *(1913-1918)*, *Those Winter Sundays*, p. 416
17. James Hillman, *In Search*, p.57
18. Judith Harris, *Chocolat.*
19. D.H. Lawrence, *ibid*, p.209
20. Mary Oliver, *Dream Work*, p.18
21. James Joyce, *Portrait if The Artist*, p.243

Chapter 6.
1. Margaret Drabble, *The Peppered Moth*, p.200
2. Mary Oliver, *Leaf & Cloud*, p.4
3. Virginia Woolf, *The Waves.*
4. Rumi, *ibid*, p.106
5. Rabindronath Tagore,"The Message," quoted in R.Bly, *The Soul is Here For Its' Own joy*, p.150
6. Anthony de Mello, The Heart of The Enlightened,"Human nature," p.106
7. Clarissa Pinkola Estes, *Women Who Run with Wolves*, Seal Skin/Soul

Skin. p.261

8. Michael Ondaatje, *The English Patient*.

9. Rumi, *Open Secret, Versions of Rumi*, Trans Coleman barks. Quoted in, Jack Kornfield, *After the Ecstasy the Laundry*, p.67

10. Edward Edinger, *Ego & Archetype*, p.26

11. Parker Palmer, *The Active Life, A Spirituality of Work, Creativity and Caring.* ps,6,21, 24

12. Parker Palmer, *ibid*

13. D. H. Lawrence, *Healing*, p.216

14 From, *Teachings of The Buddha*, by Jack Kornfield. Excerpt from *the Fire Sermon*, from Mahavagga, p.42

15 James Hollis, *On This Journey We call Our Life*, p.112

16. C.G. Jung, *The Archetypes and the Collective Unconscious*, Vol 9:420

17. Dorothea Matthews, in *Parabola*, vol.V111 #1.p.4

18. Dorothea Matthews, in *Parabola*, Vol V111 #1 p.10

19. Eileen Caddy, quoted in Ann Bancroft, *Weavers of Wisdom, Women Mystics of the Twentieth Century*, p.149

20. Michael Cunningham, *The Hours*.

21. Sally Vickers, *Miss Garnet's Angel*.

22. Sally Vickers, *ibid*, p3

23. Sally Vickers, *ibid*, p.330

24. Joseph Campbell, Quoted in an Essay by Jean Houston, *Living in One 's and Future Myths*, in *The Fabric of The Future*, p. 30

25. Frederich Holderin, *All The Fruit is Ripe*, in R.Bly, *The Soul Is Here For its Own Joy*, p.247

Chapter 7

1. Thich Nhat Hanh, *ibid*, p.154

2. Rumi, quoted in R Bly, *The Soul Is Here For It's Own Joy*, p.166

3. e.e cummings, *Poem#29*, in *100 Selected Poems*.

4 H. Luke quoting Borges, *Such Stuff As Dreams Are Made On*, p.234

5. Robert Bly, an article,"The Long Bag We Drag Behind Us," in *Meeting Shadow, The Hidden Power of the Dark Side of Human Nature*.p.6 Editors, Connie Zweig & Jeremiah Abrams.

6. J. Krishnamurti, *On Love*, a short pamphlet, taken from one of K's

talks, created by the Krishnamurti Foundation Trust, 1981.

7. e.e cummings, *ibid*, #95.
8. Boiling chick peas was a favorite metaphor of Rumi's, he even offered contemplative recipes! From, *The essential Rumi*, p.292. Also in, *Heart Ravishing Beloved*, p.61
9. Gospel of St.John. 14:27 p.168
10& 11. James Hillman, *In Search*, p.35
12. Saying, attributed to Girhault de Borneillh, in Joseph Campbell, *A Noble Heart*, in, *Transformations of Myth through Time*, p.231
13. William Shakespear, *Romeo & Juliet*, Act 2. sc. 131-35,quoted in Harold Bloom, *Shakespeare, the Invention of The Human*. p.92
14. Carl Sandburg, from, *"Explanations of Love,"* in *Harvest Poems*, p.84
15. Joseph Campbell, tells the story of, *" The Trial of The Perilous bed,"* In *Transformations of Myth Through time*, p.235
16. John Grey, *Men Are from Mars, Women Are From Venus. The Classic Guide to Understanding The opposite Sex.*
17,18. & 19. Robert Johnson, *We*, p.44, & p.55
20. C.G. Jung, in *Psychological commentary on Kundalini Yoga*, Spring 1976, p. 10-11.
21. William Shakespeare, *Loves Labors Lost*, act 2 sc. 1.
22. William Shakespeare, *Much Ado About Nothing*, Act 4, sc 3.
23. C.G. Jung, the essence of this statement is summarized in Johnson, *We*, p.192
24. Rollo May, *Love & Will*, p.276
25. Denise Levertov, *Literature of the 20th century*, p.743
26. Robert Johnson, *We*, p.103
27. Robert Johnson, *ibid*, p.31
28. Rainer Maria Rilke, *Letters To A Young Poet*, p.53-54.
29. John Welwood, *Journey of The Heart, The Path of Conscious Love.*
30. Michael Ventura, in *'Meeting The Shadow,'*p. 76
31. Michael Ventura, *ibid*, p.79
32. Rainer Maria Rilke, from *Letters to a Young Poet*, in, *On The Way To The Wedding*, by Linda Leonard, p.163
33. Ken Wilber, *Grace & Grit*, p. 366
34. Ken Wilber, *ibid*, p.401
35. T.S. Eliot, *Little Gidding*, in *The Four Quartets*, p.144
36. Rainer Maria Rilke, *Again, Again!*,*ibid*, p.167

Chapter 8

1. T.S. Eliot, *The Dry Salvages,* from *The Four Quartets,* p.130.
2. David Abram, *The Spell of The Sensuous,* p.128
3. Thich Nhat Hanh, *ibid,* "In The Forest," p.140
4. Laurens van der Post, *About Blady,* p.120
5. Sharon Butala, *ibid,* p. 87 & 92.
6. James Kale McNeley, quoted in The *Spell of The Sensuous,* p.233
7. Chogyam Trungpa Rinpoche, quoted in Pema Chodron, *Start Where You Are.* p.88.
8. Octavia Pay," Words."
9. Stephen Mitchell (translator), *The Tao te Ching.* #81.
10. Virginia Woolf, *The Waves,* p.67
11. Don Miguel Ruiz, *The Four Agreements,* p.26
12. Robert Bly, *Morning Poems, "Thoughts,"* p.86
13. David Abram, *ibid,* p.263
14. Rumi, *Word Fog,* from *Songs of the Soul Meeting,* p.22.
15. Sharon Butala, *ibid,* p.96
16. James Hollis, *ibid,* p.61
17. Rolf Jacobsen quoted in Robert Bly, *ibid,* p.250.
18. Herman Hesse, *Siddartha*
19. Mundaka Upanishad III-I-1, in R. Panikar.
20. Thomas Merton, *Zen and the Birds of Appetite,* p.23.
21. Jacques Lacan, in *"Narcissism And The Empty Word of The Ego,"* by A. Fayek, in *Melanie Klein Journal of Object Relations,* Vol.# 7 No.1 June 1989.
22. Pema Chodron, *Start Where You Are,* p.12
23. Virginia Wolf, *The Waves,* p.159.
24. Jaques Lacan, *ibid,* p.58.
25. Virginia Woolf, *The Waves,* p.198

Chapter 9

1. Mary Oliver, *The Leaf and The Cloud, " Flare,"* p.5
2. Sharon Butala, *Wild Stone Heart.*
3 Emily Carr, quoted in Doris Shadbolt, *The Art of Emily Carr,* p.206.
4. Jacques Maritain, see *The Degrees of Knowledge.*

5. Emily Carr, *ibid*, p.60
6. Emily Carr, *Klee Wyck*, p.52
7. Ken Wilber, *The Essential Ken Wilber*, p.145
8. Raimon Panikar, *Invisible Harmony*, p.93
9. Wei Wu Wei, quoted in The Essential Ken Wilber, p.124.
10. Joseph Campbell, *The Hero with A Thousand faces*, p.28
11. Rainer Maria Rilke, in *Selected Poems*, p.141.
12 Naomi Ozaniec, *Chakras for Beginners*(one of the first chakra books Which is a gem as the author studied Eastern sources.) p.54
13. Lao-Tse, translated by Arthur Whaley, in *Parabola*, vol 25 #4 Winter 2000, p.80.
14. Richard Smoley interview with Z'ev ben Shimon Halevi, *Parabola*, vol 25 #4 Winter 2000, p.60
15. Thich Nhat Hanh, "Sunflower," *ibid*, p.166
16. J. K. Rowlins *Harry Potter & The Philosopher's Stone*.
17. Simone Weil, in *Ideas*, a CBC production, April 8-12th 2002.
18. Margaret Atwood, "There is Only One of Everything," in Selected Poems.
19. Margaret Vanier, *Beyond Fate*, The Massey Lecture, 2002. p.133.
20. Thomas Moore, *Care of The Soul*, p.160.
21. Joseph Campbell, *The Hero with A Thousand faces*, p. 64.
22. Stephen Mitchell, translator, *The Tao te Ching*, p.68. 21.& p.57
23. Laurence Fisher, from an essay presented at the Lasqueti Island Writers Festival, July 2003.
24. Ancient Zen text quoted in Hubert Benoit, *The Supreme Doctrine*.

Chapter 10
1. Walt Whitman, *These Are The Days*, in Collected Poems, p.146.
2. Quoted by Thich Nhat Hanh, in *The Plum Village Chanting Book*.
3. C.G. Jung, *Letters*, vol. 1 p. 483
4. e.e. cummings,#79, p.96.
5. Jack Kornfield, "The Heart As Mother of The World"in *After The Ecstasy, The Laundry*, p.63,
6. Rainer Maria Rilke, *Duino Elegies*, p.19.

7. Translator, Kuno Meyer, *The Deer's Cry on St. Patrick's Breastplate*,
8. Joko Beck, *Everyday Zen*, p. 114
9. James Hollis, *On This Journey We Call our Life*, p.100
10. Mary Oliver, *west wind*, p.46
11. Mary Oliver, "When death Comes."in *New & Selected Poems* p.10
12. Susan Vreeland, *Girl In Hyacinth Blue*.
13. Ken Wilber, *The Eye of Spirit*, p.239
14. Adrianne Rich, "What is Possible," *Your Native Land , Your Life*."
15. WilliamBlake, "Auguries of Innocence," preface to," Jerusalem," quoted
   in Robert Johnson, *Balancing Heaven & Earth*, p.4
16. Rumi, *the essential Rumi*, p.109.

Chapter 11.
1. Thich Nhat Hanh, *call me by my true names*, p198
2. Marie Louise von Franz, *Man and His Symbols*, p.215
3. Barry Lopez, *Conversation*, in *Crossing Open Ground*, p.39
4. Thomas Merton, *The Way of Chuang Tzu*, p.130
5. Sogyal Rinpoche, *The Tibetan Book of Living and Dying*, p. 52
6. D.T. Susuki, *Zen Buddhism & Psychoanalysis*, p.91
7. Virginia Wolf, *The Waves*, xiii
8. Mary Oliver, *The Leaf & The Cloud*, p.35
9. C.G. Jung, *The Psychology of The Transference*, in,
   The Practice of Psychotherapy, p.454
10. Tony Packer, *What Is The Me?* In 'The Newsletter,' Springwater
    Center for Meditative Inquiry, Oct 1977
11. China Galland, *The Bond Between Women*, p.52
12. Antonio Machado, from *Proverbs and Tiny Songs*,p.248, in Bly, The
    Soul is Here for its Own Joy.
13. Mary Oliver, *west wind*, p.14

End Page
1. Mary Oliver, *Leaf & Cloud*, p.41

Bibliography

Abram, David,   *The Spell of The Sensuous, Perception & Language in a More than Human World*. Random House 1997.

Arrien, Angeles,   *The Tarot Handbook*, Archer/Putnam, N.Y.1997.

Atwood, Margaret,   *Selected Poems*, McClelland & Stewart, 1976.

Audi, Robert, ed.   *Dictionary of Philosophy*, Cambridge University Press,1995

Baker, Lynne,   *Art Therapy with Emotionally Disturbed Children*,an M. Ed. thesis, University of Alberta,1982.

Bancroft, Anne,   *Weavers of Wisdom, Women Mystics of the Twentieth Century*. Penguin Group, London, 1989.

Beck, Joko,   *Everyday Zen*, Harper San Fransisco,1989.

Benoit, Hubert,   *The Supreme Doctrine*, Pantheon, N.Y., 1955.

Black Elk & John Gneisenau Neihart,
      Black Elk Speaks, Being the Life Story of the Oglala Sioux, University of Nebraska Press2003.

Bloom, Harold,   *Shakespeare, The Invention of The Human*, Riverhead Books, Penguin Putnam, N.Y. 1998.

Bly, Robert,   *Morning Poems*, Harper Collins, N.Y. 1997.

Bly Robert,   *The Soul Is Here For It's Own Joy, Sacred Poems from Many Cultures*, The Eco Press. 100 West Broad St., Hopewell, New Jersey 08525. 1995.

Bly, Robert in   *Meeting the Shadow*, see Connie Zweig & Jeremiah Abrams.

Bly, Robert & Woodman Marion,
      The Maiden King, Henry Holt & Co. Inc.,N.Y.1998

Bly, Robert & Woodman, Marion, *On Men & Women, A Six part Video Series* produced by Communications Inc. Applewood, Box 148, Belleville, Ontario, K8N 5A2

Burleigh, Mutan,   *Return of The Great Goddess*, Stewart, Tabori & Ching, N.Y Div of U.S. Media Holdings Inc.,1997.

Butala, Sharon,   *Perfection of The Morning*, Harper Perennial,1992.
Butala, Sharon,   *Wild Stone Heart*, Harper Collins, 2000.
Campbell, Joseph, *The Hero with A Thousand Faces*, Bollingen Fdation,
                 N.Y., Princeton University Press,1973.
Campbell, Joseph, *Thou Art That*, New World Library, Novato, Cal. 2001.
Campbell, Joseph, *Myths To Live By*, Bantam Books, 1973.
Campbell, Joseph, *Transformations of Myth Through Time*, Harper &
                 Row,1990, (also a television series, by Dr. Stuart
                 Brown and William Free.)
Campbel, Joseph, *The Power of Myth*, Doubleday N.Y., 1988
Eliade Mircea,   *Yoga, Immortality & Freedom*, Bollingen Series, LV1,
                 Princeton University Press, 1969.
Carr,Emily,   *Klee Wyck*, 5th Ed.Toronto, Clarke, Irwin & Co.1971.
Chodron,Pema,   *The Places That Scare You, A Guide To Fearlessness
                 in Difficult Times*, Shambala Publications Inc.,2001
Chodron,Pema,   *Start Where You Are, A Guide To Compassionate
                 Living*, Shambhala Publications,Inc.,1994.
Cope Stephen,   *Yoga And The Quest For The True Self*, Bantam Books,
                 2000.
Cook,Roger,   *The Tree of Life*,Thames and Hudson, London 1988.
Cousineau,Phil,   *The Art of Pilgrimage, The Seekers Guide to Making
                 Travel Sacred*, Conari Press,California,1998.
Crawford, Saffi, & Sullivan Geraldine,
                 The Power of Birthdays, Stars and Numbers,
                 Ballantine Books, 1998.
Cummings,e.e.,   *100 Selected Poems*, Grove Press, N.Y.1954.
Cunningham,Michael,
                 The Hours, Picador, N.Y., 1998.
De Mello, Anthony, *The Heart of The Enlightened*, Doubleday N.Y.1989.
Doctorow, E.L.,   *City of God*, Penguin Putman Group. N.Y.,2001.
Drabble, Margaret, *The Peppered Moth*, McClelland & Stewart Ltd.,2001.
Edinger,Edward F, *Ego & Archetype*, Penguin Books Inc.,U.S.A. 1973.
Eliade,Mircae,   *Patterns in Comparative Religion*, London &
                 Sidney,1958.
Eliot,T.S.,   *The Complete Poems & Plays, 1909-1950*,
                 Harcourt, Brace &World Inc., N.Y.1956.
Eswaren Eknath (trans) *The Upanishads*, Nilgiri Press, 1987.

Fletcher, Colin,   *The Man Who Walked Through Time*, Random House. U.S.A. Vintage Books, 1997.

Galland,China,   *The Bond Between Women, A Journey To Fierce Compassion*. Riverhead Books N.Y. 1999.

George, James,   *Asking For the Earth, Waking Up To The Spiritual Ecological Crisis*, Element Inc, Rockport, MA.1995.

Gary Goldshneider and Joost Elfers,
    The Secret Language of Destiny, A Personology Guide to Finding your Life Purpose: Viking Studio, Penguin Group NY. 1999.

Grey, John,   *Men Are from Mars, Women Are from Venus, A Classic Guide To Understanding The opposite Sex*, Quill Press, 2004.

Hanh, Thich Nhat, *call me by my true names*, Parallax Press,Unified Buddhist Church, California.1999.

Harris, Joanne,   *Chocolat*, Penguin Putnam inc., N.Y. 2000.

Hillman, James,   *Insearch, Psych & Religion*, Spring Publications Inc. 1994.

Hillman, James & Michael, Ventura; *We've Had A Hundred Years of Psychotherapy And The World Is Getting Worse.* Harper Collins, N.Y.,1998.

Hollis, James ,   *Creating A Life, Finding Your Individual Path*, Inner City Books, Toronto, Canada, 2001.

Hollis, James,   *On This Journey We call Our Life,* Inner City Books, Toronto, 2003.

Johari, Harish,   *Chakras, Energy Centers of Transformation*, Destiny Books, Vermont, Inner Traditions International.2000.

Johnson Yvonne & Rudy Wiebe, *Stolen Life, The Journey of A Cree Woman*, Vintage Canada,, Alfred A. Knopf, 1998.

Johnson, Robert,   *Balancing Heaven & Earth*, Harper Collins, San Francisco,1998.

Johnson, Robert,   *He, Understanding Masculine Psychology*, Harper & Row, U.S,1974.

Johnson, Robert,   *We, Understanding The Psychology of Romantic Love*, Harper & Row, Publishers, San Francisco,1983.

Joyce, James,   *Portrait of the Artist*, in, *The Portable James Joyce*, ed., Harold Levin, Penguin Books Ltd.,1966.

Jung, C.G.,   *Man & His Symbols*, Doubleday & Co. Inc.Garden City, N.Y., First published,1964, reprints to,1976.

Jung, C.G.,   *Psyche & Symbol*, Anchor Books Edition, 1958. Copyright Bollingen Foundation.

Jung, C.G.   in Kundalini Yoga, Spring 1976,

Jung, C.G.,   *Memories, Dreams & Reflections*, Vintage Books. Alfred A.Knopf & Random House, Inc., Canada. 1963

Jung, C.G,   *The Archetypes and the Collective Unconscious*,The Collected works, Vol. 9, p.400.

Jung C.G,   *Modern Man in Search of A Soul*, translated by W.S. Dell,Harcourt, Brace, Jovanovich,1933.

Kennedy, X.J,   *Literature, An Introduction to Fiction, Poetry and Drama*. Little Brown & Co.,1987.

Konfield, Jack,   *After The Ecstasy The Laundry*, Bantam Books N.Y. & Canada.2000.

Kornfield, Jack,   *Teachings of The Buddha*, Shambala Publications inc., Boston N.Y. 1992

Jayakar, Pupul,   *J. Krishnamurti, A Biography*, Penguin Group,1986

Krishnamurti, J.   *On Love*, Krishnamurti Foundation trust, 1980.

Lacan,Jaques,   Ecrits: A Selection. Trans. Alan Sheridan. N.Y. Norton,1977.

Laurence, Margaret,   *A Jest of God*, McLelland & Stewart, 1966.

Lawrence D.H.,   *Poems, Selected and Introduced by Keith Sagar*, Penguin Books Ltd., London, England,1972.

Lopez, Barry,   *Crossing Open Ground*, Charles Schribner's Sons, N.Y.,1988,

Low, Albert,   *the butterfly's dream, in search of the roots of zen*, Charles Tuttle & Co., Vermont. 1993

Luke, Helen,   *Such Stuff As Dreams Are made On, The Autobiography & Journals of Helen M. Luke*, Parabola Books, The Society of Myth & Tradition, NY.2000

Luke, Helen,   *the way of woman*, Bantam Doubleday Dell Publishing Group Inc.,1995.

Matthews, D,   *A Flash of Living Fire*, in Parabola, vol.V111 #1. Jan,1983.

May, Rollo,   *Love & Will*, Dell Publishing Co. Inc.,N.Y.,1969

May, Rollo,   *The Cry For Myth*, Delta publishing N.Y. 1991.

Macleish, Archibald,
               Collected Poems, 1917-82, Harper Collins, 1985.

Meritain,Jaques,   *Creative Intuition in Art & Poetry*, Charles Schribner's
               Sons, 1959.

Merton, Thomas,   *Zen and the Birds of Appetite*, New Directions 1968.

Ming-Dao, Deng, *365 Daily Meditations*, Harper San Francisco,1992

Mitchell, Stephen, (trans), *The Tao te Ching*, Harper Collins Inc.,1988.

Moore, Thomas,   *Care of The Soul*, Harper Collins,1993.

Muten, Burleigh,   (Ed.) *Return of The Great Goddess*, Stewart, Tabori &
               Chang NY.1997

Myss, Caroline,   *Anatomy of The Spirit, The Seven Stages of Power and
               Healing*, Crown Publishers Inc., NY.1996.

O' Donahue, John, *conamara bues*, Bantam Books 2001.

Oliver, Mary,   *West Wind*, Houghton Mifflin Co.,1997.

Oliver, Mary,   *The Leaf & The Cloud*, Da Capo Press,2000.

Oliver, Mary,   *New & Selected Poems*, Beacon Press, US.,1992.

Oliver, Mary,   *Dream Work*, The Atlantic Monthly Press, NY, 1986.

Ondaatje, Michael, *The English Patient*, McClelland & Stewart CA.1996.

Ozaniec, Naomi, *Chakras For Beginners*, Hodder & Stouton, Bookpoint
               Ltd,39 Milton Park, Oxon, OX14 4TD,U.K.1994

Nomenology Project *The Hidden Truth of Your Name*, Ballantine
               Books,1999.

Packer, Tony,   *What Is The Me?* In The Newsletter Springwater
               Center for Meditative Inquiry, Oct 1977.

Palmer, Parker,   *The Active Life, A Spirituality of Work, Creativity and
               Caring.* John Wiley & Sons, Cal, U.S.A.1990.

Panikkar, Raimon, *Invisible Harmony*, Augsburg Fortress Press, 1995.

Pinkola Estes, Clarissa,
               *Women Who Run with Wolves, Myths and Stories
               of the Wild Woman Archetype*, Ballantine Books,
               N.Y. 1992.

Rich, Adrianne,   *Of Woman Born*, Norton Press N.Y, 1986.

Rilke,Rainer Maria, Duino Elegies, trans, David Young, Norton &
               Co.,N.Y. 1978.

Rilke,Rainer Maria, *Letters To A Young Poet*, trans. Stephen Mitchell,
               Vintage Books, N.Y. 1987.

Rilke, Rainer Maria, Selected Poems, Trans & Commentary by Robert Bly.

Harper & Row N.Y. 1981

Rinpoche Sogyal,   *The Tibetan Book of Living & Dying*, Harper
                    San Francisco,1993

Ruiz,Don Miguel,   The Four Agreements, A Wisdom Book, 1997.

Rumi,   *Like This,* by Coleman Barks, Maypop,1990

Rumi,   *The Essential Rumi* ,Coleman Barks,
                    Castle Books,1995.

Rowlins, J.K.   *Harry Potter& The Philosopher's Stone*, Bloomsbury
                    Publishing 1997.

Ryan M. J., Editor, *The Fabric of The Future, Women Visionaries
                    Illuminate the Path of Tomorrow*, Conari Press,1998

Sams Jamie & Carson, David
                    Animal Medicine Cards, St. Martins Press N.Y.199

Sandburg,Carl,   *Harvest Poems,*1910-1960, Harcourt, Jovanovitch,
                    1966.

Scaravelli, Vanda, *Awakening The Spine*, Harper Collins, N.Y.,1991.

Shadbolt, Doris,   *The Art of Emily Carr*, Douglas & McIntyre, Ltd.,1979.

Some, Sobonfu   *Welcoming Spirit Home, Ancient African teachings to
                    Celebrate Children & Community*, Novato Cal.1999.

St. John's Gospel, *The New American Standard Bible,*The Lockman
                    Foundation(eds.) Creation House Inc.,1973

Thacker Vimala,   *On An Eternal Voyage,*1989 Vimala PrakashanTrust,
                    Navrangpura, Ahmadabad 380 009,Gujarat,India,

Thich Nhat Hanh,   *The Plum Village Chanting Book.* Plum Village,
                    13, Martineau, 33580 Dieulivol, France.

Thoreau, Henry David,
                    Walden, Modern Library Paperback Ed.,
                    Random House, inc., 1992.

Van der Post, Laurens,
                    About Blady, A Pattern Out of Time,
                    Penguin Books, 1993.

Vanier, Margaret,   *Beyond Fate,* The Massey Lecture,2002,C.B.C.,
                    House of Anansi Press Inc., 2002.

Vickers, Sally,   *Miss Garnet's Angel,* Harper Collins, London, 2000.

Von Franz, Marie-Louise,
                    The Cat, A tale of Feminine Redemption, Inner
                    City Books, Toronto, 1999.

Vreeland, Susan,   *Girl In Hyacinth Blue*, Penguin Books, 2000.
We-Moon,   *Poem by Felix*, in 2003 calendar, Mother Tongue Inc.
    PO Box1395A, Estacada, Oregon 97023
Weil, Simone,   *Gravity & Grace*, G.P. Putnam's Son, 1952.
Weil, Simone,   Ideas, *"Enlightened by Love, The Thought of Simone
    Weil,"* CBC Ideas, Toronto, April 8-12, 2002.
Welwood, John,   *Journey of The Heart, The Path of Conscious Love*,
    Harper Collins Perennial, 1996.
Whitman, Walt,   The Completer Poems, Viking Press, 1990.
Wilber, Ken,   *Grace & Grit, Spirituality & Healing in the Life and
    Death of Treya Kilam Wilber.* Shambahala, 2001.
Wilber, Ken,   *The Essential Ken Wilber,*Shambhala,1998.
Wilber, Ken,   *The Eye of Spirit*, Shambhala, 1997.
Wilhelm Richard,   (trans),*The I Ching or Book of Changes*, Bollingen
    Series XIX, N.Y. 1950
Wolf, Virginia,   *The Waves*, Vintage edition, Random House Ltd.1992.
Zweig, Connie & Abrams, Jeremiah,
    *Meeting The Shadow, The Hidden Power of the Dark
    Side of Human Nature.*   Putnam's Sons 1991.

Slowly up the hill
Like a thicket of white flowers
forever
is coming.   ¹

ISBN 1-412025935-1

9 781412 025935